# Report Creation

## Using
## SQL Server Report Services

### with

Microsoft Dynamics GP

by
**Richard L. Whaley**
**Senior Business Consultant**
**Microsoft Dynamics GP MVP**

*Accolade Publications, Inc.*
Documentation for Software Users

The Dynamics GP Series
Report Creation using SQL Server Reporting Services

Published by:
Accolade Publications, Inc.
Altamonte Springs, Florida USA 32714


Library of Congress Card Number:   pending

ISBN: 1-931479-07-0

Manufactured in the United States of America

# *Introduction*

Sales transactions are keyed in to the application, shipped and invoiced, Purchase Orders are created, received, vouchered, and paid. Inventory movements are recorded and tracked. But if the firm cannot view the results of the business transactions and analyze the results, what good is all of this data?

SQL Server Reporting Services provides a collection of tools that allows a firm to report on the data generated and retained by their business. Table reports, charts, graphs, gauges, indicators and a number of other tools can take thousands and thousands of transactions and reduce them to easily seen trends. Executive dashboards showing open orders, orders invoiced today, purchase orders outstanding, PO's received today, inventory dollar values, transactions per month compared to last month or this same month last year are all easy to build.

SSRS is delivered a part of the MS-SQL Server and only needs to be installed an configured. The installation and configuration we will leave to the technical teams. In this book you will learn how to create, deploy, and run high quality, information packed reports using the SSRS tools.

**Disclaimer:** This document was NOT written by Microsoft Corporation who has no responsibility for its contents. The author is a seasoned business consultant who has made reasonable efforts to ensure the correctness of the information herein. However, as the author of this document was not the author of the software product on which this manual is written, and where the publisher of the software is constantly evolving and changing the software product, the author cannot guarantee the accuracy of any statements made here. The author, and Accolade Publications, Inc. specifically disclaim any warranty of correctness of the information herein and cannot be responsible for any errors or omissions or any damages, either direct or indirect, consequential or otherwise that may result or be alleged to result from the use or dependence on this material.

# Table of Contents

# IV. Accessing Data...................... 49

# V. Basic Report Creation.................. 95

# VI. Formatting Text and Data.................. 145

# VII.  Sub-reports, Charts, Et Cetera ............ 185

# VIII. The Report Manager ............................ 211

# IX.   Report Prep and Planning ................... 245

# I.    *SSRS - Introduction*

# Report Development / Deployment Tools

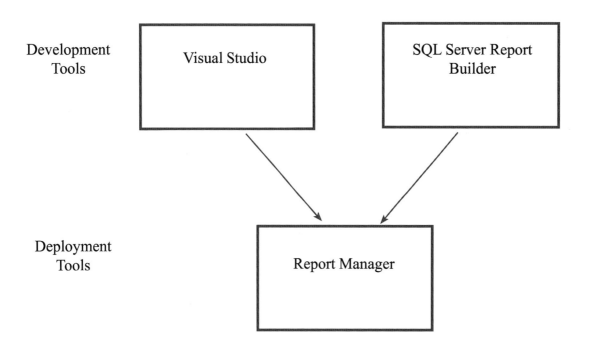

Development
Tools

Visual Studio

SQL Server Report
Builder

Deployment
Tools

Report Manager

# I. SSRS - Introduction

SSRS (SQL Server Reporting Services) is a collection of components that allow users to build and deploy reports to run against MS Dynamics and other databases. While primarily designed to retrieve and format data in MS-SQL databases, data from other sources can be used. In this text, however, we are going to focus only on retrieving data from MS-SQL databases.

Microsoft is advancing SSRS rapidly and there are several development platforms with significant differences. For example, some firms may have Visual Studio 2008 installed while others have Visual Studio 2010 or newer. There is also a simplified SQL Server Report Builder. The desktop and wizard features of these different versions are significantly different but the basic concepts behind the tools are the same.

The SQL Server Report Builder is a basic tool used to design and deploy reports. It provides users a simplified tool with a limited tool set. However, for most users, it provides quite a robust ability to generate well formatted reports.

The Visual Studios allow complete development of reports as well as other types of projects. Visual Studio uses the concept of projects to contain common components such as shared Data Sources, Datasets, and reports. Multiple reports with common features can be developed and stored in source format in a project.

Report models can also be created using Visual Studio that allow a less experienced user to open a model in the SQL Server Report Builder and format the data as desired. The model defines the data available to the user.

The Report Manager is a web based component that supports the distribution of reports to users. Users can be assigned rights and restrictions and provided access to selected reports. The report can be grouped into folders and executed on demand. Reports can also be executed by subscription. Subscriptions allow users to specify that selected reports are to be run at specific times and distributed as desired.

MS Dynamics GP also provides a method of executing SSRS reports through its My Reports menus, and reports can be deployed to SharePoint as well.

Before diving into the operations of these components, lets look at some basic concepts and the standard development process.

# I.A.    General Development Flow

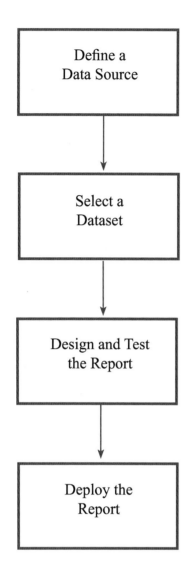

To create a report from scratch, the user must first select or create a data source. The data source defines the databases, tables and views that are exposed to the report designer. Data sources can be defined and shared among reports or created specifically for the current report. In some other reporting environments, an ODBC is created. The creation of a Data Source definition is roughly similar to creating an ODBC.

A Dataset is then defined. The Dataset takes a Data Source and selects specific tables, columns, and, potentially, rows of information. The Dataset allows queries to be defined INSIDE the report objects. This allows very complex data relationships to be defined, often eliminating the need to create special views in the SQL database. This collection of information is then passed to the report.

Once a Dataset is developed, the designer then creates the actual report itself using one of several tools. This involves selecting the specific fields to control grouping of the data, selecting the fields to be displayed, creating titles and totals, and otherwise formatting the report.

The report can be tested in most of the development tools. However, to allow other users to run the report, most firms want to deploy the reports to a tool that will allow users access to appropriate reports but not allow them to modify or change the reports. This is the job of the Report Manager. Reports created in the visual studio or other tools are deployed to the Report Manager. Folders, rights and restrictions are defined in the Report Manager that specifies which users can run what reports.

# I.B.    Data Sources / Datasets

Data Providers are just what the name suggests, the source of data to be printed in reports. A Data Provider is generally a database that contains the information that is to appear on the reports.

A Data Source is like an ODBC for other reporting tools. It establishes a connection to the Data Provider, allowing the report rendering program to obtain information (data) from the Data Provider. A Dataset then selects specific tables, columns, and rows from a Data Source and presents the selected objects to the report.

Both Data Sources and Datasets come in two general forms, Shared and Embedded. Shared objects can be used over and over again in different reports. Once defined, a new report can be written and a Shared Data Source or Shared Dataset simply selected.

Embedded Data Sources and Datasets are not available to be used in subsequent reports. When a report designer (the person that creates the report) writes a new report and does not want to use a Shared object, they must create the data connectivity completely. Embedded Data Sources and Datasets are contained completely inside the report definition and cannot be used by other reports.

Data Models can be developed and used as a shortcut to report creation. Basically, a Data Model is a report with a defined Data Source and Dataset. Users open the Data Model in the SQL Server Report Builder and place the provided data items (fields, calculations, et cetera) onto the report pasteboard, easily and quickly creating a new report without needing to know the structure of the Data Provider.

For example, customers are frequently stored in two different tables, with basic information in a table containing one row per customer and a second table holding one or more address records for the customers. To access address information, a report designer must expose both the customer master and customer address table and establish a link between the tables using the appropriate fields. For a report designer with reasonable knowledge of the database, this is easy (and will be discussed later in this book). For novices that have little knowledge of the database structure, starting with a Report Model that provides the appropriate information makes report creation simple.

Shared data objects make the writing of a series of reports easier. If a report designer will be writing a series of sales analysis reports, perhaps with different data being provided to different sales reps, creating and saving shared data objects makes writing the second and additional reports much easier.

If shared data objects are used in a new report and they do not contain the desired fields, they must be modified. Modifying the shared data objects can be OK. However, it can also expose additional fields to the other reports created using the shared data objects. If a report model uses the Shared Data Set, the users of the model will suddenly find additional fields available. Sometimes this is acceptable, sometimes not. Consider the sensitivity of the fields being added to an existing shared data objects. If necessary, create a new embedded data object.

One of the differences between Visual Studio and SQL Server Report Builder is the storage of Shared Data Sources and Shared Data Sets. Visual Studio will hold shared objects in the local project only available to the report designers. SSRB requires shared objects be published to the Report Manager. Once a Data Source or Dataset is found in the Report Manager, the SSRB can reference those objects. Note that the Report Manager is a public tool used by end users. This requires some security to keep the casual user from accidentally changing a shared object.

# I.C.    Building and Testing Reports

Once the report is connected to the data provider, the report designer can then create the data layout. The various report generation tools provide several different ways to create the layouts. In Visual Studio, a Report Wizard can walk a new designer through the process step by step. Experienced users can skip the wizard and create reports manually. The SSRB provides a standard pasteboard ready for objects to be placed upon.

During the definition of the report layout, the report designer (the person creating the report) can execute the document to examine the design. Data will be pulled from the Data Provider and displayed as specified by the layout. The report designer can then make any corrections to the layout and continue checking their results.

In all of the tools, quite a bit of formatting can be applied to the selected data. Parameters can be defined that allow end users to refine the selections. For example, a report listing customers by Sales Rep can have a parameter that lets a user run the report selecting only customers for one sales rep.

Totals, subtotals, grouping of data, highlighting, underlining, and quite a number of other effects can be applied to make a report more readable. The data can also be organized into charts and graphs in a number of formats.

# I.D.    Deploying Reports

Once the report is completed, it must be deployed to tools that will allow the appropriate users to easily run it. The Report Manager is an SSRS tool designed specifically for this purpose.

The Report Manager allows reports to be grouped into folders and sub-folders. Users can be given permissions to run reports or prevented from running a report.

Reports can also be deployed to SharePoint and directly to MS Dynamics GP.

# I.E.     *Launching Reports*

The Report Manager allows reports to be grouped into folders and security established limiting the rights of some users in some folders. Once a user locates a report in the Report Manager, simply clicking on the report launches the report. If a login or parameters are required by the report, the user enters the requested information and the report will be displayed.

The Report Manager also allows users to subscribe to reports, have those reports generated on a schedule, and emailed or filed as desired.

# I.F.     *Projects*

A project is a container in the Visual Studio report development tools that contains all of the pieces of the reports. The Date Sources, Datasets, and the report layouts are stored in Projects. When they are published, the objects are copied to the Report Manager but still remain in the Project.

Projects are convenient containers for the storage of common components. For example, several Shared Data Sources may be defined for sales reports and then a group of sales reports created using those Data Sources. A different project can be created for purchasing reports and the objects (Data Sources and Reports) contained in the Sales Reports Project will not be listed.

Some firms have hundreds or even thousands of custom reports. Knowing where to find a particular report or its components requires some organization. Placing groups of like reports into Projects provides this organization. Also, when writing purchasing reports, for example, the report designer does not need to wade through the data objects and report files of the sales department since those are in a different project.

Yes, some lines can become blurred. For example, manufacturing reports often require data from inventory tables. This is not an issue since the Project places no limitation on the data objects or the databases or tables it accesses. The limitations of Projects are solely the standards adopted by the report designers.

When creating Projects, consider the users that will need access to the reports held in the project. Again, any report when published can be deployed to any user or any folder in the Report Manager. However, when maintenance needs to be performed on a report or changes are required, having all of the reports in the Sales Reports Folder located in the Sales Reports Project makes locating the report easier.

The SQL Server Report Builder does NOT use Projects. Instead, reports are saved to folders on the disk and deployed almost immediately. Smaller firms with only a few different reports may not need the organizational facilities provided by Projects.

# I.G.    Our Approach

In this manual, both the SQL Server Report Builder and the Visual Studio tools for building reports will be examined. Throughout the book we will attempt to clearly label functions available only in one or the other of the tools.

The following icons will be used to distinguish feature sets in one or the other of the tools:

 -- This icon will appear if the function is available in the SSRB Report Builder.

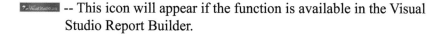 -- This icon will appear if the function is available in the Visual Studio Report Builder.

Chapter II will present an introduction to the SSRB Report Builder. Chapter III will present an introduction to the Visual Studio Report builders. The remaining chapters will discuss report formatting options.

# II.    *SQL Server Report Builder*

# II. SQL Server Report Builder

## II.A. Overview

The SQL Server Report Builder was first introduced with SQL 2005. Version 2.0 was released with SQL 2008 and the latest version, 3.0 provides significant additional features.

Version 2.0 of the Report Builder introduced a new user interface that conformed to the then current Office 2007 look and feel. It supports running the reports locally or on the server and does not require Report Models. It also introduced the concept of a Tablix, a combination of a table and a matrix report format. (Tablix will be discussed later.)

The version 3.0 of Report Builder delivers additional features. It is provided as a Click Once enabled application with SQL Server 2008 R2 and as a separate installation package with the SQL Server 2008 R2 Feature Pack. Additional features in 3.0 include support for maps and geospatial visualizations, integration to BING maps, new display types such as indicators, sparklines, and data bars, among other things.

## II.B. Starting the Report Builder

The Report Builder can open with the Getting Started window displayed. This opening window is optional and can be turned on or off with a switch setting in the Report Builder Options window. The Getting Started window offers 8 options:

**New report** -- Allows a report designer (a user that is creating or modifying a report design) to create a new report from scratch.

**New Dataset** -- Allows a report designer to create a new Dataset. Datasets are connections to Data Providers for a defined set of tables and columns. Datasets will be described later in this text

**Open** -- Opens a previously created and saved report, allowing the report designer to save their work and return to it to make more changes later.

**Recent** -- Displays a list of recently created reports. The report designer can select one of the recently worked reports and open it for modification.

**Table or Matrix Wizard** -- Starts a wizard that walks the report designer through the steps of creating a table or matrix report.

**Chart Wizard** -- Starts a wizard that walks the report designer through the steps of creating a Chart style report.

**Map Wizard** -- Starts a wizard that walks the report designer through the steps of creating a Map style report.

**Blank Report** -- Starts a wizard that walks the report designer through the steps of creating a report without any specific predefined formatting.

All of these tasks can be performed from the desktop of the SSRB, but the Getting Started window provides a good shortcut.

Before jumping into an actual report, however, let's take a quick look at the SQL Server Report Builder (SSRB).

The top of the SSRB supports a typical Office style ribbon with groups of functions designed to support the formatting of the report data. The functions are grouped into three tabs: Home, Insert and View.

The Home tab hosts a number of pure formatting functions. These allow different type fonts and sizes to be selected, borders to be placed around data, paragraph alignment to be selected, numbers to be formatted, et cetera.

The Insert tab allows different objects to be inserted into the report. Objects include the Table layout, the Matrix layout, the List layout, charts, gauges, maps lines, rectangles, sub reports, et cetera. As well, headers and footers can be added to the report using selections in the Insert tab.

The View tab defines the panes that are displayed on the SSRB Desktop. The five different panes can be turned on or off in three groups (Report Data, Groups and Properties). Turning off the display of any pane will allow more room for the pasteboard area. A fourth option on the View tab allows the rulers surrounding the pasteboard area to be turned off, again allowing more room if needed.

The Pasteboard is the central area of the SSRB where the actual report layout is created. It is called a Pasteboard after the layout boards used by newspaper and book publishers to create pages. Items (pieces of text, images, et cetera) are placed on the pasteboard in the desired position. Pieces of reports (called report objects) are placed on the pasteboard in the same manner, only electronically today.

The Report Data pane (left side of the SSRB) contains the various report objects. Included in the list of objects are:

> **Built-In Fields** -- A collection of special fields such as page numbers, dates, print times, et cetera.

> **Parameters** -- Fields defined to allow the users running the reports to enter values used to control the information printed on the report. For example, a report parameter can be defined to select a range of dates and only transactions within that range will be printed.

> **Images** -- A group of images can be loaded into this section and used in the report.

> **Data Sources** -- Connections to data providers (data bases, generally) are defined in this folder.

> **Datasets** -- A Dataset defines columns and rows to be defined that will be pulled from the data provider and placed on the report. Field names from the various columns are placed on the pasteboard to represent the desired location of the data in the report.

The Properties Pane is displayed on the right side of the SSRB desktop. A different set of properties is displayed in this area for each object on the report pasteboard. Selecting an object on the pasteboard causes the properties of that object to be displayed. Most of the properties for an object can be edited using windows or functions in the ribbon. A few properties can only be edited in the Properties pane. Properties will be defined completely in our companion book *SSRS Advanced Functions*.

The Group panes are found across the bottom of the SSRB desktop. Groups allow data to be grouped and, if desired, subtotaled by a common value. For example, all records for a specific customer can be displayed, followed by totals for that customer, and then the next customer group. Groups will be discussed later in detail.

**Properties
Pane**

The Properties Pane includes
some useful settings. For this
exercise, it will not be used.
Properties will be discussed in the
chapters on report formatting and
in the companion book *SSRS
Advanced Functions*

## II.C.  *That First Report*

It has always been easier to learn a new report writer by just diving in
and writing reports. We are going to do exactly that. In this chapter
we will design and create a basic report using a couple of tables and the
SSRB. We will create a simple Data Source/Dataset and use the fields
from that Dataset in the report. Our report will list customers and their
several addresses.

In later chapters, we will create a report using the Visual Studio tool
and explain the many options for creating Data Sources, report layouts,
embedded reports, the formatting of fields, grouping, and much more.
But, like is often said, we must learn to walk before we can run.

## II.C.1.  Getting Started

For this exercise, SQL Server Report Builder (SSRB) will be used.
Various different versions of SSRB exist and while features differ,
many of the basics can be performed in any of them. At the time of this
writing, the preferred version is Version 3. We will use that version in
this exercise and are assuming that the SSRB is already installed on the
desktop. If it is not installed, have the IT department of the firm install
the software.

1.  Open SSRB. If the Microsoft SSRB Getting Started Page is
    displayed, close it. The SSRB desktop will be displayed.

2.  Different panes may be displayed as the desktop is configu-
    rable. For this exercise, click on the Views tab. Check Report
    Data, Grouping, and Ruler. Leave Properties un-checked at this
    time.

## II.C.2.  Defining the Data Connections

A Data Source is an object that specifies a data provider (typically a database), that houses the information to be displayed on the report. Data
Sources establish a connection to the data provider and can be shared
between reports or can be embedded within the report and used only for
the current report.

Data Sources are similar to ODBCs that also provide a connection to
a data provider (such as MS-SQL). However, Data Sources are more
specific, selecting specific databases, tables, and fields. Further, Data

Sources can be built on top of ODBC's if desired although most of the Data Sources used with MS Dynamics applications will be built directly connecting to an MS-SQL server.

A Dataset is built upon a Data Source. The Dataset defines the specific tables, columns, and, optionally, rows of data that will be available to be displayed on the report.

Note that within the SSRB there are many ways to perform the same job. For example, to create a Data Source, the report designer can click on New in the Report Data window and select Data Source. If the report designer selects Dataset, an option is provided on the Dataset window to create a new Data Source. When a report object such as a table is placed on the pasteboard and no Dataset has been defined for the report, an option will be presented to select an existing Dataset or to create a new one, and for that matter create a new Data Source.

In this exercise, we will create each component individually. Just keep in mind that there are valid shortcuts that can be used successfully.

To create a new Data Source for the report:

1.      In the Report Data pane, click the New prompt. A pull down menu will be displayed.

2.      Select the Data Source option. The Data Source Properties window will be displayed.

3.      If there are any existing Shared Data Sources or Report Models, one can be selected, providing a short cut and instantly creating a connection to a specific Dataset. In this example, we will skip this option and create an Embedded Data Source, one specific to this report.

4.      Enter a Name for the Data Source. For this example, use GP-CustomerData.

5.      Select the Use a Connection Embedded in My Report option.

6.      Select a Type for the Data Source. A variety of different data providers can be used. In this book we will focus primarily on the MS-SQL Server provider. Chapter IV on Data Sources will discuss some of the other types available. For this exercise, select Microsoft SQL Server.

7.      An MS-SQL expert may elect to key in a Connection String. For most people, assistance in creating the Connection String is needed. For help building the Connection String, click the Edit button. The Connection Properties window will be displayed.

8.     The Data Source field will be filled in with the Data Type selected in the prior window. This should not need to be changed. If an error was made in selecting the data type, click on the Change button. For our exercise, do not change this value but leave it set to Microsoft SQL Server.

9.     Enter or select the name of the SQL server in the Server Name field. Any server that has already been used in the current report can be selected in the pull down list. Since this report is new, there are no selections and the name of the server must be keyed in. Server names are created by the consultant that installs the server software and application and will differ from site to site. Contact the IT department or the firm's support consultant to obtain the name of the database. Alternately, the Microsoft SQL Management Studio can be opened. The name of the server will appear in the top line of the Object Explorer.

10.    Select whether access to the data will be controlled by the user's windows credentials (Windows Authentication) or by a user ID established in SQL (SQL Server Authentication). Windows Authentication requires a SQL administrator to establish rights for a user to specific databases each time a user is created and given a Windows or Network user ID. SQL Authentication requires the user to specify an ID established in MS-SQL that has the rights necessary to access the data. Again, a SQL Administrator needs to setup this user ID and provide the appropriate access. Frequently, SQL Administrators will create a common SQL user ID such as Reports that is used to gain access to most of the tables needed in most reports. In our example, we have used the user ID sa and the sa password with SQL Server Authentication selected. The sa user and password is a special login with significant rights. Obtain a usable ID and password from the IT department.

11.    Check the Save My Password check box if the user ID and password entered is to be saved and used to modify the report. Saving the password makes editing the Connection Properties easier as the password will not need to be entered each time.

12.    In the Connect to a Database window, check on the Select or enter a Database Name option. Use the pull down list to show a list of databases in the specified Server. If no list of databases is presented, the Server Name and/or User Name/Password is incorrect. Select the desired database from the list provided. A database is created for each company supported by MS-SQL and MS Dynamics GP. An MS Dynamics database is included in the list but none of the company data is stored in this database. Select a database that contains the company data desired.

13. Do not use the Attach a Database File option.

14. Click on the Test Connection button to test the connection. If everything was specified properly, a Test Results window will announce Test Connection Succeeded.

15. Click OK to save the Connection String. (Additional options in the Connection Properties window will be discussed in Chapter IV-Accessing Data).

16. Generally speaking, leave the Use Single Transaction When Processing the Queries unchecked. This option will be discussed in the chapter on Accessing Data.

Shared Data Sources and Data Models can be used in the SSRB but cannot be created here. Later, the creation and use of Data Models will be discussed. The creation of Shared Data Sources is discussed in the Visual Studio reports builder chapters of this book.

To create a Dataset:

1. In the Report Data pane, click the New prompt. A pull down menu will be displayed.

2. Select the Dataset option. The Dataset Properties window will be displayed.

3. Enter a name for the Dataset. For our example, use CustomerInformation.

4. Select Use a Dataset Embedded in My Report for this example.

5. In the Data Source pull down window, the Data Source created earlier in this exercise should already be selected. If not, use the pull down list to locate the GPCustomerData Data Source.

6. For the Query Type, select the Text option.

7. Advanced users with experience writing SELECT statements can simply type in a Query String. Most users will want assistance in creating the Query String. Click the Query Builder button to open the Query Designer window.

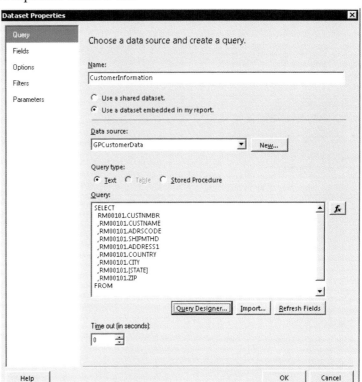

8. If the Query Designer window does not appear as shown below, click on the Edit as Text button on the menu bar of the window to toggle the display.

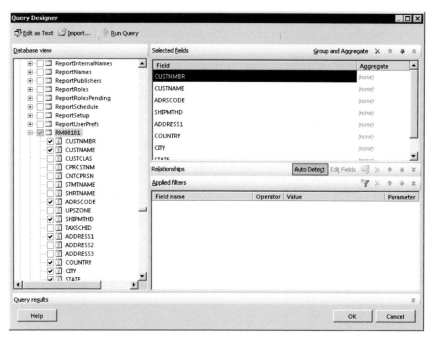

9. A list of tables available in the Data Source will be displayed in the Database View pane on the left side of the window. Locate the Customer Table (RM00101) and click the plus sign in front of the table name.

10. The fields in the RM00101 table will be shown. Check the fields to be included in the Dataset. These fields will be available for placement on the report. The Selected Fields pane will be completed automatically as fields are selected.

11. For this exercise, the Applied Filters pane will not be used. It will be explained later in this manual.

12. The SELECT statement can be tested by clicking on the Run Query icon in the top menu bar. The SELECT statement will be executed and the results shown in the Query Results pane at the bottom of the Designer window. This test is not necessary and the SELECT statement will be executed each time the report is executed to pull current data.

13. Click OK to close the query designer. A SELECT statement will be added to the Dataset Properties pane.

14. Additional features of the Dataset will be discussed in Chapter IV-Accessing Data. Click the OK button on the bottom of the Dataset Properties window to save the Dataset.

**What is a Pasteboard?**

Originally, and for hundreds of years, printers laid out pages by placing wood or lead type in a frame. When printing moved from the old flatbed presses to offset, pages were designed by printing strips of paper and pasting these strips onto a board, forming the pages. This board was called a pasteboard. As typesetting became completely electronic, the term pasteboard was retained, referring to the space on the designer's screen where elements to be printed were placed.

# II.C.3.    Creating the Report Body

SSRB allows users to create Table, Matrix, or List style reports easily. For this exercise, we are going to create a Table style report.

In the Ribbon, click on the Insert tab. A display of report objects appears in the ribbon. The objects are grouped based on their use.

In the Data Regions section of the Ribbon, locate the Table object. Click on the object and a drop down menu appears. Select Insert Table. Move the cursor over the Pasteboard and it changes form to a set of cross-hairs with a table attached. Place the cross-hairs at the upper left corner of the place on the pasteboard where the table is to be located and click.

A two row by 3 column table will be dropped onto the pasteboard. The top row is labeled Header and the bottom row is labeled Data. Click in the table area and the Table Frame appears.

Different menus can be displayed by clicking in different places on the Table. The column cells of the Table Header shows a menu with several column management options such as insert or delete columns. Clicking on the row cell of the Table Header shows a menu with several options for rows such as inserting or deleting rows. The upper left corner box produces a menu with options for the entire table such as access to the table properties menu. Right clicking in the various fields of the table produces menus with options for the table as well as the text box (the "cell" that holds data or header labels).

Lets generate a quick and easy report to start and then we will add more and more features to it.

Hover the cursor over a Text Box in the Data row. An icon appears that looks like a pull down list. Click on this icon and a list of fields in the Dataset is displayed. Select a field and the field data placeholder will appear in the Data Text Box and a default column label in the Header Text Box.

For the sample report, select Customer Number, Customer Name, and City for columns one, two and three.

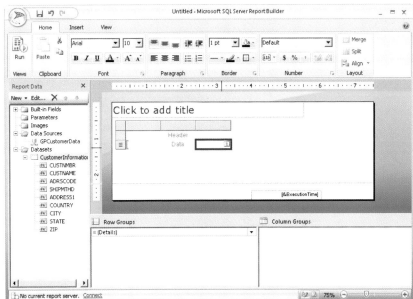

In addition to the drop down list of fields, the report designer can drag and drop a field name from the Dataset display in the Report Data pane. Click on the Plus Sign ( + ) icon in front of the Dataset folder and again in front of the actual Dataset to expand the Dataset and show the list of fields.

Click on the Click to Add Title. The cursor will change to a text cursor. Type a title such as "My Customer Address List".

In the Ribbon, click on the Home tab and click the Run icon to preview the report to date.

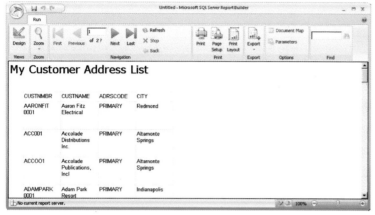

The Ribbon changes to one containing a single tab: Run. Options for viewing the report and locating data are found in this Ribbon. The report as designed is displayed in the central pane of the window.

On the far left end of the Ribbon is a button that will return to the Designer views. Reading left to right, the user will find Zoom buttons to control the size of the view, page controls (also called VCR buttons), printing buttons, several additional options, and a Find window. The Options allow the Document Map (to be discussed later in this book) to be shown or hidden and parameters to be re-entered, selecting different sets of data.

Looking at the quick and easy report that has been rendered, the reader will notice that several fields have wrapped into two or more lines. This causes each record on the report to use additional lines vertically and, if the report designer is trying to fill a pre-printed or predefined form, elements below the wrapped data will be placed in unexpected places. This action can be controlled in several ways.

Return to the Report Design mode by clicking on the Design button.

Hover the cursor over the Customer Number field (the data field, not the title) and right click. The Text Box/Tablix menu will be displayed. All of the options of this menu will be discussed in Chapter V-Basic Report Formatting.

From the menu, select Text Box Properties. The Text Box Properties window will be displayed for the selected Text Box. There are 9 screens to this window: General, Number, Alignment, Font, Border, Fill, Visibility, Interactive Sorting, and Action. These screens will all be discussed in Chapter V-Basic Report Formatting.

On the General screen of the Text Box Properties window, there is a check box named Allow Height to Increase. By default, this box is marked. Un-check the box and click OK. Repeat this for each of the fields and then re-run the report.

All data should occupy only one line. However, if the data is too long for the allowed space, the Text Box will not grow in width.

To adjust the width of fields, return to the Design view and click on the table, allowing the Table Frame to be displayed. Click on the line in the top of the Table Frame that marks the right end of the desired field and drag the line to the right. This will increase the width of the field.

# II.C.4.     Saving the Report

Saving the report allows a report designer to stop working, possibly publish the report to users, but also keep the source material in the event that changes are needed later.

To save a report, click on the SSRB icon in the upper left corner of the window. The SSRB menu will be displayed with options to save the report, create a new report or open existing reports.

Select the Save icon and save the report under the name of MyCusto-merList. The system will add an extension of .RDL to the title. This stands for Report Definition Language. For the technically inclined, reports are stored in XML.

# *II.D.   Multi-Table Report With Groups*

The report example above is a simple single table report.  Most frequently, reports will need to pull data from more than one table.  Totals, subtotals and groups are also common requirements.  This next exercise will demonstrate the creation of a report with multiple tables and provide grouping and totals as well.  In this exercise, we will also use the reports wizard.

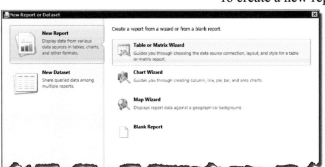

To create a new report, open the SSRB menu by clicking on the SSRB icon ( ) in the upper left of the window.  From the menu displayed, select New.  The Report Wizard will be displayed.

To create a new table or matrix report using a wizard, select the Table or Matrix Wizard option.  (To create a new report without using the wizard, select Blank Report).

For this exercise, select the Table or Matrix Wizard.

The New Table or Matrix -- Choose a Dataset window will be displayed.  In this window, click the Create A Dataset option and then click Next.  The New Table or Matrix -- Choose a Connection to a Data Source window will display.  Click the New button.

The Data Source Properties window as seen in Section II.C.2. above will be displayed.  Create a new Data Source as described in Section II.C.2. Name this Data Source *Customer Aging*.

Once the Data Source has been built, it will be displayed in the Choose a Connection to a Data Source window and will be selected by default.  Click the Next button.  The New Table or Matrix Design a Query window will be displayed.

This window was discussed briefly in Section II.C.2. above.  In this exercise, we are going to use multiple tables and build a relationship between the tables.

Click the Plus Sign ( + ) icon to the left of the word Tables in the database View pane of the window to expand the list of tables.  Scroll down to the RM00101 and RM00103 tables.  Check the box to the left of the two tables. This will select all fields from the two tables and add those fields to the Selected Fields pane.

In between the Selected Fields and the Applied Filters pane can be found the Relationship pane. Typically, this pane is collapsed. Click on the Line Expansion Arrows ( ⊗ ) icon to open the pane.

Click on the Auto Detect button at the top of the Relationships pane to delete the automatically detected relationship. Click on the Add Relationship icon at the top of the Relationships pane to add a new relationship. The Left and Right Table and Join Fields for the new relationship will be blank.

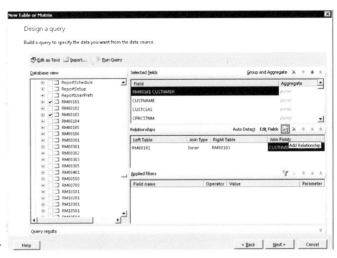

Click in the Left Table area in the new relationship to show a list of available tables. Select RM00101 to select the Customer Master table. Click in the Right Table area in the new relationship to show a list of available tables. Select RM00103 to select the Account Balances table. The Join Type should be set to Inner. See Chapter IV-Accessing Data for more information on the Join Types.

Double click in the Join Fields area of the new relationship to open the Edit Related fields window. Click in the field name space under the Left Join Field label to display a list of fields in the left table (RM00101 in our example.) Select the CUSTNMBR field. By default the Operator is set to = . Click in the field name space under the Right Join Field label to display a list of fields in the right table (RM00103 in our example.) Select CUSTNMBR from that table. This relationship will connect the two tables by the customer number field and when a record is pulled from the Customer Master table, records with the same customer number will be pulled from the Customer Account Balances table.

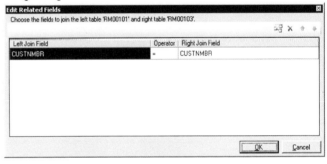

Click OK to save the related fields and return to the Design a Query window. The Relationship should look like the one in the example shown. Click Next on the New Table or Matrix wizard to display the Arrange Fields window.

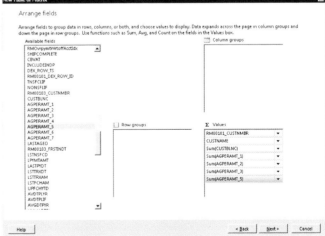

The Arrange Fields window allows the report designer to place fields in either a table style or a matrix style report. If fields are simply placed in the Values pane of the window, a simple table style report is created. If one or more fields are placed in the Row Groups pane, a table report grouped by those fields is created. (Groups will be discussed in detail later in this book). If fields are placed in both the Row and Column group panes, then a Matrix report is generated.

For this exercise place the following fields in the Values pane and leave the Row and Column Groups panes empty:

- RM00101.CUSTNMBR
- CUSTNAME
- CUSTBLNC
- AGPERAMT_1
- AGPERAMT_2
- AGPERAMT_3
- AGPERAMT_4
- AGPERAMT_5
- AGPERAMT_6
- AGPERAMT_7

Note that the amount fields will be converted to Sum aggregations under the assumption that some grouping will be performed.

Click the Next button to move to the Choose the Layout window. Accept the default layout and click the Next button to display the Choose a Style window. Accept the default and click the Finish button.

The report is basically ready to run. Of course, the amount columns need better headers and need to be formatted for currency. The 8 amounts selected are the customer balance and 7 aging buckets.

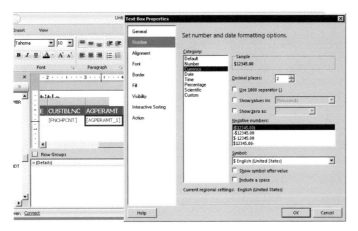

Hover the cursor over each of the numeric data fields individually and right click. From the Text Box/Tablix menu that appears, select Text Box Properties. On the Text Box Properties window, click on the Number screen. In the Category pane, click on Currency. Make any other adjustments desired to show the data with a leading currency symbol and the appropriate number of decimal places. Click OK.

Re-run the report to see all of the data properly formatted.

Aged account reports are frequently grouped by sales reps, allowing management to have the appropriate sales rep make necessary collection calls to late accounts.

To group rows of accounts by sales rep, hover the cursor over the Row Groups pane of the design desktop and right click. The menu that appears will have an Add Group option. Select Add Group and a second level menu will appear. Select Parent Group. The Tablix Group Properties window will appear.

In the Group Properties window, use the pull down list next to the Group By field to list all of the fields in the Dataset. From the list, locate and select the sales person ID (SLPRS-NID.) Also Mark the Add Group Header and Add Group Footer check boxes.

Click OK to close the Tablix Group Properties window and add the group to the report. Checking the Group Header and Group Footer boxes adds two rows to the report, one above the group and one below the group. The row below the group is used for group totals.

Before adding the group totals, create a row at the end of the report for grand totals. Hover the cursor over the tablix and right click. From the Text Box/Tablix menu, select Insert Row and from the sub-menu displayed, select Outside Group-Below. Clicking on this option will add a row to the bottom of the report.

To add totals to the report easily, hover the cursor over the two groups in the Row Groups area and right click. Select from the menu the Add Total option and select to place the totals after the data. Do this for each group (the Sales Person Group just created and the original Details Group). Totals are now found on the report.

Of course, the total amounts need to be formatted as currency just as the other amounts were.

## II.E.    *Formatting Options*

Designing a report is often more than just putting information on paper. To make a report more readable, lines, footers, bolding, images and other effects are required. Of course, the SQL Server Report Builder provides these options.

## II.E.1.    Page Header and Footers

Page headers and footers appear at the top and bottom of each page respectively. As with other formatting options, these objects are easy to add to any report.

In the SSRB, if a Wizard is used to create a report, by default a Page Footer is included and a common field ExecutionTime is displayed on the footer. To add a Page Header (or a Page Footer if one does not exist on the current report) hover the cursor over the report body and right click. From the menu that appears, select Insert. A list of objects that can be inserted into the report is displayed.

At the bottom of the list/menu, Page Header is listed (Page Footer will also appear if it does not already exist for the report).

Once the selection is made from the menu, a space will appear on the report pasteboard for the page header. Text Boxes can be dropped into the header and titles applied. Fields from the Built-In Fields in the Report Data pane can be dragged and dropped onto the Page Header and/or Footer. Parameters used to drive the report can also be dropped into the Page Header to document the entries made.

# II.E.2.    Text Formatting, Bolding, Underlining, Etc.

Text formatting options can be found on the Home tab in the Ribbon in the Design view. Any Text Box can be selected and formatted, including both labels and database provided information.

To apply formatting to a Text Box, select the Text Box by clicking on it. The formatting options in the Home tab become active.

In the Font area of the Home Tab, different type faces and sizes can be selected. The information in the selected Text Box can be bolded, underlined, or set as Italics.

In the Paragraph area of the Home Tab, the Text Box data can be centered, right justified, left justified, indented, numbered, et cetera.

Borders can be applied to a Text Box using the Border section of the Home tab.

Numbers can be formatted using the Number section of the Home tab. A pull down menu allows numbers to be set as Currency, Dates, Times, Percentage, pure numbers, Scientific Notation, or custom formatted. Buttons on the Ribbon turn on percent signs, currency symbols, thousands separators, et cetera.

The Layout section of the Home tab allows multiple cells to be merged, split, aligned, et cetera.

Formatting of data on the report can also be performed using the Properties pane. When multiple cells need to be formatted, they can be selected by holding the Shift Key and clicking on more than one cell. The Properties can then be set for all cells at one time. See our companion book *SSRS Advanced Functions* for information on properties managed in the Properties panes.

Right clicking on a Text Box opens a menu. One of the options on the menu is the Text Box Properties window. This window can be used to format the individual Text Box. Use of the Text Box Properties window is covered in detail in Chapter VI.

## II.E.3.     Total and Other Lines

Other than Page Headers and font management, lines are one of the most used objects for dressing out reports.  Lines allow sections to be visually split, column labels to be separated from the columns of data, totals to be separated from the list of values, et cetera.

Lines can be placed on SSRB reports in two manners:  as a graphic image using the line or rectangle tool, or as a border to a Text Box.

The Line and the Rectangle tools are found on the Insert tab of the Ribbon in the Design view.   Click on the Insert tab and look into the Report Items section.

Lines and Rectangles can be dragged and dropped onto the report.  However, they cannot span multiple Text Boxes.  Either object can be placed inside a Text Box or outside of a group of Text Boxes.  Using the Line or Rectangle object actually places a Text Box on the report pasteboard containing the line or outlined by the Rectangle.

To span a series of Text Boxes, the Border attribute is easier.  First, use the View tab to display the Properties panes.  Then select a group of Text Boxes using the Shift key and clicking in each of the cells to be selected.  Typically, a user will select several Text Boxes in a line to place a horizontal line on the form or several in a column to place a vertical line.  Once all of the desired Text Boxes have been selected, search in the Properties pane for Border group.  (If the Border group is not displayed, it is possible that the data inside the Text Box has been selected rather than the Text Box itself).  Expand the Border options (Border Color, Border Style, and Border Width.)  Each parameter can be set for each of the four sides of the Text Box.  Set the appropriate side to the desired style and weight of line.

Note:  By default, Text Boxes are placed on the report with a Light Gray line surrounding them.  To delete this line, the border must be cleared.

## II.E.4.     Summary

Many more formatting options are available.  Those discussed above are the most commonly used features.  Other formatting functions, including charts and graphs are discussed in Chapters V., VI., and VII..

# III. Reporting With Visual Studio

# III. Reporting With Visual Studio

Software Versions Used

Visual Studio 2008 is used in this exercise.

Visual Studio is a software development platform designed for developers. One of the types of objects that can be built using Visual Studio is reports built against the SQL databases. These reports can be created either by developers or by sophisticated report designers.

While most of the data retrieval and formatting functions found in Visual Studio are also found in the SQL Server Report Builder, the Visual Studio is a Project based tool. Projects allow common objects to be stored in a container called a Project and shared among other objects in the Project. For example, a Data Source can be created, stored in the Project as a Shared Data Source, and used by many different Datasets and/or reports.

Let's take a look at how reports are built using Visual Studio and then examine in detail the concept of Projects.

## III.A. That First Report

In these next few pages we will design and create a basic report using a couple of tables. We will create a simple Data Source and Dataset and use the fields from those objects in the report.

In later chapters, we will explain the many options for creating Data Sources, Datasets, report layouts, embedded reports, the formatting of fields, grouping and much more. But, like is often said, we must learn to walk before we can run.

### III.A.1. Getting Started

For this exercise, Visual Studio 2008 will be used. Various different versions of Visual Studio exist and while features differ, many of the basics can be performed in any of them. At the time of this writing, the current (as of this writing) preferred version is 2008.

1.    Open Visual Studio 2008. The Microsoft Visual Studio 2008 Start Page will be displayed.

2.    On the menu bar at the top, select File, then New, then Project to create a new project folder. The New Project window will be displayed.

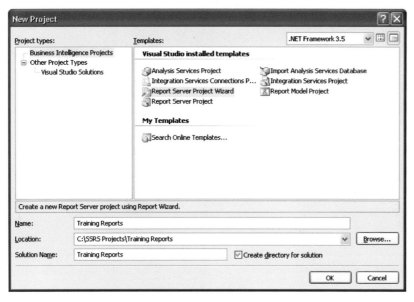

3.    In the Project Types window on the left, Highlight the Business Intelligence Projects. A variety of BI templates will be displayed in the Templates window on the right. In this text, we will be primarily interested in the Report Server Project Wizard, the Report Server Project, and the Report Model Project.

4.    Select Report Server Project Wizard. This wizard will step us through the various steps required to produce a report. The Report Server Project requires that the user knows the appropriate steps and can make the necessary selections in the proper sequence. The Report Model Project is used to create Report Models, allowing less technical users to build final layouts from preselected data sets.

5.    Provide a name for the new project in the Name field in the bottom section of the New Project window.

6.    Select a location where the project components will be stored. This location should be different from the final deployment location. If the project needs to be shared between multiple developers, select a shared folder on the server. By default, the system will select the user's document folder on the local machine.

7.    The Solution Name defaults to the Name of the Project. This can be changed if necessary. Leave the "Create Directory for Solution" box checked to create a new folder for the project. Otherwise, the location specified must already exist.

8.    When everything in the New Project folder is correct, click OK. The "Welcome to the Report Wizard" splash screen may be displayed. This screen can be disabled by checking the "Don't Show this Page Again" check box on the splash screen. Click Next to move to the Select the Data Source window.

# III.A.2.    Defining the Data Source

As mentioned earlier, a Data Source is an object that specifies a data base, set of tables and fields that are available to be used in the report. Data Sources can be defined and shared between reports within the same project or can be embedded within the report and used only for the current report.

Data Sources are similar to ODBC's that also provide a connection to a data provider (such as MS-SQL). However, Data Sources are more specific, selecting specific databases, tables, and fields. Further, Data Sources can be built on top of ODBC's if desired although most of the Data Sources used with MS Dynamics applications will be built directly connecting to an MS-SQL server.

When using the Report Wizard to select a data source, the Select Data Source window will be displayed.

In the Select Data Source window shown, the Shared Data Source option is greyed out and not available. We have just created a new project and there is no shared Data Source in the new project. Later, when this window is displayed again, users will have the option to select a Shared Data Source, assuming that some user creates a Shared Data Source.

To create a new Data Source:

1.     Select the New Data Source option.

2.     Enter a Name for the Data Source. For this example, use GPCustomerData.

3.     Select a Type for the Data Source. A variety of different data providers can be used. In this book we will focus primarily on the Microsoft SQL Server provider. Chapter IV on Accessing Data will discuss some of the other types available. For this exercise, select Microsoft SQL Server (which should be the default.)

4.   A MS-SQL expert may elect to key in a Connection String. For most people, assistance in creating the Connection String is needed. For help building the Connection String, click the Edit button. The Connection Properties window will be displayed.

5.   The Data Source field will be filled in with the Data Type selected in the prior window. This should not need to be changed. If an error was made in selecting the data type, click on the Change button. For our exercise, do not change this value but leave it set to Microsoft SQL Server.

6.   Enter or select the name of the SQL server in the Server Name field. Any server that has already been used in the current project can be selected in the pull down list. Since this project is new, there are no selections and the name of the server must be keyed in. Server names are created by the consultant that installs the server software and application and will differ from site to site. Contact the IT department or the firm's support consultant to obtain the name of the database. Alternately, the Microsoft SQL Management Studio can be opened. The name of the server will appear in top line of the Object Explorer.

7.   Select whether access to the data will be controlled by the user's windows credentials (Windows Authentication) or by a user ID established in SQL (SQL Server Authentication.) Windows Authentication requires a SQL administrator to establish rights for a user to specific databases each time a user is created and given a Windows or Network user ID. SQL Server Authentication requires the user to specify an ID established in MS-SQL that has the rights necessary to access the data. Again, a SQL Administrator needs to setup this user ID and provide the appropriate access. Frequently, SQL Administrators will create a common SQL user ID such as Reports that is used to gain access to most of the tables needed in most reports. In our example, we have used the user ID sa and the sa password with SQL Server Authentication selected.

8.   Check the Save My Password check box if the user ID and password entered is to be saved and used to execute the report. Saving the password makes editing the Connection Properties easier as the password will not need to be entered each time.

9.   In the Connect to a Database window, check on the Select or enter a Database Name option. Use the pull down list to show a list of databases in the specified Server. If no list of databases is presented, the Server Name and/or User Name/Password is incorrect. Select the desired database from the list provided.

10.   Click on the Test Connection button to test the connection. If everything was specified properly, a Test Results window will announce Test Connection Succeeded.

11.  Click OK to save the Connection String. (Additional options in the Connection Properties window will be discussed in Chapter IV-Data Sources).

12.  To make the new Data Source shared, or available to be used in additional reports in the project, check the Make this a Shared Data Source check box. For this exercise, check the box.

13.  Click the Next button on the bottom of the Select the Data Source window to move to the Design the Query window.

14.  Advanced users with experience writing SELECT statements can simply type in a Query. Most users will want assistance in creating the Query String. Click the Query Builder button to open the Query Designer window.

15.  If the Query Designer window does not appear as shown below, click on the Edit as Text button on the menu bar of the window to toggle the display.

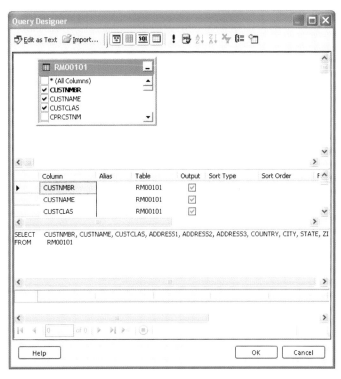

16.  Place the cursor in the upper panel and right click. From the menu that appears, select Add Table. From the list of tables that is displayed, locate and select RM00101. This is the MS Dynamics GP customer table.

17.  The RM00101 table will be placed in the pane as shown. Check the fields to be included in the Data Source. These fields will be available for placement on the report. The second and third pane will be completed automatically as fields are selected in the table. For the example, select the same list of fields shown in the third pane.

18.  The SELECT statement can be tested by clicking on the ! icon in the top menu bar. The SELECT statement will be executed and the results shown in the fourth pane. This test is not necessary and the SELECT statement will be executed each time the report is executed to pull current data.

19.  When the SELECT statement is constructed as desired, click the OK button to return to the Design the Query window. Additional features of the Query Designer will be discussed in Chapter IV-Accessing Data.

# III.A.3. Forming the Report

Typically, the majority of time is spent by designers in the report layout. Here, the data elements available in the Data Source are placed on the report itself. Totals, groups and subtotals, as well as headings, page numbers, and other formatting operations are specified here.

Our example report at this point is going to be a simple listing of customers. Many of the features available in this section will be discussed in detail in Chapter V-Basic Report Creation. Many additional parameters will be found in our companion book ***SSRS Advanced Functions.***

When using the Report Wizard, upon completing the Data Source, the Select the Report Type window will be shown. For our example, select the Tabular report and click Next. The Design the Table window will be shown.

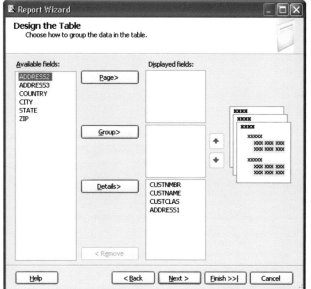

While SSRS developers like to think their tabular reports are a new design and in no way emulate banded reports, if it looks like a duck, walks like a duck, and quacks like a duck, it is a banded report. Banded reports, and SSRS tabular reports, work like this:

1.      Each time the page is turned, the page header is printed again.

2.      Detail lines are printed for each record returned from the database by the SELECT query.

3.      Whenever a Group By field changes, a group footer and header is printed.

The Design The Table window allows a designer to pick the fields to control and/or appear in each band or area of the report.

The fields selected in the Data Source will be shown in the Available Fields area. Fields can be moved into the other areas by highlighting them and clicking on the Page, Groupb or Details button.

Data fields that are to be printed in the page header are moved into the Page area. Fields that are to be printed in the body of the report are placed in the Details area by highlighting them and clicking the Details area.

If Detail records are to be grouped, insert the field to group by into the Group area. In some cases, more than one field is desired in the Group area but the data is only to be grouped on one of the fields. Only select the Group By fields at this point. For example, if a new group is needed for each customer number and the designer also wants the Customer

Name to appear in the group header, only select the Customer Number field at this point. Adding the Customer Name to the Group box at this point will cause the report to be grouped first by customer number and then grouped by customer name, as if there might be more than one customer name per customer number.

Multiple fields are added to the group box when multiple tiered grouping is desired. For example, the designer may want to first group customers by state and then by city. With this sorting, each time a city changes, totals for the city can be printed. Later, when the state changes, totals per state can be printed.

When additional fields such as the customer name need to be printed in the same band as the customer number, these fields are added in the Design Tab for the report.

For this example report, add each of the fields to the Details section. Do not add any fields to the Page or Group areas at this time.

Click the Next button to open the Choose the Table Style window. Several color schemes are provided and can be applied to the report by simply selecting the desired scheme. A preview of the sample on the right side of the screen shows the results of applying the color scheme to the report. Note that the Generic option removes all color formatting from the report.

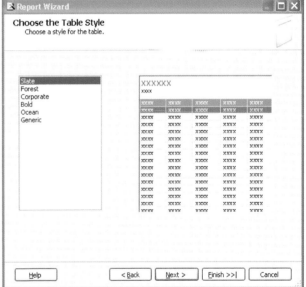

Select a color scheme for the example report and click Next to open the Completing the Wizard window.

In the Completing the Wizard window, enter a name for the report. This name will not only be used to file the report in the project but will be the default report title. For the example report, enter "Customer List" in the Report Name field.

The Completing the Wizard window shows a summary of the selections made for the report. There is also an option to Preview the Report. Check the Preview check box to open a preview when the Finish button is clicked. Leaving the box un-checked will open the Report Design tab when the Finish button is clicked.

Leave the Preview box unmarked and click the Finish button to open the new report in the project desktop.

# III.A.4.    The Report Design Desktop

When the Report Wizard is complete, the report is rendered in both a Design tab and a Preview tab in a Report Design Desktop. Technically, this is a version of the Project Desktop with a Report Design opened.

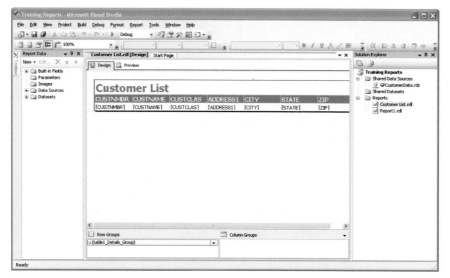

The Report Data pane at the far left of the window shows the fields that can or do appear on the report. This includes Built In Fields, Parameters, Images, Data Sources and Datasets.

The Solution Explorer on the far right of the window shows all of the components of the current project. The Customer List report is shown at the bottom of the Solution Explorer screen. That report is highlighted and displayed in the center of the window.

The pane in the center of the window has two tabs: Design and Preview. The Design tab shows the report in designer mode, allowing the user to make modifications to the layout of the report. The Preview tab executes the query and renders the report as users will see it.

The lower section of this area shows two group panes: the Row Groups and the Column Groups. Typically, tabular reports or simple lists may have row groups, pulling, for example, all customers in a single state, printing a subtotal break and then continuing with customers in the next state. Matrix reports will have groupings by both rows and groups.

Most of the work of designing reports will be performed in this area. Data Sources designed elsewhere and used in the current report can actually be modified from this desktop. Parameters, allowing users to select the specific sets of records from the Data Source to be displayed are defined in this area. Built In fields such as page numbers, execution times, User ID, et cetera can be added to the report layout from this area. Images and other fields from the Data Sources can be added to the layout.

A significant amount of formatting can be applied to the fields on the report and the report itself using the Report Design Desktop. The Toolbox on the far left expands to offer formatting tools such as lines, tables, rectangles, et cetera. Individual fields have property pages that can be manipulated as desired.

All of these formatting options will be discussed in Chapter V-Basic Report Creation.

# III.A.5.    Previewing A Report

To preview a report in the Report Design Desktop, click on the Preview tab. If the report was designed with a user ID and password recorded, providing immediate access to the information, the report will be rendered. Otherwise, the user will be requested to enter a user ID and Password and click a View Report button before the report is rendered.

Designers can switch back and forth between the Design and Preview tabs. Changes can be made, previewed, and then additional changes applied until the report is rendered as desired.

Preview the example report Customer List. Data in several of the fields is too long to be displayed in the space automatically provided and word wraps by default. Some of the formatting functions discussed in Chapter V will explain how to control this.

# III.A.6.    Publishing A Report

When the report is complete, the components of the report need to be published to the Report Manager.

If the Project is new, some configuration settings are required to tell the system the location of the Report Manger or SharePoint server. Click on Project and select Properties to open the Project's Property Pages. Complete the Target fields to specify the destination folders in the Report Manager for the various components and the Report Server's URL. Once these fields are properly completed, report objects can be deployed.

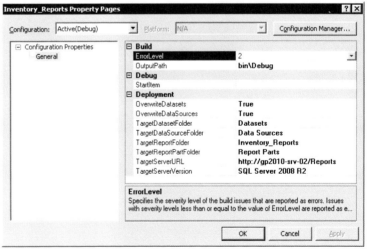

To deploy or publish all of the report objects in a project, right click on the Project Name in the Solution Explorer. To deploy only selected components, right click on those components. It is important to note that deploying a report also requires the Data Source, Dataset and any other components required by the report to be deployed.

From the menu displayed, select Deploy and the selected object(s) will be built and deployed to the destination Report Server.

See Chapter VIII of this manual on configuration of the Report Manager.

# III.B.  Projects

A project is a container in the report development tools that contains all of the pieces of the reports.  The Date Sources, Data Sets and the report layouts are stored in Projects.  When they are published, the objects are copied to the Report Manager but still remain in the Project.

Projects are convenient containers for the storage of common components.  For example, several Shared Data Sources may be defined for sales reports and then a group of sales reports created using those Data Sources.  A different project can be created for purchasing reports and the objects (Data Sources and Reports) contained in the Sales Reports Project will not be listed.

Some firms have hundreds or even thousands of custom reports.  Knowing where to find a particular report or its Data Source requires some organization.  Placing groups of like reports into Projects provides this organization.  Also, when writing purchasing reports, for example, the report author does not spend time ignoring the Data Sources and Report Files of the sales department since those are in a different project.

Yes, some lines can become blurred.  For example, manufacturing reports often require data from inventory tables.  This is not an issue since the project places no limitation on the Data Sources or the databases or tables it accesses.  The limitations of Projects are solely the standards adopted by the users.

When creating Projects, consider the users that will need access to the reports held in the project.  Again, any report when published can be deployed to any user or any folder in the Report Manager.  However, when maintenance needs to be performed on a report or changes are required, having all of the reports in the Sales Reports Folder located in the Sales Reports Project makes locating the report easier.

The Visual Studio project can be used to create a variety of code sets.  Only a few of these are SQL Server Report Service projects.  Many of the features in the project menus apply to types of projects outside of the realm of this book.  Many of these features will not be discussed and otherwise ignored in this book.  After all, we are focused on generating SSRS reports.

# III.B.1.    Creating a Project

When Visual Studio is first launched, the Start Page is shown with several different panes. One pane, the Recent Projects pane shows recent projects and provides a link to open an existing project or create a new one.

To create a new project:

4.       On the menu bar at the top, select File, then New, then Project to create a new project folder. The New Project window will be displayed. The  Create Project link can also be clicked in the Recent Projects pane. This link accomplishes the same result as the New Project window will be displayed.

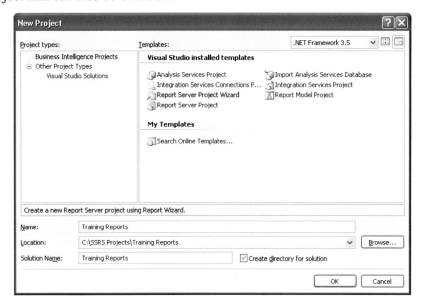

5.       In the Project Types window on the left, Highlight the Business Intelligence Projects. A variety of BI templates will be displayed in the Templates window on the right. In this text, we will be primarily interested in the Report Server Project Wizard, the Report Server Project and the Report Model Project.

6.       Provide a name for the new project in the Name field in the bottom section of the New Project window.

7.       Select a location where the project components will be stored. This location should be different from the final deployment location. If the project needs to be shared between multiple developers, select a shared folder on the server. By default, the system will select the user's document folder on the local machine.

8.       The Solution Name defaults to the Name of the Project. This can be changed if necessary. Leave the "Create Directory for Solution" box checked to create a new folder for the project. Otherwise, the location specified must already exist.

9.       Select a template for the first objects to be contained in the project. Templates for SSRS reports include The Report Server Project Wizard, the Report Server Project, and the Report

Model Project. Selecting the template defines the remainder of the creation process for the first object. Actually, the project folder is created as soon as the user clicks OK on this page. The template selection tells the software how to move forward.

10. When everything in the New Project folder is correct, click OK. The "Welcome to the Report Wizard" splash screen may be displayed. This screen can be disabled by checking the "Don't Show this Page Again" check box on the splash screen. Click Next to move to the Select the Data Source window.

The three report templates work this way:

**Report Server Project Wizard** -- This creates a project and then steps through a series of windows that lead the user through the creation of a report. This is the template that was used in the exercise in the prior chapter.

**Report Server Project** -- This template creates an empty project. The user needs to then specify which objects (Data Source, Data Set, Report, et cetera) is to be added to the project.

**Report Model Project** -- This special template walks the user through the creation of a report model. Report Models provide a predefined Data Source/Data Set that allows users to create customized reports without any understanding of the underlying data structures.

# III.B.2.    Opening an Existing Project

Projects can contain multiple Data Sources, Data Sets, and Report Definitions. Existing projects can easily be modified and new items added to the project.

When Visual Studio 2008 first opens, the Start Page contains a pane listing Recent Projects. Clicking on one of these projects will open that project.

If a project is not listed, click on File in the top menu and select Open, Project/Solution. A windows folder browser window will open. Browse to the folder where the desired Project is stored. Locate a file with a name that matches the desired Project and an extension of .sln. Select that file and click Open to open the project.

Depending on how the Project was closed, the Solution Explorer may not be displayed. This pane appears generally on the far right of the desktop and shows a list of all of the objects contained in the Project. To show the Solution Explorer window, select from the top menu View→Solution Explorer.

## III.B.2.a.    Editing Existing Objects

To edit an existing object in a Project, locate the object in the Solution Explorer and double-click it. The appropriate panes will open depending on the object selected.

Editing Data Sources, Data Sets, and Report Definitions will be discussed in the chapters that follow.

## III.B.2.b.    Creating New Objects

To add new objects to an existing Project, select from the top menu Project → Add New Item. The Add New Item window will open.

Four templates will be offered. To add a new Data Source, select the Data Source template. To add a new Dataset, select the Dataset template. A new report can be added by selecting either the Report or the Report Wizard template. The Report Wizard will walk the designer through a series of screens to create a new report. The Report template will expect the user to know the steps to follow.

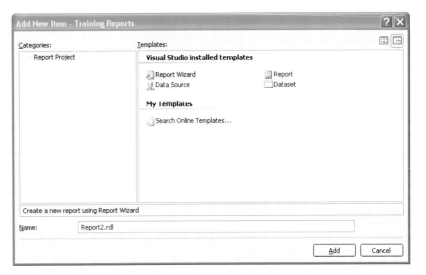

The chapters that follow will cover the process of creating these objects in detail.

## III.C.   *Panes and Views*

Visual Studio is designed to support a variety of development efforts. SSRS reports are but one of those efforts. Many of the panes and views available in Visual Studio do not apply to the creation or modification of reports and will be ignored in this discussion. Those listed below, however, can be useful to report developers.

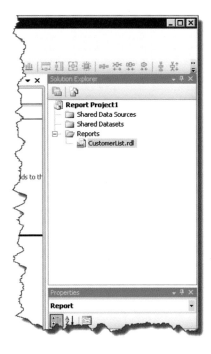

## III.C.1.   Solution Explorer

The Solution Explorer pane provides a view of the shared resources contained in the Project. If Shared Data Sources, Shared Data Sets, or Reports have been defined, they will be listed in the appropriate folder in this pane. Clicking on the appropriate object opens that object for editing.

## III.C.2.   Designer View

The Designer view is actually a series of panes typically selected by the report designer (the person creating the report) to show the information they desire. The center pane of the Designer view is the Design tab, where objects, Text Boxes, and data placeholders are organized into the desired format for the report.

## III.C.3.   Preview View

The Preview View executes the report as it is defined in the Design View and allows the report designer to see the effects of the layout specifications.

## III.C.4.   Code View

The Code View pane (View → Code Definition Window) allows source code for the current project to be examined and edited. Visual Basic programmers may find this view helpful. For most report designers, this may be an interesting pane to examine but will not be discussed in this text.

# III.C.5. Server Explorer

The Server Explorer lists the Data Connections (similar to Data Sources) that have been defined by the developer using this Project. Data Connections present the database in a manner similar to viewing the database in the SQL Management Studio.

# III.C.6. Output View

This pane is useful to report developers. When building or deploying the final version of the report, any errors generated will be displayed in this pane. The pane will automatically open to show the errors. The pane may be closed once the errors have been addressed.

# III.C.7. Properties Pane

Most of the properties of objects used in reports can be edited through the various property windows and tool bars. However, a slightly more technical Properties Pane can be displayed for each object.

The Properties Pane for each object lists all of the properties assignable to that object. For example, Text Boxes have properties such as Font, Alignment, type and fill colors, et cetera.

Unlike the Properties Windows, several objects of the same type can be selected at once and their common properties adjusted at one time. For example, several Text Boxes in a row can be selected and the top border defined for all of the selected Text Boxes using the Properties Pane.

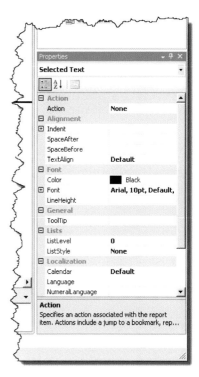

# III.C.8.    Document Outline View

Document Outlines are useful constructions for large reports that are normally displayed to screen rather than being printed. In the Document Outline View, selected fields are listed in sorted order. Clicking on one of the values scrolls the report directly to the data for that object.

For example, in a report listing open sales transactions for customers grouped by customer, one or more customers may have several pages of transactions while others have only one or two. Manually scrolling through the report to locate the customer can be time consuming. And, if the customer number or name can be repeated in addresses or in numeric fields, a Find operation may not locate the correct customer. By marking the customer number field as the outline field, a list of customer numbers will be displayed. Clicking on the customer number will scroll the body of the report directly to the customer's information.

# IV. Accessing Data

# IV.  Accessing Data

Before data can be placed on a report, the report must be told where to find the data, how to connect to the data, and what information must be provided. This involves three constructions: Data Providers, Data Sources and Datasets. It doesn't matter whether Visual Studio or SSRB is being used to create reports as these objects are common to both.

Data Providers are the holders of the data. An MS-SQL database and the MS-SQL software that provides access to that data is a Data Provider. SQL reports can also access data from additional Data Providers such as flat tables, Excel worksheets et cetera.

Data Sources are used to define the connections to the Data Providers. When a Data Source is defined, the instructions and drivers used to connect the report software to the Data Provider are selected. Creating a Data Source is somewhat like defining an ODBC connection. The report designer selects a connection type or driver and specifies the database and credentials needed to connect to the database.

If the report designer is using Visual Studio, Data Sources can be stored in the Project and shared. Shared Data Sources can be used in more than one report while non-shared data sources are only available to the one report contained in the project. In SSRB, a Data Source must be published to the Report Manager before it can be shared.

Datasets are collections of fields pulled from a Data Provider (or database) using a Data Source. The Data Source defines the connection to the data provider (a database, an ODBC et cetera) while a Dataset defines a query that pulls specific columns (including formulas) and rows from the Data Provider.

Data Sources were discussed briefly in the introduction chapter of this manual and used in the examples in the earlier chapters. In this chapter we split the definition of Data Sources and Datasets properly and explore more of the options available for the creation of these objects.

There are two other tools that will also be discussed in this chapter: The Query Designer and the Expression Builder. These tools are instrumental in the extraction of data from the provider and the presentation of that data to the report designer.

The Query Designer builds a SQL Select statement that will be used by the report to extract raw data from the Data Provider.

The Expression Builder allows the report designer to use extracted data, common fields, constants and functions to create calculated fields. For example, while simple formatting can extract the date only from a SQL date/time field, the Expression Builder can calculate a date 30 days from the date contained in the data.

**Software Versions Used**

Visual Studio 2008 and Sql Server Report Builder Version 3.0 are described in this chapter. Throughout the chapter, the following icons will be used to specify the report development tool being discussed:

 SSRB

This icon will appear next to any discussion that is unique to the Sql Server Report Builder Version 3.0

Microsoft® Visual Studio 2008

This icon will appear next to any discussion that is unique to the Visual Studio 2008 development environment.

All of these objects are common to both the SSRB and Visual Studio. However, some of the objects (the Query Designer in particular) look different in the two different tools. Watch the icons described above and be sure to review the material appropriate to the tool in use.

# IV.A.   Defining Data Sources

During the exercises in Chapters II & III, we walked through the process of creating a Data Source. Let's take a deeper look at the creation of a Data Source.

As stated earlier, Data Sources can be specific to and embedded in a report or, if Visual Studio is being used, the Data Source can be shared. Shared Data Sources can be used by any report generated inside the Project that contains the Shared Data Source. Embedded Data Sources are only used in the one report where they are defined.

Both Shared and Embedded Data Sources are created the same way. The difference between the two is the availability of the Shared Data Source to be used in other reports.

Data Sources can be created in a project by adding a new item and selecting Data Source as the item to add or by using the Report Wizard to create a new report and defining the Data Source as part of that process.

## IV.A.1.   SSRB Data Sources

Interestingly enough, while a Wizard is provided in Visual Studio for the creation of a Data Source, no Wizard is provided in the SSRB Version 3.0. Don't Panic! Data Source creation is very easy and can be completed in a few keystrokes.

In addition to an Embedded Data Source, a Report Model can be selected by the report designer that contains a predefined Data Source and Dataset.

# IV.A.1.a    SSRB Manual Creation

To create a new Data Source using the SQL Server Report Builder, either right click on the Data Sources folder in the Report Data pane and select Add Data Source or click on the New pull down menu and select Data Source. In either event, the Data Source Properties window will open. Two screens are available: General and Credentials.

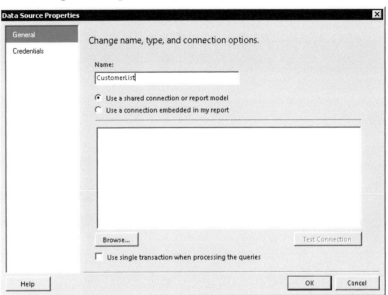

The General screen allows a report designer to select a Data Source already published to the Report Server or to create a new connection embedded in the current report.

To use a published Data Source, select the Use a Shared Connection option and click on the Browse button. Locate the report server and select the desired Data Source. A report model can also be selected from the current Report Server.

To create a new embedded Data Source, select the Use a Connection Embedded in My Report. The face of the Data Sources Properties General window will change slightly.

To create a new embedded connection:

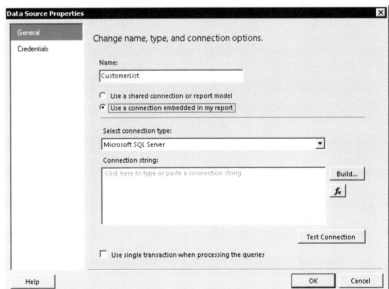

1.    Enter a Name for the Data Source. The name will be used to reference the Data Source.

2.    Select a Type for the Data Source. A variety of different data providers can be used. In this book we will focus primarily on the Microsoft SQL Server provider.

3.    An MS-SQL expert may elect to key in a Connection String. For most people, assistance in creating the Connection String is needed. For help building the Connection String, click the Edit button. The Connection Properties window will be displayed.

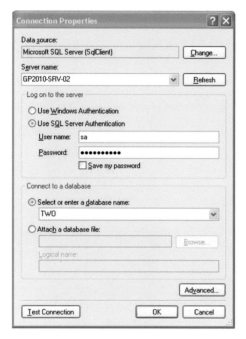

4. The Data Source field will be filled in with the Data Type selected in the prior window. This doesn't need to be changed. If an error was made in selecting the data type, click on the Change button. For our exercise, do not change this value but leave it set to Microsoft SQL Server.

5. Enter or select the name of the SQL server in the Server Name field. Any server that has already been used in the current project can be selected in the pull down list. Since this project is new, there are no selections and the name of the server must be keyed in. Server names are created by the consultant that installs the server software and application and will differ from site to site. Contact the IT department or the firm's support consultant to obtain the name of the database. Alternately, the Microsoft SQL Management Studio can be opened. The name of the server will appear in top line of the Object Explorer.

6. Select whether access to the data will be controlled by the user's windows credentials (Windows Authentication) or by a user ID established in SQL (SQL Server Authentication). Windows Authentication requires a SQL administrator to establish rights for a user to specific databases each time a user is created and given a Windows or Network user ID. The user's login to windows then provides access to MS-SQL. SQL Authentication requires the user to specify an ID established in MS-SQL that has the rights necessary to access the data. Again, a SQL Administrator needs to setup this user ID and provide the appropriate access. Frequently, SQL Administrators will create a common SQL user ID such as Reports that is used to gain access to most of the tables needed in most reports. In our example, we have used the user ID sa and the sa password with SQL Server Authentication selected.

7. Check the Save My Password check box if the user ID and password entered is to be saved with the Connection Properties. Saving the password makes editing the Connection Properties easier as the password will not need to be entered each time.

8. In the Connect to a Database window, check on the Select or enter a Database Name option. Use the pull down list to show a list of databases in the specified Server. If no list of databases is presented, the Server Name and/or User Name/Password is incorrect. Select the desired database from the list provided.

9. Click on the Test Connection button to test the connection. If everything was specified properly, a Test Results window will announce Test Connection Succeeded.

10. Click OK to save the Connection String.

# IV.A.2.    Visual Studio Data Sources

Visual Studio allows the creation of Data Sources using either a Wizard or manually. Additionally, a Data Model, containing a Data Source and Dataset can be defined in the Visual Studio and published, allowing SSRB users to begin report definition with a pre-defined set of data objects.

## IV.A.2.a.    DS Creation using a VS Wizard

During the exercise in Chapter II, we created a Data Source using the Report Wizard. We are going to review that process here, provide some additional details and look at some additional options available.

When using the Report Wizard to create a report, the first steps involve the selection of an existing Data Source or the creation of a new one. The Select Data Source window is displayed, allowing this selection.

To use an existing Data Source in the new report, select the Shared Data Source option button and then open the pull down list box. All of the Shared Data Sources stored in the current Project will be listed. Select the desired Data Source.

To create a new Data Source:

1.      Select the New Data Source option.

2.      Enter a Name for the Data Source. The name will be used to reference the Data Source. It is especially important if the new Data Source will be shared as the name assigned to the Data Source will appear in the pull down list of sources.

3.      Select a Type for the Data Source. A variety of different data providers can be used. In this book we will focus primarily on the Microsoft SQL Server provider.

4.      An MS-SQL expert may elect to key in a Connection String. For most people, assistance in creating the Connection String is

needed. For help building the Connection String, click the Edit button. The Connection Properties window will be displayed.

5. The Data Source field will be filled in with the Data Type selected in the prior window. This doesn't need to be changed. If an error was made in selecting the data type, click on the Change button. For our exercise, do not change this value but leave it set to Microsoft SQL Server.

6. Enter or select the name of the SQL server in the Server Name field. Any server that has already been used in the current project can be selected in the pull down list. Since this project is new, there are no selections and the name of the server must be keyed in. Server names are created by the consultant that installs the server software and application and will differ from site to site. Contact the IT department or the firm's support consultant to obtain the name of the database. Alternately, the Microsoft SQL Management Studio can be opened. The name of the server will appear in top line of the Object Explorer.

7. Select whether access to the data will be controlled by the user's windows credentials (Windows Authentication) or by a user ID established in SQL (SQL Server Authentication). Windows Authentication requires a SQL administrator to establish rights for a user to specific databases each time a user is created and given a Windows or Network user ID. The user's login to windows then provides access to MS-SQL. SQL Authentication requires the user to specify an ID established in MS-SQL that has the rights necessary to access the data. Again, a SQL Administrator needs to setup this user ID and provide the appropriate access. Frequently, SQL Administrators will create a common SQL user ID such as Reports that is used to gain access to most of the tables needed in most reports. In our example, we have used the user ID sa and the sa password with SQL Server Authentication selected.

8. Check the Save My Password check box if the user ID and password entered is to be saved with the Connection Properties. Saving the password makes editing the Connection Properties easier as the password will not need to be entered each time.

9. In the Connect to a Database window, check on the Select or enter a Database Name option. Use the pull down list to show a list of databases in the specified Server. If no list of databases is presented, the Server Name and/or User Name/Password is incorrect. Select the desired database from the list provided.

10. Click on the Test Connection button to test the connection. If everything was specified properly, a Test Results window will announce Test Connection Succeeded.

11. Click OK to save the Connection String.

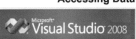

12. To make the new Data Source shared, or available to be used in additional reports in the project, check the Make this a Shared Data Source check box.

When a user runs a report using this data source, they may be required to provide credentials to gain access to the MS-SQL data. Credentials can be embedded in the data source and automatically submitted to MS-SQL. Using embedded credentials, the system will always sign on with the specified user ID and password, and users will not need to provide their own. To embed credentials in a Data Source:

1. On the Select the Data Source window, click on the Credentials button. The Data Source Credentials window will be displayed.

2. There are 4 options. Select the method to be used to authenticate the user when this Data Source is used:

   **Use Windows Authentication** -- Select this option to use ONLY windows authentication to gain access to the data. The SQL administrator will need to manage which user can access what data.

   **Use a specific user Name and Password** -- Using this method, a user ID and password are specified and always used by the Data Source to gain access to the data. This allows unchallenged access to run the report.

   **Prompt for Credentials** -- This option tells the system to prompt for a user ID and password. However, the developer can specify the prompt to be displayed.

   **No Credentials** -- This option tells the system to prompt the user for an ID and password using the default prompts.

3. Click OK to close the Data Source Credentials window and return to the Select the Data Source window.

When all information is entered as desired, click the Next button to save the Data Source and advance in the Wizard to the Data Set Definitions. See Section IV.B.1. below for information on creating a Data Set using the Report Wizard.

# IV.A.2.b.    VS Manual Creation

A Shared Data Source can be added to an existing project by selecting Project on the menu bar then Add a New Item.  From the Add New Item window that is displayed, double click on Data Source.  The Shared Data Source Properties window will be displayed.

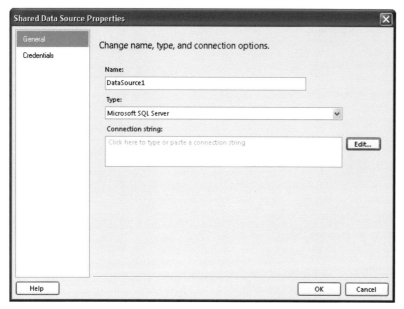

This window works very similar to the Select Data Source window in the wizard, except that there is no option to select an existing Data Source.  Also, it is assumed that the user is creating a Shared Data Source since this window is independent and not built into the Report Wizard.

There are two faces to the window: General and Credentials.  The set of fields to be shown is selected by clicking on the desired option in the list on the left.  By default, General is selected and the general fields are shown.

To create a Shared Data Source using this window:

1.    Enter a Name for the Data Source.  The name will be used to reference the Data Source.  It is especially important if the new Data Source will be shared as the name assigned to the Data Source will appear in the pull down list of sources.

2.    Select a Type for the Data Source.  A variety of different data providers can be used.  In this book we will focus primarily on the Microsoft SQL Server provider.

3.    An MS-SQL expert may elect to key in a Connection String. For most people, assistance in creating the Connection String is needed.  For help building the Connection String, click the Edit button.  The Connection Properties window will be displayed.

4.    The Data Source field will be filled in with the Data Type selected in the prior window.  This should not need to be changed. If an error was made in selecting the data type, click on the Change button.

5.    Enter or select the name of the SQL server in the Server Name field.  Any server that has already been used in the current project can be selected in the pull down list.  Since this project is new, there are no selections and the name of the server must

be keyed in. Server names are created by the consultant that installs the server software and application and will differ from site to site. Contact the IT department or the firm's support consultant to obtain the name of the database. Alternately, the Microsoft SQL Management Studio can be opened. The name of the server will appear in the top line of the Object Explorer.

6. Select whether access to the data will be controlled by the user's windows credentials (Windows Authentication) or by a user ID established in SQL (SQL Server Authentication). Windows Authentication requires a SQL administrator to establish rights for a user to specific databases each time a user is created and given a Windows or Network user ID. The user's login to windows then provides access to MS-SQL. SQL Authentication requires the user to specify an ID established in MS-SQL that has the rights necessary to access the data. Again, a SQL Administrator needs to setup this user ID and provide the appropriate access. Frequently, SQL Administrators will create a common SQL user ID such as Reports that is used to gain access to most of the tables needed in most reports. In our example, we have used the user ID sa and the sa password with SQL Server Authentication selected.

7. Check the Save My Password check box if the user ID and password entered is to be saved with the Connection Properties. Saving the password makes editing the Connection Properties easier as the password will not need to be entered each time.

8. In the Connect to a Database window, check on the Select or enter a Database Name option. Use the pull down list to show a list of databases in the specified Server. If no list of databases is presented, the Server Name and/or User Name/Password is incorrect. Select the desired database from the list provided.

9. Click on the Test Connection button to test the connection. If everything was specified properly, a Test Results window will announce Test Connection Succeeded.

10. Click OK to save the Connection String and return to the Shared Data Source Properties window.

11. Click on Credentials to change the Shared Data Source Properties window to show the credentials fields.

12.   There are 4 options.  Select the method to be used to authenticate the user when this Data Source is used:

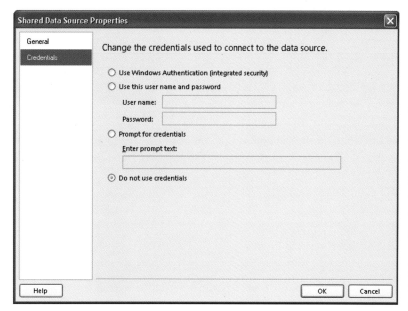

**Use Windows Authentication** -- Select this option to use ONLY windows authentication to gain access to the data.  The SQL administrator will need to manage which user can access what data.

**Use a specific user Name and Password** -- Using this method, a user ID and password are specified and always used by the Data Source to gain access to the data.  This allows unchallenged access to run the report.

**Prompt for Credentials** -- This option tells the system to prompt for a user ID and password.  However, the developer can specify the prompt to be displayed.

**Do Not Use Credentials** -- This option tells the system to prompt the user for an ID and password using the default prompts.

13.   Click OK to close the Shared Data Source Properties window and save the new Shared Data Source.

# IV.A.3.   Common Data Source Properties

A few of the properties found in the Data Source definitions are identical regardless of the tool used to create the Data Source.  Those are discussed here.

# IV.A.3.a.    Other Connection Types

The Data Connection Type window allows connections to be created to a wide variety of Data Providers. When the Connection Type pull down list is opened, a list of the registered provider types is displayed. This list can be different on each server, depending on the type of data providers installed in the environment. Listed below are some of the common provider types.

Each connection type requires it's own formatted Connection String. In all cases, either the Build button or the Function Builder will assist the report designer in selecting the appropriate components of the connection string and will then generate and display the connection string. The definitions below will identify the type of information required for each connection.

**Microsoft SQL Server** -- For reports written against MS Dynamics ERP applications, this will be the connection type selected. The Connection Properties window has been discussed in detail for this connection type in the preceding pages.

**Microsoft SQL Azure** — Azure is Microsoft's cloud based service, allowing database and infrastructure to be hosted remotely and accessed by any workstation with proper credentials. Azure Data Source Connection Properties are almost identical to the MS SQL Data Connection Properties. An Azure server should be selected.

**OLE DB** -- Use this option to create a connection to an OLE DB data provider. A link is first created to the data provider, a user ID and Password entered for testing and then an initial catalog selected.

**Microsoft SQL Server Analysis Services** -- This connection type is available only if MS SQL Server Analysis Services are installed. The report designer selects an analysis server, enters the appropriate user ID and Password to gain access to that server, and then selects a database in the analysis server.

**Oracle** -- This connection type allows access to data stored on an Oracle server. The Server name and a user ID and Password are entered to establish a connection to the database.

**ODBC** -- This connection type allows use of an already created ODBC connection on the local workstation. The Connection Properties require the selection of the ODBC as well as specification of a Login User Name and Password for testing. (ODBC connections can, among other things, retrieve data from an Excel Spreadsheet for use in an SSRS Report.)

**XML** -- This connection type allows data to be retrieved from an XML table. See the notes later in this section on creating a conection to an XML table.

**Microsoft SharePoint List** -- This connection type allows data to be retrieved from an Sharepoint List. See notes later in this chapter on creating a connection to a SharePoint List.

**TERADATA** -- This type of connector allows the report designer to extract data from a Teradata style data warehouse.

## IV.A.3.b.    Credentials

The second screen of the Data Source Properties window allows the report designer to record login credentials that will be used to run the report. Unless these credentials are recorded with the report, the end user will be required to provide credentials to access data in the data provider.

When using Visual Studio, user credentials can be stored in the project and published with the report. When using SSRB, the credentials are never stored with the report source definitions. They can, however, be entered into the Data Source just before publishing the report to the Report Server where they will be retained.

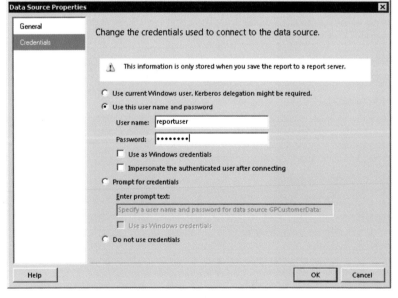

The report designer has four options:

**Use Current Windows User** -- The current windows user's credentials are used to log into the data provider.

**Use This User Name and Password** -- A special user name and password is provided in the next two fields and that user ID and password are passed to the data provider to gain access to the data.

**Prompt for Credentials** -- The end user will be asked to enter a user ID and password when the report is executed. Typically a special user ID and password are defined in the data provider and used to gain access. A field is provided where the report designer can specify a prompt string to be displayed when the user ID and password are requested.

**Do not Use Credentials** -- The end user is not asked to login. This is selected when the data provider is not secured.

# *IV.B.    Datasets*

Datasets, as has been stated earlier, define the rows and columns of data that are extracted from the Data Provider. Typically, Datasets are created by defining the query that will extract the data.

## IV.B.1.    Datasets for SSRB

Datasets for the SQL Server Report Builder are typically created for each report from the Data Source embedded in the report. A Data Model can be selected or a Dataset published to the Report Server can be selected. Since the SSRB does not use a Project to hold components of a report, a shared Dataset is not available other than those already published to the Report Server.

### IV.B.1.a.    SSRB Manual Creation

To create a Dataset in the SSRB:

1.      In the Report Data pane, click the New prompt. A pull down menu will be displayed. Select the Data Set option. Alternately, the report designer can right click on the Datasets leaf of the Report Data explorer and select Add a Data Set.

2.      Enter a name for the Dataset. For our example, use Customer-Information.

3.      Select Use a Dataset Embedded in My Report for this example.

4.      In the Data Source pull down window, the Data Source created earlier in this exercise should already be selected. If not, use the pull down list to locate the GPCustomerData Data Source.

5.      For the Query Type, select the Text option.

6.      Advanced users with experience writing SELECT statements can simply type in a Query String. Most users will want assistance in creating the Query String. Click the Query Builder button to open the Query Designer window.

7. If the Query Designer window does not appear as shown below, click on the Edit as Text button on the menu bar of the window to toggle the display.

8. A list of tables available in the Data Source will be displayed

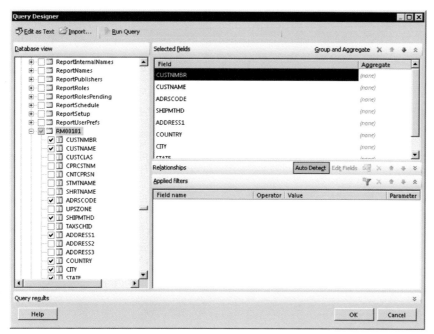

in the Database View pane on the left side of the window. Locate the Customer Table (RM00101) and click the plus sign in front of the table name.

9. The fields in the RM00101 table will be shown. Check the fields to be included in the Dataset. These fields will be available for placement on the report. The Selected Fields pane will be completed automatically as fields are selected.

10. For this exercise, the Applied Filters pane will not be used. It will be explained later in this manual.

11. The SELECT statement can be tested by clicking on the Run Query icon in the top menu bar. The SELECT statement will be executed and the results shown in the Query Results pane at the bottom of the Designer window. This test is not necessary and the SELECT statement will be executed each time the report is executed to pull current data.

12. Click OK to close the query designer. A SELECT statement will be added to the Dataset Properties pane.

# IV.B.2. Datasets for Visual Studio Reports

When using the Visual Studio to create reports, opening a wizard starts the entire process of creating a report, from building the Data Source, through the Dataset, to formatting the report. The Report Wizard section below discusses continuing the creation of a Dataset through the wizard.

Of course, a Dataset can be created manually using the Add Item → Dataset menu option as discussed in a few pages.

## IV.B.2.a Using the Report Wizard

From inside an existing Project, the Report Wizard is started by selecting Project on the menu bar then Add New Items. From the Add New Items window, double click on the Report Wizard icon. The Report Wizard starts by defining or selecting a Data Source and continues through the definition of the Dataset.

1.  The definition of a Dataset in the Report Wizard begins when the Design the Query window is displayed. Advanced users with experience writing SELECT statements can simply type in a Query String. Most users will want assistance in creating the Query String. Click the Query Builder button to open the Query Designer window.

2.  If the Query Designer window does not appear as shown below, click on the Edit as Text button on the menu bar of the window to toggle the display.

3.  Place the cursor in the upper panel and right click. From the menu that appears, select Add Table. From the list of tables that is displayed, locate and select the desired table. Multiple tables can be selected if desired. The selected tables will be placed in the top pane of the Query Designer window.

4.  When more than one table is selected, they must be linked or related by common fields. For example, the RM00101 table (the GP Customer Master Table) and the RM00102 table (the GP Customer Address Table) both contain a field called

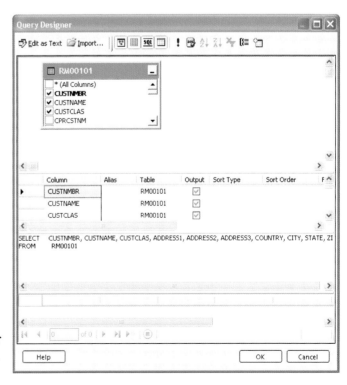

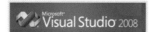

CUSTNMBR. This field holds the Customer Number by linking the RM00101 table to the RM00102 table by the Customer Number field, records from RM00101 - RM00102 pair with matching customer numbers will be pulled. See the comments below for information on the various relationships between tables.

5.  Check the fields to be included in the Data Source. These fields will be available for placement on the report. The second and third pane will be completed automatically as fields are selected in the table.

6.  The SELECT statement can be tested by clicking on the ! icon in the top menu bar. The SELECT statement will be executed and the results shown in the fourth pane. This test is not necessary and the SELECT statement will be executed each time the report is executed to pull current data. However, complex data relationships can be built using the Query Designer and multiple tables. It is best to test the query and ensure the results obtained are those desired. If not, simplify the query by removing tables and add them back in one by one, testing the results each time.

7.  When the SELECT statement is constructed as desired, click the OK button to return to the Design the Query window.

8.  Click the Next button to move on to the next step in the Report Wizard.

# IV.B.2.b    Manual Creation of a Dataset

Shared Data Sets are built using the Add Item → Dataset option. Click Project on the Desktop menu then Add Item and click the Dataset icon.

The Shared Dataset Properties window provides a number of additional features, allowing for the creation of a robust data set ready for placement on the report. Formulas can be defined, combining multiple fields and generating new values.

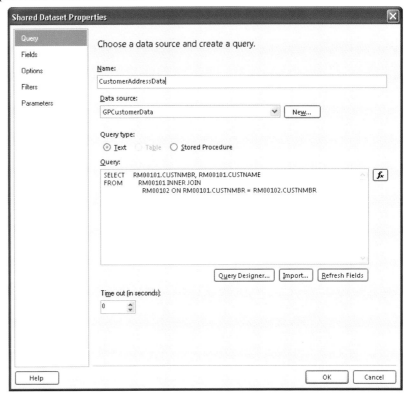

The Shared Dataset Properties window contains 5 screens: Query, Fields, Options, Filters and Parameters. The Query screen is used to define the query used to pull information from the Data Source. The Fields screen allows fields in the query to be renamed. The Options screen allows changes to Collation, Case Sensitivity et cetera to be made. The Filters screen allows restrictions to be applied to the data retrieved and the Parameters screen allows user parameters to be defined.

The definition of a Dataset begins with the Query screen of the window. The other screens are described in Section IV.B.3. Common Features of Datasets.

First, a **Name** is assigned to the new Dataset. This name will be used to refer to the Dataset in the project and assign the Dataset to reports.

Next, a **Data Source** must be selected. Use the Pull Down list to display a list of all shared Data Sources in the project and select the desired one. If necessary, the **New** button can be clicked to open the Shared Data Source Properties window, allowing the creation of a new Data Source to be used in the Dataset. See Section IV.A.2. above for information on using the Shared Data Source Properties window.

Three types of Queries are supported:

**Text** -- A typical query formed by building a SELECT statement is a text query. The Query Designer assists in building this type of query.

**Table** -- Some forms of Data Sources provide data in tables. A Table Query can then be built.

**Navigating To Select the Data Source using the Wizard**

To get to the Select the Data Source window in an existing project, select Project → Add New Item and select Report Wizard from the Add New Items window.

**Stored Procedure** -- SQL Stored Procedures can be segments of code that perform functions (such as aging the customer accounts) or code blocks that return collections of data. These later stored procedures can be used to provide data for an SSRS report.

To keep life simple, in this book we'll focus on Text Queries only!

As we have mentioned in several other places in this text, a qualified SQL developer might wish to write their own SELECT statement in the Query box. For most people, the Query Designer offers significant assistance in building a query through it's graphical interface. To use the Query Designer, click on the Query Designer button at the bottom of the Query text box. The Query Designer window will be displayed.

1. If the Query Designer window does not appear as shown below, click on the Edit as Text button on the menu bar of the window to toggle the display.

2. Place the cursor in the upper panel and right click. From the menu that appears, select Add Table. From the list of tables that is displayed, locate and select the desired table. Multiple tables can be selected if desired. The selected tables will be placed in the top pane of the Query Designer window.

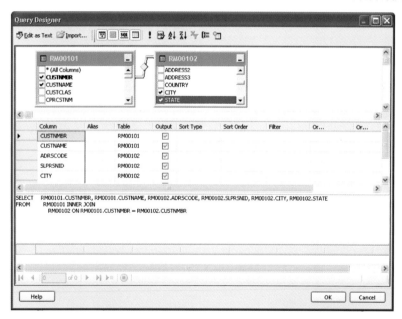

3. When more than one table is selected, they must be linked or related by common fields. For example, the RM00101 table (the GP Customer Master Table) and the RM00102 table (the GP Customer Address Table) both contain a field called CUSTNMBR. This field holds the Customer Number. by linking the RM00101 table to the RM00102 table by the customer number field, records from RM00101 - RM00102 pair with matching customer numbers will be pulled. See the comments below for information on the various relationships between tables.

4. Check the fields to be included in the Data Source. These fields will be available for placement on the report. The second and third pane will be completed automatically as fields are selected in the table.

5. The SELECT statement can be tested by clicking on the ! icon in the top menu bar. The SELECT statement will be executed and the results shown in the fourth pane. This test is not necessary and the SELECT statement will be executed each time

the report is executed to pull current data. However, complex data relationships can be built using the Query Designer and multiple tables. It is best to test the query and ensure the results obtained are those desired. If not, simplify the query by removing tables and add them back in one by one, testing the results each time.

6.  When the SELECT statement is constructed as desired, click the OK button to return to the Shared Dataset Properties window. The text query will be shown in the Query text field.

The **Import** button on the Query screen allows pre-written queries to be imported directly into the Query text field. Clicking on the Import button opens a file browser window that allows the user to locate .SQL or .RDL files to be imported. Select the appropriate file that contains a pre-written query and click the Open button to import the query.

The **Refresh Fields** button updates the list of fields provided by the Data Source. Frequently, in development environments, data tables will be updated by one developer while a second developer is working on SSRS reports. Alternately, the tables used in a Dataset may have changed since the Dataset was built and new fields added. Clicking on the Refresh Fields button updates the fields available in the Data Source.

The **Time Out** field is used when the Data Source is an MS-SQL type to provide a limit the amount of time the Dataset will wait for the provider to return data. Leaving the value at 0 will allow the system to wait indefinitely. Other values will cause the Dataset to time out after the specified number of seconds. Unless reports are hanging without an explanation, leave the Time Out value set to 0.

The Query screen is the only screen that is required. However, developers of reports usually find the Filters and Parameters screens very useful. All of the remaining screens are defined in the next few pages.

**Connection String Format**

Connection strings can be quite complex. The Connection Properties window makes the writing of a connection string easy and also generates a simple two component string.

# IV.B.3.    Common Features of Datasets

Whether a Dataset is defined in Visual Studio or the SSRB, several additional screens are available as part of the Dataset Properties window. These include the Fields, Options, Filters and Parameters screens.

## IV.B.3.a.    Fields

The Fields screen provides a list of all of the fields selected in the Dataset's query, allows the report designer to add more fields from the query and allows the report designer to create calculated fields.

The **Field Name** for a field retrieved from the Data Source's query cannot be changed. When new fields are added or calculated fields are created, the report designer can specify the name of the field. This field name will be used in the report.

The **Field Source** is as the name suggests, the source of the field. Fields in the Data Source's database can be entered or expressions created. Click on the Function ( $fx$ ) icon to open the Expression Builder to assist in creating an expression.

# IV.B.3.b.    Options

Typically, the values on the Options screen do not need to be changed. For most report designers, these values may even be a mystery. Do not change the values if the changes are not completely understood.

For reference, here is a definition of each of the fields on the Options screen:

**Collation** -- Basically, this is the sorting order for the data in the table being used. There are other schemes in the report writer that can easily be used to sort data without changing the collation. Collation goes deeper than simply sorting by considering special characters needed in some alphabets et cetera.

**Case Sensitivity** -- This setting determines if characters in the data returned from the data set should be considered different if they are uppercase or lower case. In other words, should 's' and 'S' be considered the same or different. Options include:

> **True** -- Upper and lower case letters are considered different.

> **False** -- Upper and lower case letters are considered the same.

> **Auto** -- Use the setting of the database.

**Accent Sensitivity** -- This indicates whether the data is accent sensitive or not. Possible answers are:

> **True** -- Accent sensitivity is used.

> **False** -- Accent sensitivity is not used (accents are ignored).

> **Auto** -- The accent sensitivity of the database is used. If the data provider does not support accent sensitivity, it is treated as false.

**Kanatype Sensitivity** -- This value is used to specify whether the data is Kanatype sensitive. It is used to specify whether the Dataset needs to different between the two types of Japanese Kana characters Hiragana and Katakana. Options are:

**True** -- Data is to be treated as Kanatype sensitive.

**False** -- Do not treat the data as Kanatype sensitive.

**Auto** -- The setting of the data provider is used. If the data provider does not support Kanatype sensitivity, the report runs as if the value is set to False.

**Width Sensitivity** -- This setting determines whether the data is width sensitive. Width sensitivity applies to the space characters consumed on screen or on paper. For example, the letter 'i' requires less width than the letter 'W'. Options are:

**True** -- Indicates that the data is width sensitive.

**False** -- Indicates that the data is NOT width sensitive.

**Auto** -- This tells the report server to attempt to recover the setting from the data provider (the Data Source). If the data provider does not support the width sensitivity type, the report runs as if the setting is False.

**Interpret Subtotals as Detail Rows** -- A Dataset query can be configured to return aggregated or subtotal rows. This setting instructs the report to treat aggregated rows or subtotals as details.

**True** -- Treat aggregated rows as detail rows.

**False** -- Do not treat aggregated rows as detail rows.

**Auto** -- If the report does not use the Aggregate function, the report should treat subtotal rows as detail rows.

# IV.B.3.c. Filters

The Filters Screen allows restrictions to be placed on the rows of data returned by the Dataset. For example, if a report is to be created that only lists customers assigned to a specific sales rep, a restriction can be defined that will return ONLY those desired customer records.

Multiple filters can be defined for a single Dataset. In the example shown, three filters are defined. The first filter restricts the data to customers whose sales person is RLW. The second restricts the returned data to customers in the state of FL while the third filter restricts data to customers in the city of Orlando. When the report using this Dataset is run, only the customers of RLW in Orlando, Florida will appear on the report.

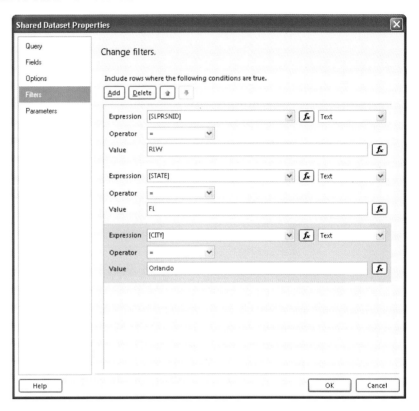

The Filters screen has significant power, up to a point. There are numerous ways to define filters and the fields or values used to select data. However, when more than one filter is defined, as in the example shown, all comparisons must be true for a record to be selected from the Dataset. For example, using the filters shown in the example, if a customer is located in Orlando, Florida but is assigned to a sales representative other than RLW, that customer will not appear on the report!

Let's look at some of the other features of the Filter screen.

The **Add** button adds a filter to the list. When the Filter screen is first displayed, there are no fields available for the definition of a restriction. Clicking the Add button adds a set of filter fields to the list.

The **Delete** button will remove a filter from the list. Highlight the filter set to be deleted and then click the Delete button.

The **Up Arrow** button will move a filter up in the list. Highlight the filter to be moved and click the Up Arrow icon.

The **Down Arrow** button works exactly the same as the Up Arrow, only moving the filter down in the list.

For each filter, there are four fields and two function buttons.

The **Expression** field is used to select the Dataset field to be matched. Using the pull down list box, a list of fields selected in the query is shown. Select the desired field.

The Function Icon ( $f_x$ ) allows a function to be written around the data fields. For example, the report designer may want to select all records where the ZIP code starts with "3". Clicking on the function icon opens the Expression window. See the section below on the use of the Expression window.

The Comparison Type field tells the filter how to compare the Expression to the Value. For example, when using Greater Than or Less Than operators, considering the expression to be Text versus an Integer can yield different results. Valid Comparison Types are:

**Text** -- The field or expression is considered to be text, even if the text is composed of numbers.

**Boolean** -- The field or expression is evaluated as either true or false. Any value that equals 0 is considered false, other values are considered True.

**Date/Time** -- The field or expression is considered to be a SQL Date/Time value.

**Integer** -- The field or expression is considered to be an integer.

**Float** -- The field or expression is considered to be a float value with decimal points.

An example of the importance of the Comparison Type field is seen when lists of numbers are used. If a text comparison is performed, the text 2 is considered greater than the text 15. However if an integer comparison is performed, the number 2 is less than the number 15.

The Operator field determines how the Expression is compared to the Value. Valid operators are:

**=** -- The Expression must equal the value for the filter to be evaluated as True.

**<>** -- The Expression must be different from the value for the filter to be evaluated as True.

**Like** -- The Expression must match the fixed portion of the value. For example, if the value is expressed as RL%, any Expression starting with RL followed by any characters will cause the comparison to be evaluated as True.

**>** -- The Expression must be greater than the Value field for the filter to be evaluated as true.

>= -- The Expression must be greater than or equal to the Value field for the filter to be evaluated as true.

< -- The Expression must be less than the Value field for the filter to be evaluated as true.

<= -- The Expression must be less than or equal to the Value field for the filter to be evaluated as true.

**Top N** -- The data is sorted by the Expression field and a specified number of records is selected from the top of the list. The number of records to be returned by the Data Source is specified in the Value Field.

**Bottom N** -- The data is sorted by the Expression field and a specified number of records is selected from the bottom of the list. The number of records to be returned by the Data Source is specified in the Value Field.

**Top %** -- The data is sorted by the Expression field and a percentage of the total number of records is selected from the top of the list. The percentage to be returned by the Data Source is specified in the Value Field.

**Bottom %** -- The data is sorted by the Expression field and a percentage of the total number of records is selected from the top of the list. The percentage to be returned by the Data Source is specified in the Value Field.

**In** -- The data found in the field specified in the Expression field must appear in the list of values entered into the Value field.

**Between** -- The Value field is split into two fields and the value found in the field specified in the Expression field must be between the first and last values entered in the two Value fields.

Data can be manually entered into the Value field for the comparisons or the Function button can be clicked, opening the Expression window where a calculation can be built to generate the value(s).

# IV.B.3.d.  Parameters

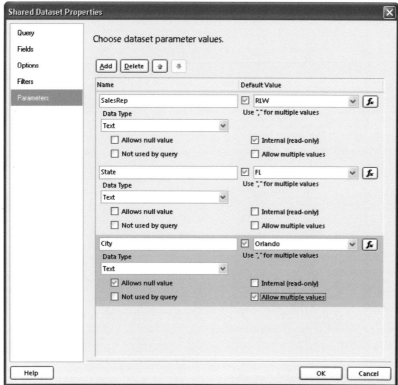

When a query is created, the query is parsed and for each query parameter defined, a matching parameter is created in the Parameters screen. This screen can be used to add, edit or delete any parameters from the query.

Note: Parameters in Datasets can be left unchanged. Report parameters will make all of the necessary connections.

For each query parameter that is parsed, a report parameter is created. When the query is changed, new parameters are created as needed.

To add a parameter, click the Add button and then complete the following fields. One set of fields is created each time the Add button is clicked.

**Parameter Name** -- The parameter name is case sensitive and cannot contain any blanks.

**Default Value** -- Enter a value for the query parameter. This can be a static value (meaning that only rows will be returned that match the fixed value) or a reference to a report parameter. (This is only available for Shared Datasets.)

**Data Type** -- Specify the type of data for the query. The type of data defines the way the comparisons work. If, for example, numbers are entered in the value fields, numeric data is compared different than strings of digits.

**Allow Nulls** -- If this box is checked, the report designer can leave the value empty and the user, if the parameter is related to a report parameter, can leave the report parameter empty. (This is only available for Shared Datasets.)

**Read Only** -- This marks the parameter as read only. When a shared Dataset is added to a report, this field will not be shown and the default value cannot be changed. (This is only available for Shared Datasets.)

**Omit from Query** -- When a reference to a report parameter is an expression in the shared dataset filter and not actually in the query, select this option. A default value is not required. (This is only available for Shared Datasets.)

# IV.C. Query Designer Options

We have talked briefly about the Query Designer window in earlier sections of this book. This graphical window assists novices and even most experienced users in creating a SQL SELECT statement, ensuring that the syntax of the statement is correct. There are quite a number of options and features in this window providing significant power.

The Query Designer is different for Visual Studio and SSRB Version 3.0. Each of these performs the same function but with slightly different screens.

# IV.C.1. SSRB Query Designer

The SSRB Query Designer window is divided into five panes, most of which can be collapsed or expanded as needed to provide more room for the report designer to work. The Line Expansion Icon ( ) on the right edge of four of the panes control the display or hiding of the pane.

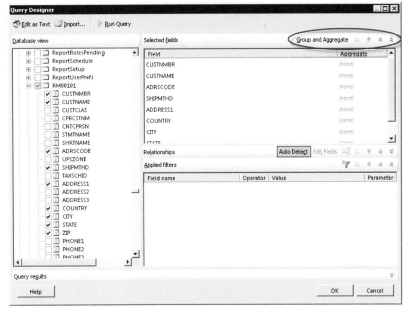

Three of the panes (the Selected Fields, the Relationships and the Applied filters panes) have a collection of buttons that allow the contents of the pane to be built, edited or deleted.

Generally, objects in the Data Source (found in the Database pane) are selected to be used in the report. These fields then appear in the Selected Fields pane.

Relationships between different tables are defined in the Relationships pane to make sure that the properly matching records are retrieved. Then filters are added using the Applied Filters pane to restrict the data returned. Parameters entered by the user at the time the report is executed are defined elsewhere.

When the query is tested, the results are displayed in the Query Results pane.

# IV.C.1.a.    The Database Pane

The General Pane of the Dataset Properties has selected a connection to a Data Provider.  In the Database Pane, all of the types of objects that can provide information for the report are listed in an explorer form.  For MS SQL Server databases the objects are:

**Tables** -- The collection of native data tables contained in the databases.  The tables have columns or fields defined and hold the data for the application.

**Views** -- Views are structures in MS-SQL that combine one or more tables in a prescribed manner and pre-select fields from those tables or create new fields through formulas.  Views appear as tables to a report designer but some combinations of data tables are best performed by creating a view.

**Stored Procedures** -- Stored Procedures are snip-its of SQL code that are stored and pre-compiled for faster execution.  Some stored procedures perform functions on tables while others define sets of data.  When a Stored Procedure that defines a set of data is selected, the available fields of that Stored Procedure can be exposed and used in the report.

**Table Value Functions** -- Table Value Functions are user defined functions that return tables of data.  These tables can be used in reports just like a native table or Stored Procedure table.

Expanding one of these types of data shows the available objects of that type.  For example, expanding the Tables object by clicking on the Plus Sign Icon ( + ) to the left of the Tables folder will show a list of Tables.  Expanding a Table by again clicking on the Plus Sign Icon will show a list of fields in the table.  Either the Table as a whole or individual fields in the table can be added to the Dataset by clicking the check box to the left of the table or field.

Use the Database Pane to select the fields and/or tables (views, stored procedures, and/or Table Valued functions) to provide data columns to the report.

# IV.C.1.b.    The Selected Fields Pane

Initially, the Selected Fields pane displays the fields marked in the Database pane. However, a number of additional functions can be performed on these selected fields.

The Line Expansion Icon ( ⊗ ) to the far right on the top of the pane hides or exposes the Selected Fields pane. This is used to make additional room in the Query Designer to work in other panes.

The Up and Down arrows in the group of icons at the top of the Selected Fields pane allows a field to be moved up or down in the listing. Select a field and then click on either the up or down arrow to move that field.

The Group and Aggregate button changes the selection of fields from details to summary data grouped by one or more fields. For example, if a report designer wants to list the open documents for all customers and group them by the customer number and document type, then display only the total of the documents for each customer by each type, the Group and Aggregate button will be used.

In the example shown, three fields are selected: The customer number, the receivables document type and the current transaction amount. The Group and Aggregate button was clicked, turning the query from a detail query to one that returns summary information.

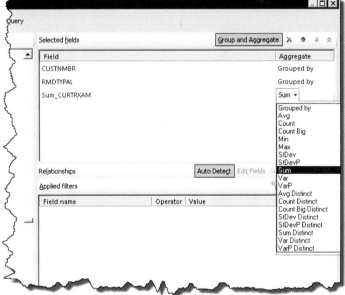

Two fields are marked as Group By fields: The customer number and the document type. This will group data first by the customer number and then, for each customer, by the document type. To group first by the document type and then by the customer, the placement of the two fields in the list would be reversed.

Any field that is not a Group By field must be aggregated. That means that one of the grouping or aggregation functions must be selected for each remaining field. In this display, the only remaining field is the Current Transaction Amount (CURTRXAM). Notice that it is marked with a SUM function, indicating that all values for each of the records will be summed together for each grouping.

Other aggregation functions include:

**Avg** -- The average of the values encountered will be calculated and displayed.

**Count** -- The count of the records encountered will be displayed. For example, if records are aggregated by customer and the document numbers are aggregated using the count function, the count of the number of documents will be displayed.

**Count Big** -- This works the same as the Count but a Big integer is used, allowing for an accurate count of a large number of records to be displayed.

**Min** -- The minimum value encountered for the selected field is displayed.

**Max** -- The maximum value encountered for the selected field is displayed.

**StDev** -- The standard deviation of the values of the fields grouped is calculated and displayed.

**StDevP** -- This is a special form of the StDev function. The StDev function can perform a Standard Deviation calculation on other functions. The StDevP only performs Standard Deviation calculations on pure numeric data.

**Sum** -- The sum of all of the values in the group is calculated and displayed.

**Var** -- This function returns the variance of all non-null values in the group. The variance is the difference between the individual values and the standard deviation.

**VarP** -- This function performs the Variance function only on pure numeric data.

**Distinct Functions** -- Several Distinct functions are provided. These perform the same function as the non-distinct functions but only use one occurrence of a value. For example, if the value 15 appears more than one time in a group, only one occurrence of 15 is used in the calculation.

## IV.C.1.c.    The Relationships Pane

The Relationships Pane is used when more than one table has been selected to provide data to the report. It is vital that the relationships between the tables be defined. Unless a relationship is defined, when the query is executed, each record from the first table would be matched with each and every record in the second table. And if there were multiple tables defined, millions of false records would be defined. Fortunately, SSRB will return an error if the tables are not related, preventing such an obvious problem.

Relationships between tables must be meaningful. For example, in a report listing open receivable items, the open item table often contains only a customer number and then details about the transaction, but nothing else about the customer. To get the customer name, the open items table must be related to the customer table. The customer number field exists in both tables and is the natural way to establish the relationship.

In MS Dynamics GP, most tables contain a field called DexRowID. Every table contains one. To relate the tables by the DexRowID does not work. While the field name is identical, the data in the DexRowID for the customer record does not necessarily match the DexRowID for the open items. For that matter, each open item has a different DexRowID value, meaning that while most customers can have multiple open items, using the DexRowID will result in only one match, if any, and the open item probably will not match the customer.

Just because field names match does not mean the data in the fields will create a proper relationship. The fields selected to relate records must contain meaningful data. For example, the customer number in the customer table is a unique identifier and selects one customer from that table. Each open item in the open item table must be related to one customer. Using the customer number to relate these tables makes perfect sense and works.

Some table pairs require more than one field to establish a relationship. The customer address table can contain several different addresses for one customer. Relating the customer table to the customer address table by the customer number will return every address for the customer. If this is what the report designer wants, this works. However, if the report designer only wants the billing address, then the customer table must be related to the address table by both the customer number and the address ID. In the customer record, a special field is used to record the address ID of the billing address. In the customer address table, one field is named the Address ID field. Relate the two tables first by the customer number then match the customer's billing address ID to the address table's Address ID field. (The match of customer number to customer number is required since the address IDs are not unique. More than one customer, for example, might have an address with an ID of PRIMARY).

Relationships between tables are defined in the Query Designer in the Relationships pane. Click on the Line Expansion Icon ( ⊻ ) at the far right edge of the top of the pane to expand the pane and display any contents. Up and Down arrows for the pane allows entries to be moved up or down in the list.

The Auto Detect button instructs the SSRB to attempt to automatically detect relationships between the tables. For MS Dynamics products, this most often fails. Click the button to remove the Auto Detect attempts.

The Add Relationship ( ) icon adds a new table relationship to the pane and allows the report designer to enter or edit the parameters for the relationship. To edit any existing relationship, highlight that line in the pane and click on the Edit Fields button.

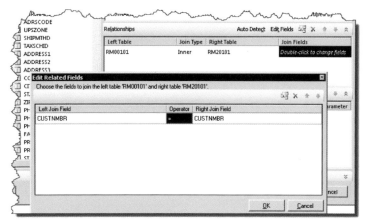

In the Relationships pane, in the new row, click in the Left Table space. A list of available tables will be displayed. Select the table to become the Left table.

Click on the Join Type to select the appropriate relationship. In most cases, either an Inner Join or a Left Outer Join will be used. The join types are defined below:

Next, click in the Right Table space and select from the list displayed the table that will become the Right Table.

The Left and Right table positions are important in the processing of the relationship (called a Join in SQL). Records are first pulled from the Left table one at a time and then for each record in the Left Table matching records are pulled from the Right Table. When all matching records have been pulled from the Right Table, the next record is pulled from the Left Table. Which records are pulled from the two tables depends on the Join Type and the Join Fields. Let's look at the different types of Joins and the way they work.

### Fields in a Relationship

The two different fields in each line of a relationship must match in both data content as well as data type.

Data stored in a table can be stored in several forms. Characters, Strings, Integers, Floating Numbers and Dates are general examples of the different data types.

When creating a relationship, fields of the same type must be compared. For example, strings should be compared to strings. If a string is compared to a date, even if the string contains data that looks like a date, SQL will not find a match.

**Inner** -- A record is pulled from the left table and then each matching record from the right table is pulled. If more than one matching record exists in the right table, one line is displayed for each match. If no matches exist in the right table, no data is returned from either table. After attempts to locate matching records in the right table are complete, the next record in the left table is pulled and the process repeats.

**Left Outer** -- A record is pulled from the left table. The system then attempts to pull matching records from the right table. If no matching records are found in the right table, one row is returned with information only from the left table. If one or more matching records are found in the right table, one line is returned for each match.

**Right Outer** -- This works just like the Left Outer except the left and right tables are reversed.

**Full Outer** -- Records from either the right or the left table that do not have matching records in the other table are returned.

How the left and right tables are related depends on the Join Fields. To enter join fields, click on the space in the Relationship under the Join Fields prompt. The Edit Related Fields window opens, allowing the report designer to select the fields and the operator.

Clicking in the space under the Left Join Field displays a list of fields found in the left table. Select the desired table. Clicking in the space under the Right Join Field displays a list of fields found in the right table. Again, select the desired fields. The operator defaults to the equals operator, meaning that the data in the right field must be equal to the data in the left field for a match to exist.

# IV.C.1.d.    The Applied Filters Pane

Establishing relationships between tables and selecting fields will produce a list of records to be presented on the report. It is possible that more records than desired will be returned. Applied Filters is one way of restricting the rows presented to the report.

There are two types of filters that can be applied: constant and parameter based. Constant filters are always applied and always restrict the records selected to those allowed by the filter. Parameter based filters use a User Entered value to restrict the data selected.

Click on the Add Filter ( 𝗬 ) icon to add a new Applied Filter.

Click under the Field Name prompt to display a list of fields available in the selected tables. Select the field to be used in the restriction.

Click in the space under the Operator prompt to select the comparison operator. Allowable operators are:

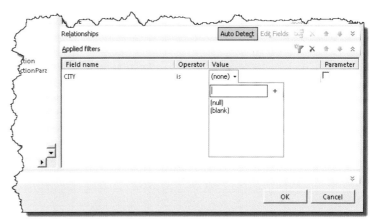

**Like** -- The contents or the value in the Field are compared to the contents of the Value field. The information entered in the Value field (or for the parameter, if the parameter field is marked) can contain the wild card character %. For example, if the value is "Alta%" then it is considered a match for "Altamonte".

**Not Like** -- The contents or value of the Field are not like the data in the value field (or parameter).

**Is** -- The contents or value of the Field must match exactly the specified Value or the contents of the Parameter (if the parameter box is checked).

**Is Not** -- The contents or value of the Field is NOT equal to the contents or value in the Value field or the data entered in the Parameter.

**Is Any Of** -- A list of several values can be specified in the Value field or in the Parameter. If the contents of the Field specified match any one of the values, the record is included.

**Is None Of** -- The contents of the Field are not found in the list of values.

**Is More Than** -- If the contents or value in the Field is greater than the value specified or the value entered in the Parameter, then the record is selected.

**Is More Than or Equal To** -- If the contents or value in the Field is greater than or equal to the value specified or the value entered in the Parameter, then the record is selected.

**Is Less Than** -- If the contents or value in the Field is less than the value specified or the value entered in the Parameter, then the record is selected.

**Is Less Than or Equal To** -- If the contents or value in the Field is less than or equal to the value specified or the value entered in the Parameter, then the record is selected.

Click under the Value prompt to enter the value to compare to the Field. The report designer can select from two special values (null) and (blank) or can enter a value. The contents of the field will be compared to the value and, based on the comparison operator, if a true match is found, the line is returned to the report.

This type of filter is considered a constant filter. It will always be applied to the data each and every time the report is run and can only be changed by the report designer.

To create a parameter driven filter, check the box in the Parameter column. A parameter must be created with the same name as the field. (The creation of Parameters will be discussed later.) When the report is executed, the user will be allowed to enter a value in the defined parameter field and that value will be used in the comparison with the data in the field to select records for inclusion in the report. This allows the user to change the selection of records each time the report is rendered.

If a value is entered into the Value field and the Parameter box is checked, the information entered into the Parameter field becomes the default value and the report will render immediately using that value. The user can then change the value if desired and re-render the report.

Multiple filters can be applied.  For example, one filter can select records greater than a certain value while a second filter selects records less than a specified value.  The result is that records with a value between the two different filters is selected.

## IV.C.1.e.   The Query Results Pane

To make sure that a Query will return the desired records, there needs to be a way to test the query and filters.  The Query pane and the Run Query button provide this.

When the query is built as desired, click the Run Query button to test the query.  The results will be displayed in the Query Results pane.  If the records pulled are not the ones desired, re-examine the query, the relationships and the filters.

# IV.C.2. Visual Studio Query Designer

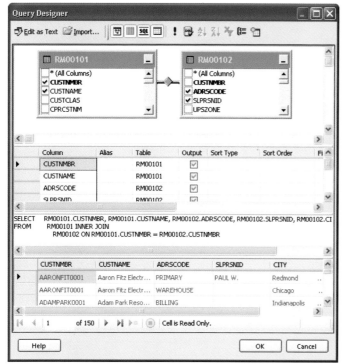

The window is split into 4 panes, not all of which need to be displayed. The 4 panes, from the top down, are called the Diagram, Criteria, SQL and Results pane.

The Diagram pane is used to graphically select tables to provide data and to establish and maintain the links between the tables. Fields in the tables can be selected as well.

The Criteria pane allows modifications to the data selected. For example, an Alias or nickname can be assigned to a field, data can be sorted by specified fields et cetera.

The SQL pane shows the actual SELECT statement in Transact SQL form that will be executed. Experienced users can edit this statement in the text window directly.

The Results pane shows the data pulled from the Data Source by the Select statement. The user must click on the Exclamation Point ( ! ) icon for the data to be pulled. This pane is useful to ensure the query is built correctly.

## IV.C.2.a. The Query Diagram Pane

The definition of a query using the Query Designer normally begins in the Diagram pane. Right clicking in this pane opens the Diagram Pane menu. Let's first look at what each of these menu selections does.

**Execute SQL** -- This option runs the SELECT statement and places the data pulled into the Results pane. This is the same action that occurs when the Exclamation Point ( ! ) icon is clicked.

**Add Group By** -- This option adds a Group By clause to the SELECT statement. Group By allows summary data to be generated, aggregating the details by the selected grouping fields. .

**UnDo** -- Reverses a change made.

**ReDo** -- Restores a change removed by the Undo command.

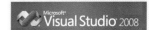

**Add Table** -- This is the most frequently used option on this menu. Clicking this button opens a list of tables available in the Data Source. The report designer can then select one or more tables to be included in the report. The tables will be placed in the Design Pane. If more than one table is selected, a default link between the tables is established. The process of adding tables to the query is discussed in detail below.

**Add New Derived Table** -- This adds a derived table to the new query.

**Pane** -- Allows users to turn on or off the display of one of the Query Designer panes.

**Clear Results** -- Clears all data currently displayed in the Results pane.

**Properties** -- Displays the Properties Window for the current query in the Query Designer window.

The primary use of the Diagram pane is to add tables to the query, establish the proper links between the tables, and to select the fields to be made available to the report.

Right clicking on the Diagram pane and selecting Add Table from the menu opens a list of tables available in the Data Source. The report designer can then locate a table and add it to the Query. A panel will be displayed in the Diagram pane for the selected table listing the fields contained in the table.

At this point, the SQL pane will be updated. If, for example, the RM00101 table was chosen, the SELECT statement will read:

SELECT    FROM RM00101

Of course, this statement is incomplete at this point.

If a second table is added the SQL pane will again be updated. For example, if the RM00102 table is added, the SQL statement will be changed to read:

SELECT    FROM RM00101 INNER JOIN RM00102 ON
        RM00101.CUSTNMBR=RMN00102.CUSTNMBR

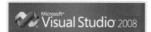

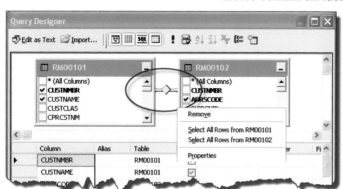

As additional tables are added to the Diagram pane, the system attempts to establish a link between the tables. In our example above, both tables contain an identical field, CUSTNMBR which is, of course, the customer number. The system "guesses" that this common field can be used to link the two tables. The user can change this.

Right clicking on the link between any two tables opens the Table Link Menu. There are four options on this menu:

**Remove** -- Selecting this option will remove the link between the two tables.

**Select All Rows from Table1** -- This will change the type of link to a Left Outer Join, pulling all records from the table on the left even if no matching records exist in the table on the right.

**Select all Rows from Table2** -- This will change the type of link to a Right Outer Join, pulling all records from the table on the right even if no matching records exist in the table on the left.

**Properties** -- This option opens the Join Properties window.

There are four different ways that SQL can relate two tables, called joins. These are the Inner Join, the Left Outer Join, the Right Outer Join and the Outer Join. By default, the Query Designer uses the Inner Join. Here is how the four joins work:

**Inner Join** -- A record in the table on the left is pulled. The system then attempts to find records in the table on the right where the link fields match. Data is added to the results for each matching pair of records.

**Left Outer Join** -- A record in the table on the left is pulled and added to the result set. IF matching records are found in the table on the right, that data is added to the result set. At least one line is displayed, representing the data in the table on the left and multiple lines are displayed if there are multiple matches in the table on the right. This join is selected by picking Select all Rows from (table on the left) the menu.

**Right Outer Join** -- This works the same as the Left Outer Join on the right and left tables are switched. This join is selected by picking Select all Rows from (table on the right) the menu.

**Outer Join** -- This type of join is seldom used and, if the report designer needs it, it must be entered into the SQL pane manually. Records are pulled from both tables even if no matches exist in the other table.

Links can be manually added between two tables in the Diagram pane. Click a field in one table and drag that field name onto a matching field in the other table. A link will be established between the two tables using the selected field.

Multiple fields can be used to relate tables. In the tables we have been using for our examples, the Customer Table (RM00101) and the Customer Address Table (RM00102), there is a field in the RM00102 table that holds the Address ID. In the Customer Table, there are several fields that reference an Address ID. For example, the Billing Address ID points to the address record where bills should be sent. Even though the fields are not named the same, we know that matching data is contained in these two fields. A link can be established between the PRBTADCD (the bill to address in the Customer Table) and the ADRSCODE (the address code field in the Customer Address Table). This link PLUS a link between the customer number fields in the two tables will produce a results table that lists the customer information and the billing address information only.

The fields of each table are listed in the panels in the Diagram pane. To add fields to the results, mark the check box to the left of the field name. If all of the fields in a table should appear in the results, mark the All Columns box at the top of the list. It will not be necessary to mark each individual field in a table if the All Columns box is marked.

Complex relationships can be built between multiple tables in the Diagram pane. Experienced users will have no problem doing this. Newer users may find, after linking several tables, that the results produced are not what is expected. We suggest building queries by adding one table at a time, adding the desired links and fields and then clicking on the Exclamation Mark ( ! ) icon to test the results before adding more tables and links.

# IV.C.2.b.  The Query Criteria Pane

The Criteria pane, the second pane in the Query Designer, is used to modify the data returned in the results set.

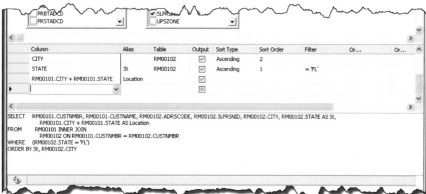

Each column selected in the tables that appear in the Diagram pane appear in the Criteria pane. Several additional columns in this pane are provided to allow modification to the results.

Additional fields can be added to the **Column** column. Any legitimate Transact SQL expression can be entered to consolidate several fields (as shown in our example) or to display only parts of the data in a field. Using the pull down list, other fields in the tables in the Diagram pane can be selected and added to the list.

The **Alias** column is used to assign a different name to a column. In the example shown, the STATE field has been renamed 'St" while the expression entered has been named 'Location'. While created fields like the expression need to have a name assigned, the Alias column can also be used to provide clearer names for fields. In some queries, duplicate columns can be pulled from different tables. The Alias allows the columns to be given different names, helping the report designer remember, for example, which customer number comes from which table.

The **Table** column lists the specific table that is the source of the field. Notice in our example that the table is listed only for the first two fields shown. The expression was built using a more fully qualified field name that includes the table name followed by a dot and then the field name. This allows fields from more than one table to be used in the expression.

The **Output** column contains a check box for each field. By default, they are all marked. It is allowable to add a column to the list and uncheck this box, removing the field from the result set. However, the field can be used to sort or filter the results.

The **Sort Type** column is used to select fields for sorting the result set and define the direction of the sort. In the example shown, the results are sorted by the STATE and CITY fields and the sort is in Ascending order.

Any field available in the Data Source can be used to sort the results. If the database is large (contains a large number of records) sorting the results on too many fields can slow down the response time, taking longer to render the report. Also, using indexed fields for sorts can speed up

the sorting process. Indexing is akin to the card catalogue in a library and allows quicker access to the data. Only a few fields in a table are typically indexed. A discussion of indexing is beyond the scope of this manual, consult with a SQL Data Base Administrator to determine the indexes that exist on the tables being used if report speed becomes an issue.

The Sort Order field defines which field will be used first to sort the data when the results are being sorted by more than one field. In the example used here, the results will be sorted first by STATE and then by CITY since STATE is marked as sort 1 and CITY is marked as sort 2.

**Filters** can be applied to the query to restrict the records returned. Filters are applied by entering an expression in the Filter field (or any of the additional fields to the right of the Filter field) that must evaluate to TRUE if a record is to be returned. In other words, looking at our example, a record is added to the results only if the STATE field is equal to 'FL'

## IV.C.2.c.    The Query SQL Pane

The SQL pane holds a text version of the graphical selections made in the first two panes of the Query Designer. As the report designer builds the query, the SQL pane is constantly updated. Examine the criteria applied in the example above and how those are manifested in the SELECT statement in the SQL pane.

The SELECT statement, of course, can be manually edited in the SQL pane. Experienced users frequently find edits in this area easier than working in the first two panes in some cases. The expression shown above can easily be entered into the SQL pane.

For most users, the SQL pane should be ignored, allowing changes made to the Diagram and Criteria pane to drive the creation of the SELECT statement in the SQL pane.

## IV.C.2.d.    The Query Results Pane

As was mentioned earlier, significantly complex queries can be created using the Diagram and the Criteria pane. Clicking on the Exclamation Point ( ! ) icon will execute the SELECT statement and display the results in the Results pane. This allows the report designer to test their query.

# IV.D.   The Expression Builder Window

Many of the fields that are available in the Query Designer (and in other places in SSRS) can be completed with an expression. For example, if the report designer wants to create a filter that shows records where the Customer ID begins with AB, there is no operator that says Begins With. However, an expression can be built that will limit the data checked to the first two characters of the customer number. Then a filter can be built where the expression is equal to "AB" to obtain the records desired.

The Function ( $f_x$ ) icon appears next to any field that can be filled by creating an expression. Clicking on this icon opens the Expression Builder window.

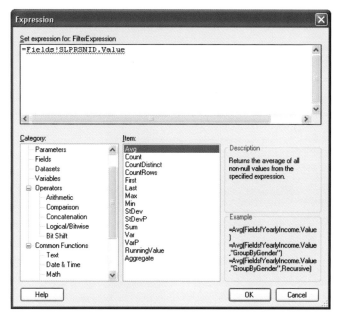

There are four sections to this window: The Expression pane, the Category Explorer, the Item list and the context sensitive help area. The expression being built is constructed in the Expression pane. A report designer can simply type in the expression if desired. Alternately, the Category, Item, and context sensitive help areas provide assistance to get the syntax of the statement correct.

The Category pane provides a list of available fields, datasets, operators and functions that can be used in creating the expression. When appropriate, the Item pane expands the list. For example, in the Categories pane, select Common Functions and then Aggregate. A list of Aggregation functions will appear in the Item list. The report designer can double click on the item to insert it into the expression (place the cursor where the item should be inserted first).

When an item is selected, the context help area will show a description of the item and an example of the usage of the item.

When the expression is built as desired, click the OK button to close the window and return the expression to the field.

# IV.E.  *Accessing Data Other Than SQL*

## IV.E.1.    Using Excel Data

Excel data (data stored in Excel worksheets) is accessed in the report builder through an ODBC connection.  Here are the steps:

1.      In Windows Administrative Tools, create a new DSN.  Select the Excel driver and point it to the Excel worksheet containing the data to be used in the report.

2.      In the Report Writer, create a new Data Source of the type ODBC.  Click the Edit button next to the Connection String box and select the ODBC created in step 1.

This data source can now be used like any other data source.  A Dataset needs to be created, of course, to select the rows and columns to be used in the report.

## IV.E.2.    Using XML Data

When creating a Data Source to retrieve data from XML tables, the connection string is simply a URL that points to the web service, web application, or XML document in HTML.  A web service format url might look like:

>                 http://mysite.com/results.aspx

The format of the URL for an XML document looks like:

>                 http://localhost/XML/myfile.xml

Credentials must be configured for Windows integrated security or no credentials.  Stored and prompted credentials are not supported.  If No Credentials is selected, Anonymous access is used.

The text based query builder must be used to create queries for Datasets and the query must return XML data.

# *IV.F. Applying Parameters to Datasets*

The creation of a parameter in a report does not automatically apply that parameter to the Dataset. When a parameter is created and the report executed, the report rendering software will ask the user for values for the parameters but it will not automatically restrict the data selected. A Filter must be applied to the Dataset based on the parameter.

Filters are used to restrict the data rows extracted from the Data Provider. Filters can be static (ie SLSPRSNID = "TOM") which will always restrict the report to the predefined filter, or a filter can compare a field to a parameter. For example, if a parameter is provided that allows a user to select a sales rep, a filter can be created that will compare the salesperson field in the data to the value entered in the parameter.

Ranges are supported by providing a starting and ending parameter. For example, a starting date and ending date parameter can be created and then two filters used to restrict data to the records that are greater than or equal to the starting date and then less than or equal to the ending date.

Report Parameters and the creation of filters is discussed in detail in Chapter V.E.3.

# V. Basic Report Creation

# V.    *Basic Report Creation*

So once a basic report is created, most people want to dress up the presentation a bit to make the report look good and easy to read. In this chapter we will discuss the basics of report formatting while in subsequent chapters more detailed formatting tools will be discussed.

Once again, both the SSRB and the Visual Studio designer will be discussed. Watch the icons to determine which set of instructions applies to the design tool in use.

## V.A.    *A Tour of the Desktops*

Before plunging into the details of formatting reports, let's take a look at the two different desktops, the SSRB and the Visual Studio desktop. It is not necessary to learn both desktops as each tool uses only one or the other. Select the appropriate section based on the tool being used to create reports.

## V.A.1.    SSRB Desktop

Designed more for the average user that can write reports but is not a developer, the SQL Server Report Builder desktop is simpler yet provides almost all of the functionality of Visual Studio. It does not use Projects but can store reports in folders to be opened and modified and components of report deployed to the Report Server can be reused.

**Software Versions Used**

Visual Studio 2008 and SQL Server Report Builder Version 3.0 are described in this chapter. Throughout the chapter, the following icons will be used to specify the report development tool being discussed:

This icon will appear next to any discussion that is unique to the SQL Server Report Builder Version 3.0

This icon will appear next to any discussion that is unique to the Visual Studio 2008 development environment.

# V.A.1.a.    Opening the SSRB

The SQL Server Report Builder can open with the Getting Started window displayed. This opening window is optional and can be turned on or off with a switch setting in the Report Builder Options window. The Getting Started window offers 8 options:

**New report** -- Allows a report designer (a user that is creating or modifying a report design) to create a new report from scratch.

**New Dataset** -- Allows a report designer to create a new Data Source/ Dataset. Data Sources and Datasets are connections to Data Providers for a defined set of tables and columns. Datasets will be described later in this text.

**Open** -- Opens a previously created and saved report, allowing the report designer to save their work and return to it to make more changes later.

**Recent** -- Displays a list of recently created reports. The report designer can select one of the recently worked reports and open it for modification.

**Table or Matrix Wizard** -- Starts a wizard that walks the report designer through the steps of creating a Table or Matrix report.

**Chart Wizard** -- Starts a wizard that walks the report designer through the steps of creating a Chart style report.

**Map Wizard** -- Starts a wizard that walks the report designer through the steps of creating a Map style report.

**Blank Report** -- Starts a wizard that walks the report designer through the steps of creating a report without any specific pre-defined formatting.

All of these tasks can be performed from the desktop of the SSRB, but the Getting Started window provides a good short cut.

# V.A.1.b.    The Main SSRB Desktop

The top of the SSRB supports a typical Office style ribbon with groups of functions designed to support the format-ting of the report data. The functions are grouped into three tabs: Home, Insert and View.

The Home tab hosts a number of pure format-ting functions. These allow different type fonts and sizes to be selected, borders to be placed around data, paragraph alignment to be selected, numbers to be formatted et cetera.

The Insert tab allows different objects to be inserted into the report. Objects include the Table layout, the Matrix layout, the List layout, charts, gauges, maps lines, rectangles, sub-reports et cetera. As well, headers and footers can be added to the report using selections in the Insert tab.

The View tab defines the panes that are displayed on the SSRB Desk-top. The five different panes can be turned on or off in three groups (Report Data, Groups and Properties). Turning off the display of any pane will allow more room for the pasteboard area. A fourth option on the View tab allows the rulers surrounding the pasteboard area to be turned off, again allowing more room if needed.

The Pasteboard is the central area of the SSRB where the actual report layout is created. It is called a Pasteboard after the layout boards used by newspaper and book publishers to create pages. Items (pieces of text, images et cetera) are placed on the pasteboard in the desired posi-tion. Pieces of reports (called report objects) are placed on the paste-board in the same manner, only electronically today.

The Report Data pane (left side of the SSRB) contains the various report objects. Included in the list of objects are:

> **Built-In Fields** -- A collection of special fields such as page numbers, dates, print times et cetera.

> **Parameters** -- Fields defined to allow the users running the reports to enter values used to control the information printed on the report. For example, a report parameter can be defined to select a range of dates and only trans-actions within that range will be printed.

> **Images** -- A group of images can be loaded into this section and used in the report.

**Textbox versus Cell**

Technically, Textbox IS the proper name for the space in Tables and Matrix structures that hold data and labels. Both Tables and Ma-trixs look very much like spread-sheets that refer to their spaces as cells. We are using the phrase cell only because so many people are familiar with this term. Be aware, later in this book we will drop the use of the word CELL!

Think of it this way: A Textbox is a structure that can be placed on a report to hold data or labels. A Table is a collection of Textboxes.

### What is a Pasteboard?

Originally, and for hundreds of years, printers laid out pages by placing wood or lead type in a frame. When printing moved from the old flatbed presses to offset, pages were designed by printing strips of paper and pasting these strips onto a board, forming the pages. This board was called a pasteboard. As typesetting became completely electronic, the term pasteboard was retained, referring to the space on the designer's screen where elements to be printed were placed.

**Data Sources** -- Connections to data providers (data bases, generally) are defined in this folder.

**Datasets** -- A Dataset defines columns and rows to be defined that will be pulled from the data provider and placed on the report. Field names from the various columns are placed on the pasteboard to represent the desired location of the data in the report.

The Properties Pane is displayed on the right side of the SSRB desktop. A different set of properties is displayed in this area for each object on the report pasteboard. Selecting an object on the pasteboard causes the properties of that object to be displayed. Most of the properties for an object can be edited using windows or functions in the ribbon. A few properties can only be edited in the Properties pane.

The Group panes are found across the bottom of the SSRB desktop. Groups allow data to be grouped and, if desired sub-totaled, by a common value. For example, all records for a specific customer can be displayed, followed by totals for that customer, and then the next customer group. Groups will be discussed later in detail.

## V.A.1.c.    The Home Tab

The Home Tab provides a significant number of formatting tools for Text Boxes in a report.

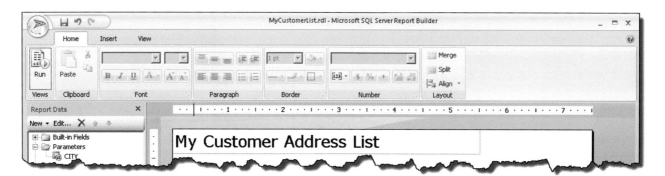

The Home Tab ribbon is broken into 7 sections: Views, Clipboard, Font, Paragraph, Border, Number and Layout.

The **Views Section** houses the Run button. The Run button displays the Run tab and executes the report in preview mode inside the SSRB. This allows the report designer to review the final report and its operation before publishing the report for users.

The **Clipboard Section** houses buttons for Cut, Copy and Paste. These functions work exactly like every other cut, copy and paste function. An area of the report is highlighted, either the cut or copy button is

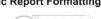

clicked and the highlighted area is copied to the Clipboard. If the cut button was clicked, the highlighted area is deleted from the paste board. The cursor can be moved to another area and the paste button clicked to paste the copied material back onto the paste board.

The **Font Section** contains a number of buttons and windows that modify the look of the information displayed in a Text Box on the report. To use these functions, highlight one or more Text Boxes on the report. Then click the desired button.

**Bold ( B )** -- Clicking this button changes the type face to **Bold**.

**Italic ( I )** -- Clicking this button changes the type face to *Italics*.

**Underline ( U )** -- Clicking this button <u>Underlines</u> the selected text.

**Text Color ( A )** -- Clicking this button opens a color picker. The report designer can then select a color for the text.

**Increase Font Size ( A )** -- Clicking this button increases the font size of the selected text by one step. Steps are defined in the Font Size pull down menu.

**Decrease Font Size ( A )** -- Clicking this button decreases the font size of the selected text by one step. Steps are defined in the Font Size pull down menu.

**Type Face ( Arial ▼ )** -- Clicking the arrow in this pull down menu displays a list of type faces installed on the local machine and available for use in the report. Be careful to select a type face that is installed on all of the workstations that will be running the report. If a special type face is used and is not available when the report is rendered, a near match will be used and the report may not appear as desired.

**Font Size ( 11 ▼ )** -- Clicking the arrow in this pull down menu displays a list of font sizes. Select the desired size for the highlighted text.

The **Paragraph Section** of the ribbon contains buttons that allow the formatting of paragraph styles and placement of text within a Text Box.

**Align Top ( )** -- Aligns the text in the Text Box with the top of the box.

**Align Center ( )** -- Centers the text in the Text Box vertically.

**Align Bottom ( )** -- Aligns the text in the Text Box with the bottom of the box.

**Decrease Indent ( )** -- Reduces any indent applied to the selected text.

**To Follow Along...**

To follow the examples in this chapter using Visual Studio 2008, create a new Dataset using the MS Dynamics GP company database. Include two tables, RM00101 and RM00102 with the default linking. Do not apply any filters, parameters or change any other settings in the dataset!

If the dataset described in Chapter IV was created following the discussion in that chapter, some settings will be invalid for this report!

**Supported Image File Formats**

At the time of this writing, the following image file formats are supported by Visual Studio:

- JPEG
- GIF
- PNG
- BMP

Other file formats may be supported as the software is updated.

**Increase Indent (⊞) --** Indents the selected text.

**Left Justify Text (≣) --** Left justifies the selected text in the Text Box.

**Center Text (≣) --** Centers the selected text in the Text Box horizontally.

**Right Justify Text (≣) --** Right justifies the selected text in the Text Box.

**Bullets (≔) --** Applies (or removes) bullets to the selected text in the Text Box.

**Numbers (≔) --** Applies (or removes) numbers to the list of text lines selected.

The **Border Section** contains buttons and tools to create and format a border around selected Text Boxes.

**Border Width ( 1 pt ▼ ) --** This pull down menu allows the report designer to select the desired weight or width of the lines that form the border.

**Fill Color ( ▼ ) --** This button opens a color picker. The report designer can select the color to be used as the background for the selected Text Box(es).

**Border Style ( — ▼ ) --** This button allows the report designer to select one of several styles for the border line. Styles include:

**Solid --** A Solid Line.

**Dotted --** A series of dots forms the line.

**Dashed --** A series of dashes forms the line.

**Double --** Two parallel lines are used as the border.

**None --** No border is applied or an existing border is removed.

**Border Color ( ▼ ) --** Clicking this button opens a color picker. The report designer can select the color to be used for the border.

**Border Side ( □ ▼ ) --** Borders can be applied to all four sides of a Text Box or to specific sides. Clicking this button opens a list of options allowing the report designer to specify the side or sides of the selected Text Box(es) to which the border will be applied.

The **Number Section** provides formatting options for numeric data. When numeric data (which includes dates and times) appears on a report, the users typically want specific formatting. These buttons and pull down menus provide most of the common options needed.

**Number Style** ( Number ▾ ) -- Opening this pull down menu allows the numeric data in the selected Text Box(es) to be formatted easily by selecting a specified format. Formats provided are:

**Default** -- The numbers are displayed in the same manner as they are stored in the table. For example, if a number is stored as a float with 8 decimal places, all 8 decimal places will appear on the report. A Date/Time field will show both the date and the time.

**Number** -- Data will be formatted as a number.

**Currency** -- Data will be formatted as currency with the default number of decimal places based on the country settings of the workstation.

**Date** -- A date time field will be reduced to a date only, stripping the time fields off the report.

**Time** -- A date time field will be reduced to a time field only, stripping the date information off the report.

**Percentage** -- A number is shown as a percentage. The number will be multiplied by 100. Thus .10 will be displayed as 10%.

**Scientific** -- The number will be shown in scientific notation (ie 1.234356E4).

**Custom** -- A custom format must be defined for this data. The creation of custom formats will be discussed later in this chapter.

**Placeholder Style** ( [123] ▾ ) -- Data is placed on a report inside a Text Box. When the report writer is in Design mode (in deference to Run mode), data is displayed in the Text Boxes using a Placeholder. This pull down list allows the report designer to specify the type of place holder to use. Options include:

**Placeholder** -- A marker represents the data. Typically, the marker is the name of the field in the table surrounded by square brackets (i.e., [CUSTNMBR]).

**Sample Values** -- A representation of the number is shown (i.e., $99,999,999.99).

**Currency Symbol ( $ )** -- Clicking this button applies or removes the currency symbol from the numeric data in the selected Text Box(es).

**Percent Sign ( % )** -- Clicking this button applies or removes the Percent Symbol from the numeric data in the selected Text Box(es).

**Thousands Separator ( , )** -- Clicking this button turns the use of thousands separators in the numeric data on or off.

**Decrease Decimals ( .00 )** -- Clicking this button reduces the number of decimal places shown in the numeric data.

**Increase Decimals ( .00 )** -- Clicking this button increases the number of decimal places shown in the numeric data.

The **Layout Section** contains buttons that help manage the layout of groups of Text Boxes.

**Merge ( Merge )** -- This button is used to merge two or more Text Boxes. Select the desire boxes then click the button. One larger Text Box spanning the original space is created.

**Split ( Split )** -- This button is used to split a Text Box into two or more pieces. Select the desired Text Box and click the button.

**Align ( Align )** -- This button brings the data in a group of selected Text Boxes into the same alignment. Data can be right, center or left aligned, et cetera.

# V.A.1.d.    The Insert Tab

The Insert Tab provides a number of objects that can be inserted into the report. The use of most of these objects will be described later in this chapter. A brief definition of each object is provided here.

**Report Parts ( ⊞ )** -- This button opens a Report Part Gallery pane. Inside the Gallery, a list of report parts published to the current report server is displayed. The report designer can select from these published report parts (such as Data Sources, Datasets, Images, et cetera) and include the part in the current report.

**Table ( ⊞ )** -- This tool is used to add a Table style report to the pasteboard. Its use is described in detail later in this chapter.

**Matrix ( ⊞ )** -- This tool is used to add a Matrix style report to the pasteboard. Its use is described in detail later in this chapter.

**List ( ⊞ )** -- This tool is used to add a List style report to the pasteboard. Its use is described in detail later in this chapter.

**Chart ( ⊞ )** -- This tool is used to place a chart on the report. Its use is described in Chapter VII of this book.

**Gauge ( ⊚ )** -- This tool is used to place a gauge on the report. Its use is described in Chapter VII of this book.

**Map ( ⊕ )** -- This tool is used to place a map on the report with addresses from the data located on the map. Its use is described in Chapter VII of this book.

**Data Bar ( ⊞ )** -- This tool is used to place a data bar style display on the report. Its use is described in Chapter VII of this book.

**Sparkline ( ⊞ )** -- This tool is used to place a sparkline representing data points on the report. It's use is described in Chapter VII of

this book. Sparklines are commonly seen in displays of stock prices, et cetera.

**Indicator (** ▦ **)** -- This tool allows a variety of symbols to be used on a report to indicate one of several states (selected, not selected, on, off et cetera) The use of indicates is described in Chapter VII of this book.

**Text Box (** A **)** -- AH! The aforementioned Text Box! Text Boxes are like the cells on a spreadsheet. However, they can be grouped into Tables, Matrixes, or List structures placed independently on the report to hold dates, page numbers, titles, et cetera. Text Boxes and many of their properties are described later in this chapter.

**Image (** 🖾 **)** -- Images are pictures or other graphics that can be placed on the report. These can include logos, signatures, images of products, et cetera. Images are described later in this chapter.

**Line (** ╲ **)** -- Lines, as the name applies, allow the placement of lines on a report. Lines span sections and are used to separate, for example, headers from the body of the report, et cetera. Lines cannot span multiple Text Boxes and if frames around a group of Text Boxes is needed, borders should be used.

**Rectangle (** ▭ **)** -- This tool places a rectangle on the pasteboard. A table, list, or matrix inside a rectangle will cause the rectangle to expand or grow as data is printed on the report inside the table, list or matrix.

**Sub Report (** 🗔 **)** -- This tool inserts one report inside a host report. Data can be passed between the two reports to control printing. For example, a list of customers can include a sub-report that displays open orders for the customer.

**Header (** 🗎 **)** -- Clicking this button adds (or removes) a header area to the report. Text Boxes placed on the header will appear at the top of each page of the report.

**Footer (** 🗎 **)** -- Clicking this button adds (or removes) a footer area to the report. Text Boxes placed on the footer will appear at the bottom of each page of the report.

## V.A.1.e.      The View Tab

The View Tab provides four check boxes.  Marking each of these boxes causes the indicated pane to be displayed in the lower section of the desktop.  The four check boxes are:

**Report Data** -- Checking this box causes the Report Data pane to be shown on the desktop.

**Grouping** -- Checking this box causes the Grouping panes to be shown at the bottom of the desktop.

**Properties** -- Checking this box causes the Properties pane to be displayed on the right side of the desktop.

**Ruler** -- Checking this box causes rulers to be displayed across the top and down the left side of the pasteboard.  Rulers can help report designers place data properly on the report.

The pasteboard section of the desktop is always shown except when the report writer is in Preview Mode (then the report designer clicks on the Run button).

## V.A.1.f.      The Run Tab

The Run Tab is displayed when the Run button is clicked on the Home tab ribbon.  This tab executes the current report, allowing the report designer to review the design and layout before publishing the report to users.

# V.A.2.    Visual Studio Desktop

Designing reports using the Microsoft Visual Studio tool provides a few more options to the designer such as the use of Project containers to hold report parts for sharing without publishing the parts. It also presents the user with a number of other options for creating other types of programs which can lead non-developer users into strange areas. Use of the Visual Studio desktop for designing reports should be reserved for developers.

The Visual Studio Report Designer desktop is very customizable. A number of windows / panes can be displayed or hidden, allowing a report designer to select the elements they want to see at any point in the project development.

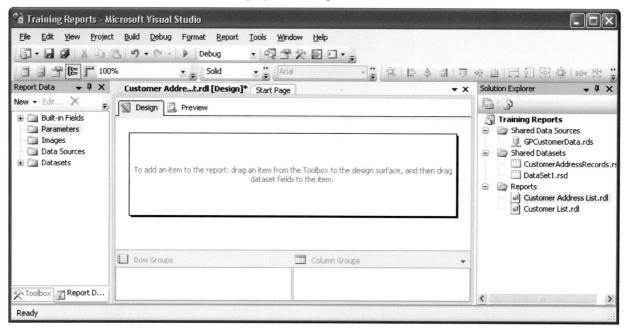

The image shown above is the default view that is seen when the report design view is first shown. If a report designer modifies the desktop, the next time the report design desktop is displayed, the designer's customized layout will be shown.

Most of the panes or windows are opened from the View menu option. Also, panes are typically opened as docked windows inside the Project window. They can be moved to other docked spaces in the Project window or can be floated onto the user's desktop, completely outside of the Project window and making more Project window space available to the report designer.

Some of the windows/panes described below are found in the default layout shown above. Others must be opened/displayed by selecting them from the View menu.

# V.A.2.a.    Solution Explorer Pane

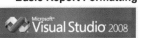

The Solution Explorer pane shows the objects contained in the current Project. This includes Shared Data Sources, Shared Datasets and Reports. Any of these objects can be opened for editing by expanding the folder containing the object and double clicking on the object itself. (Remember, the Visual Studio Project allows shared objects and stores them inside the Project.)

Selecting an object in the Solution Center and right clicking opens a menu. The contents of the menu are different for different types of objects shown in the Explorer.

Objects can easily be renamed by right clicking and selecting Rename. Change the name of the object as desired. The new name will be carried into other objects that may reference the renamed object. For example, if a Data Source is used in one or more Datasets and is renamed, the Datasets will be updated and show the new name.

Objects can be deleted from the project permanently by right clicking on the object and selecting Delete. Note that an UnDo option is not available. Objects accidentally deleted will need to be re-created.


# V.A.2.b.    Report Data Pane

The Report Data Pane (shown in our example on the left side of the Project window) shows the data elements that can be added to the report. Five folders appear in this window:

**Built In Fields** -- A set of predefined fields frequently used in refining the layout of reports can be selected from this list. These include fields such as page numbers, Execution Time, et cetera.

**Parameters** -- In this folder, parameters used to select data to appear on the report are defined. When the report is executed, the user will be asked to provide values for these parameters.

**Images** -- Images can be used in the reports. The images are first imported into the Project using this folder and then placed as desired on the report layout. Acceptable image file formats are shown in the margin notes.

**Data Sources** -- Shared Data Sources can be assigned to this report by adding the Data Source to this folder. Also, an Embedded Data Source, specific to this report can be defined if necessary.

**Datasets** -- Shared Datasets can be assigned to this report by adding the Dataset to this folder. As well, an Embedded Dataset can be designed specifically for this report.

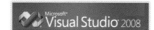

## V.A.2.c.     Toolbox Pane

The Toolbox pane is frequently hidden and may be a tab at the bottom of the Report Items window (as shown in our example) or a floating tab on the left of the Report Items window. Clicking on the tab will open or display the Toolbox window.

The Toolbox contains a number of objects that are used to design and format reports. These include:

**Pointer ( )** -- Clicking on this tool returns the cursor to the simple Pointer tool used to select other items on the Pasteboard.

**Text Box ( )** -- Text Boxes are like the cells on a spreadsheet. However, they can be grouped into Tables, Matrixes, or List structures or placed independently on the report to hold dates, page numbers, titles et cetera. Text Boxes and many of their properties are described later in this chapter.

**Line ( )** -- Lines, as the name applies, allow the placement of lines on a report. Lines span sections and are used to separate, for example, headers from the body of the report, et cetera. Lines cannot span multiple Text Boxes and if frames around a group of Text Boxes is needed, borders should be used.

**Table ( )** -- This tool is used to add a Table style report to the pasteboard. Its use is described in detail later in this chapter.

**Matrix ( )** -- This tool is used to add a Matrix style report to the pasteboard.

**Rectangle ( )** -- This tool places a rectangle on the pasteboard. A table, list or matrix inside a rectangle will cause the rectangle to expand or grow as data is printed on the report inside the table, list or matrix.

**List ( )** -- This tool is used to add a List style report to the pasteboard. It's use is described in detail later in this chapter.

**Image ( )** -- Images are pictures or other graphics that can be placed on the report. These can include logos, signatures, images of products, et cetera. Images are described later in this chapter.

**Sub Report ( )** -- This tool inserts one report inside a host report. Data can be passed between the two reports to control printing. For example, a list of customers can include a sub-report that displays open orders for the customer.

**Chart ( )** -- This tool is used to place a chart on the report. Its use is described in Chapter VII of this book

**Gauge ( )** -- This tool is used to place a gauge on the report. Its use is described in Chapter VII of this book.

**Map ( )** -- This tool is used to place a map on the report with addresses from the data located on the map. Its use is described in Chapter VII of this book.

**Data Bar ( )** -- This tool is used to place a data bar style display on the report. Its use is described in Chapter VII of this book.

**Sparkline ( )** -- This tool is used to place a sparkline representing data points on the report. Its use is described in Chapter VII of this book.

**Indicator ( )** -- This tool allows a variety of symbols to be used on a report to indicate one of several states (selected, not selected, on, off et cetera) Its use is described in Chapter VII of this book.

## V.A.2.d.     Designer Pane/Design Tab

The Report Designer Pane is actually a collection of two tabs and several areas on one of the tabs. The tabs are the Design and the Preview tab. On the Design tab, can be found, the report pasteboard and the groups area.

The Report Pasteboard in the Design Tab is used to create and format the report. Items from the Toolbox are placed on the pasteboard to format the report and then data items are inserted, providing the information to be displayed.

Right clicking on the Reports Pasteboard opens the Reports Pasteboard menu. Several options are provided:

The Insert option provides an alternate method of inserting items typically found in the Toolbox onto the pasteboard. For example, a Table or Matrix item can be dragged from the Toolbox and dropped on the pasteboard or the Insert/Table item selected from the menu, causing the Table item to be automatically dropped on the pasteboard.

The Pasteboard Menu contains a pair of options not available in the Toolbox. The pasteboard can be expanded and sections provided for a report header and/or footer by making the appropriate selection from

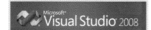

the menu. As expected, items placed in the report header will print at the top of each page of the report while items placed in the report footer will print at the bottom of each page.

The View option on the Pasteboard Menu allows Rulers to be displayed across the top and left side of the report. These rulers are frequently helpful in placing elements in the desired location on a report and ensuring that the report properly fits on the desired size sheet of paper.

The Groups Area shown at the bottom of the Designer Tab can be turned on or off using the Pasteboard menu.

## V.A.2.e.    Design Pane / Groups Areas

Report users often want their data grouped and subtotaled. For example, when printing a list of customers with balances due, the customers are frequently grouped by sales rep with a total receivables amount printed for each sales rep. This is accomplished using the Row Groups area.

Matrix reports can group data in two dimensions. Sales reps can be printed across the top of the report and states down the right side. For each sales rep/state, a total receivables amount could be printed. This requires grouping by Columns.

Row and Column groups are defined by placing the controlling field name in the Row Groups and/or Column Groups area. Using our example above, the Sales Rep ID field would be placed into the Column Groups area and the State field would be placed into the Row Groups area. Placing a SUM(AmountDue) field in the body of the report would create a matrix report as described. This example will be shown later in this manual.

## V.A.2.f.    Design Pane / Preview Tab

The Preview Tab is used to run the report inside the Designer, allowing the person designing the report to easily test the report and see the actual data display. Corrections can easily be made and the preview repeated as often as necessary until the report is correct. At that time, the report is published.

## V.A.2.g.    Error List Pane

The Error List pane is not shown in the example window shown.  It opens automatically when certain processes are run (such as publishing of reports) and reports any errors to the user.  The pane can be opened from the View menu if desired and closed whenever it is not needed.

## V.A.2.h.    Output Pane

The Output pane is another automatic pane.  While it can be opened from the View menu, it automatically opens when certain processes are executed (such as the publish report process) to show the progress of the process.  It can be closed when not needed.

## V.A.2.i    Properties Window

Properties windows show a list of properties associated with individual objects.  Every object in SSRS has a list of properties associated with it.  In some cases, for example fields on the report pasteboard, the properties window will be used to edit certain formatting settings.

Properties windows are typically opened by selecting the option from the objects right-click window.

# *V.B.    Creating a Report -- Overview*

When either tool is first started, a wizard may be presented to allow the initial creation of a new report. In this section, the creation of a new report from the menu options will be discussed. This always launches the wizard in SSRB. In both SSRB and Visual Studio, the use of a wizard is optional.

# V.B.1.    Creating a New Report in SSRB

The creation of a new report can begin when the application is first opened or by clicking on the icon at the top left corner of the ribbon and selecting New. The New Report or Dataset Wizard is opened. The user can select to use the Table or Matrix Wizard, the Chart Wizard or the Map Wizard. Also, a Blank Report can be selected, allowing the user to make all the formatting choices from scratch.

To create a report without using a wizard, either close the window or select Blank Report. The user will be dropped into the SSRB with an empty pasteboard and no Data Source or Dataset selected.

The steps to create a report using SSRB were covered in Chapter II and will not be repeated here other than in summary. Refer to Chapter II for details on creating a report.

1.    Create or select from the Report Server a Data Source to be used to connect to the desired Data Provider (see Chapter IV for information on creating Data Sources).

2.    Create or select from the Report Server a Dataset to provide the desired columns and rows to the report.

3.    Select either a Table, Matrix or List tool, place it on the pasteboard, and format the report as desired.

# V.B.2.     Creating a New Report in VS

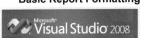

There are two ways to create a report in Visual Studio 2008, using the Report Wizard or manually creating the report components. Chapter III of this manual walked through the process of creating reports using the Report Wizard. In this section, we will create a report from the Project Add New Item templates as well as launching the wizard from within the project. Following this discussion, we will launch into a detailed discussion of the formatting features available for reports irregardless of the way the report was initially created.

In an existing Project, new reports can be added using the Reports Wizard or by individually defining the components (Data Source, Dataset and Report layout). Each of these two options is accessed from the Visual Studio desktop by clicking on Project on the menu bar and then selecting Add New Item.

The Add New Item window will be displayed. Two templates offer the report designer the option of creating a report using the Report Wizard or by simply creating a Report using shared Data Sources and Datasets.

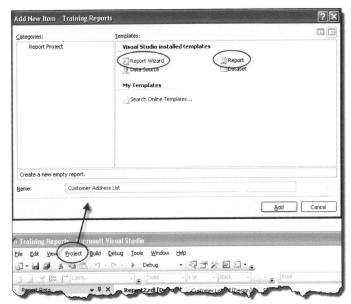

Clicking on the Report Wizard template starts the report wizard and walks the report designer through several steps to construct a new report. This process is documented in Chapter II. In this chapter, we will discuss creating a report using the Report wizard.

The creation of a report using the Report template assumes that a Data Source and Dataset have already been created. (See Chapter IV for information on creating Data Sources and Datasets.)

To start the process of creating a report, click on the Report icon in the Add New Item window. The Name field at the bottom of the window becomes active and the default name ReportX.rld is shown. Change this to the desired name for the new report. Then click OK.

# V.C.    *Creating A Table Report*

SQL Server Reports come in three forms: Table, Matrix and List. Table reports are the typical list of records, frequently grouped and subtotaled, with specific fields shown for each row of data. Matrix reports summarize data in two dimensions with one set of headings across the top and a second down the side and summary information shown in the matrix table. List reports are simple lists of rows of data.

To create a Table Report, create a new report as described earlier. Then click on the Table Report tool and place the tool on the Pasteboard in the report designer area.

## V.C.1.    **Placing the Table**

**Where is the Table Report Tool?**

SSRB

Insert Tab → Data Regions → Table

Toolbox → Table

Data elements can be placed on the pasteboard in individual Text Boxes, and the report or document formatted manually to meet almost any business requirement. To produce a clean and neat table report, with data organized into rows and columns, a Table tool is provided. The Table tool allows the report designer to specify the number of columns of data to appear on the report, the individual data elements to be printed, and the heading to appear over each column. It is a shortcut to building clean tabular reports.

Place the Table tool on the pasteboard by dragging and dropping the Table ( ▥ ) icon to the pasteboard. A table layout grid will appear on the pasteboard with two rows and three columns. The top row of the table is reserved for column headings and the second row is designated for data. The words Header and Data appear temporarily in the table grid as a reminder.

At the same time, an entry is listed in the Row Groups area labeled (*Details*). This indicates that one group of rows will be printed for each detail line returned by the query. When the table is first placed on the pasteboard, only one data row is included in the group. The header row is not repeated.

The table grid can be manipulated using the cursor. However, touching the grid in different places has different affects.

Click on the top, right, or left line of the table frame and the Move arrows appear. The table can be moved using the mouse by dragging and dropping or by pressing any of the four direction keys on the keyboard. Place the table in the desired position on the pasteboard.

Place the pointer on any cell and the Table Frame appears. Note on the left side of the table, the rows that hold data are marked with three lines and a bracket is shown. The bracket indicates the rows that are included inside the group.

To add rows or columns to the table area, place the cursor inside the table area in a Text Box and right click. The Text Box/Tablix menu appears. Place the cursor on the top row (above the header) and right click and a short form of the menu appears offering only column functions. Place the cursor on the frame right edge and right click and a short form of the menu appears showing only row functions. If the cursor is placed over the table frame right edge over a marked row, additional functions on the menu allow rows to be added inside or outside of the group.

To add a row, select one of the marked rows, place the cursor over the Table Frame, and right click. From the Table menu that appears, select Insert Row. From the Insert Row menu, select Inside Group - Below. (At this point, the table has no data and the Inside Group - Above would have the same results.)

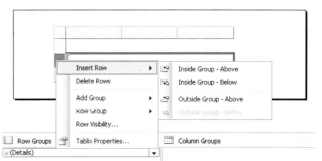

Note that rows can be added outside of the group. Adding rows above the group will add to the column headers while adding rows below the group will provide space for grand totals.

The menu that is displayed when the cursor is placed in one of the Text Box cells and right clicked was referred to as a Text Box/Tablix menu because it contains options for both the Text Box and the Tablix. A Tablix is a term that refers to the data space in the report. This data space could be a Table or a Matrix. Many of the functions for either a Table or a Matrix are common and apply to either structure. Thus, the term Tablix has been adopted to refer to these common features and functions.

Notice as well that different functions appear on each of the menus. While the Tablix menu offers options to Insert Columns and Insert Rows, the menu displayed from the right side of the Table Frame offers only the Insert Row function but also Row Group, Add Row and Row Visibility functions. The menu displayed from the top of the Table frame includes Column visibility. (Column group functions are not offered since a Table tool was selected.)

To add a column, of course, simply click and show one of the menus from a column with an Insert Column and select to insert the new column to the right or left of the selected column.

There are a large number of formatting options for the Table. These are covered in Chapter VI under Tablix Formatting Options.

# V.C.2.    Placing Data In the Table

Of course, a report is not a report without data. Data from the database is placed on the report by dragging and dropping the field name from the Dataset to the desired cell in the Table. Of course, there are several different ways to accomplish this.

Using a simple drag-and-drop, expand the Dataset menu to show the field or fields desired. Click on a field and drag it to the desired column in the Table. When the field is dropped onto the table, a label is placed in the Label row and the data field is placed into the first row of the column.

A second option uses a fields menu in the Text Box/cell. Click on the desired cell and a small menu icon appears in the top right corner of the Text Box. Clicking on this icon will display the Field List menu.

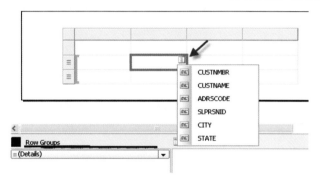

The Field List menu displays a list of all of the fields found in the Datasets assigned to the report. Simply click one of the fields and that field will be dropped into the selected Text Box/cell. If there is data above the selected cell, a column title will be placed in the header row matching the field selected. If the new field is being placed in the second data row and another data field already appears in the top data row, the label for the cell will be placed in the second header row, if it exists. If no second header row exists, no label will be displayed. (If two column data header rows are needed, create them before adding data to the Table.)

There are a significant number of formatting options available for the rows, columns and Text Boxes in a Table. Some of those options (Visibility) have been hinted at already. See Chapter VI for more details on the formatting options of Tablix (tables and/or matrixes) objects.

# V.C.3.    Adding Groups

Grouping functions allow data to be separated on the report into sections of like information, or groups. For example, management may want a list of customers assigned to sales reps. Grouping the list of customer accounts will generate a report that will first list a sales rep and then all of the customers assigned to that rep. The group is then repeated for all sales reps.

Another use for groups is to print a list of customers and all of the sales transactions for the customers. Or, using the customer list and the sales detail line history information and print a list of customers and what items they are purchasing. Turn that over and create a list of items and which customers purchased the items.

Groups add real power to designing reports. Groups within groups are even supported as will be seen below. Let's use the example of customers and their list of sales transaction documents.

For these next few examples, create a new Shared Dataset. The information on the Dataset is given in the side bar box.

Start by creating a basic table report. Drop the Table tool on the pasteboard and then put the customer number, sales order document number (SOPNUMBR) and the document amount (DOCAMNT) in the report. Preview the report.

Most probably, the customer numbers word wrapped and printed on two lines. This can be controlled. Return to the Design tab, put the cursor in the Customer Number data Text Box, right click and open the Text Box properties window. Un-check the option Allow Height to Increase. Click OK to close the window. Click again on the Text Box to show the Table Frame. Grab the right edge of the Customer Number column (in the Table Frame) and drag the divider to the right, providing more space for the customer number. Preview the report again.

Now it is time to add a group. On the report as designed so far, we have a list of customer sales transactions. We want to group those transactions by customer, allow room for some customer information at the top of each group and for totals at the bottom of the group.

Notice in the Row Groups that a group currently exists for Details. We need to add a group for Customer Number. (If the Row Group pane is not seen, right click on the pasteboard and select View → Grouping from the menu.)

Put the cursor either on the row marker in the Table Frame or in one of the Text Boxes holding the detail data. Right click. Select Add Group. The Tablix Group window will be displayed.

In the Group By field, use the pull down list to select the field used to group the data. In our example, this will be the Customer Number field (CUSTNMBR). This will cause the rows on the report to be grouped by the Customer Number.

To insert a header row (a row at the top of each group), click the Add Group Header check box.

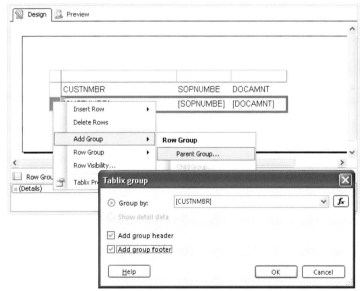

To insert a footer row (a row at the bottom of each group for subtotals, et cetera), click the Add Group Footer check box.

Click OK. This will close the Tablix Group window and create the grouping. Click on the Preview tab to review the results.

Notice that the customer number is repeated on the report. It appears in the Group By column as well as the details area. Since it is not needed in both places, delete the one in the details area. Click on the table to

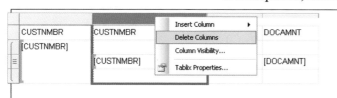

show the Table Frame. Put the cursor in the column header at the top of the detail column for the customer number and right click. Select Delete Columns.

Each sales transaction has a document date. This column and others can be added to the report in several ways. The report designer can click on the column header in the Table Frame, right click and select insert column. The designer can insert the new column to the right or left of the existing column. Click in the Text Box where the data should be displayed, click on the table icon, and select the field to be displayed in this column.

A second method of creating a new column and adding the data item allows both steps to be performed in one move. Click on the data item in the Datasets area of the Report Data pane and drag it to the pasteboard. As the cursor moves over the lines between existing columns, an Insertion Bar appears. When this bar appears in the desired spot, drop the field. A new column will be added and the selected data item displayed in that column.

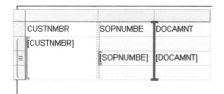

Previewing the report shows the data field including both date and time information. MS-SQL includes both date and time in a single field. Seldom, however, is the time used on transactions and it is frequently defaulted to 12:00:00 AM. The data can be limited to the date by formatting the Text Box. In the Design Tab, put the cursor in the Text Box that holds the Date/Time information. Right click and open the Text Box Properties window. Select the Number screen from the list on the left. In the Category window, select Date. Then in the Type field that appears next, select the desired format for the date. Click OK to close the Text Box Properties window. Preview the report again.

Format the dollar amounts to show only two decimal places. Right click on the Text Box. Be careful where the cursor is placed. The cursor must be in the Text Box but not on the data item. If the cursor is clicked while the data placeholder is highlighted, the Placeholder menu will be displayed rather than the Text Box menu. Select Text Box Properties, select the Number screen in the Text Box Properties window, and format the data as a number with a thousands separator but no currency symbol. To do that, select the Category Number and use two decimal places. If the Category Currency is selected, the currency symbol will be selected!

# V.C.4.   Adding SubGroups

SSRS supports groups within groups. In the example we have been using, Customers and their Transactions, we have listed all sales documents for each customer. What if management wants subtotals of quotes, orders, invoices, back orders, and returns for each customer with the detail listed.

|  |  |  |  |  |
|---|---|---|---|---|
|  |  |  | Total |  |
| VISIONIN0001 |  |  |  |  |
|  | Order | ORD1004 | 5/18/2014 | 73,947.65 |
|  |  | Total Orders |  | 73947.65000 |
|  | Invoice | STDINV2248 | 4/12/2017 | 73,947.65 |
|  |  | Total Invoices |  | 73947.65000 |
|  |  | Customer VISIONIN0001   Total |  | $147895.30 |
| WESTCENT0001 |  |  |  |  |
|  | Order | ORDPH1002 | 5/17/2014 | 99.75 |
|  |  | Total Orders |  | 99.75000 |
|  | Invoice | INVPS1007 | 4/12/2017 | 99.75 |
|  |  | Total Invoices |  | 99.75000 |
|  |  | Customer WESTCENT0001 Total |  | $199.50 |
| WESTSIDE0001 |  |  |  |  |
|  | Order | ORDST1012 | 5/27/2014 | 385.10 |
|  |  | Total Orders |  | 385.10000 |
|  |  | Customer WESTSIDE0001   Total |  | $385.10 |
| Grand Total |  |  |  | $1979113.21 |

Since we already have a report that lists the sales documents by customer, lets take the details lines and add a parent group by document type within the customer group.

Now, in MS Dynamics GP, document types are represented in the tables as numeric values (See *Information Flow and Posting* from Accolade Publications, Inc. for a listing of many of the coded fields.) That means that when a list of sales documents is grouped by document type, we get a list for type 1, type 2, type 3 et cetera. It would be better to have the groups labeled using the words Quote, Order, Invoice et cetera.

In the Text Box that is displaying the Group By field (SOPTYPE), right click. In the Text Box section of the menu, click on Expression to open the Expression builder. Use the Switch command to build an expression that will convert the numbers to words. The syntax of that expression is:

```
=Switch(Fields!SOPTYPE.Value=1,"Quote",
    Fields!SOPTYPE.Value=2,"Order",
    Fields!SOPTYPE.Value=3,"Invoice",
    Fields!SOPTYPE.Value=4,"Backorder",
    Fields!SOPTYPE.Value=5,"Return")
```

Of course, subtotals per document type would be nice as well as some labels on the total lines indicating "Total Invoice Dollars", "Total for Customer xxxxxx" and "Company Grand Totals"

Multiple levels of subgroups are supported. However, when the nesting of the groups gets too deep, readers find it difficult to follow the report.

# V.C.5.    Adding Totals and Subtotals

Totals can be displayed on a report for the entire report as well as for each group. In our example report, sales documents per customer, totals can be shown for all sales documents as well as for all documents per customer.

To add totals for the report:

1.    Place the cursor in one of the Text Boxes near the bottom of the table.

2.    Right click. From the menu select Insert Row. If this was done from a Text Box in a group, options to add the row inside or outside the group are provided. We want to add a row below the existing rows and, if appropriate, outside of the group.

3.    Select a Text Box in the new row directly below the column of numbers to be totaled. Click on the little table icon in the Text Box and select the name of the field to be totaled. By default, the system will insert a SUM(*[fieldname]*) function in the total area.

Yes, it is that easy.

There is a wide variety of aggregation functions (sum, max, min, count et cetera) that are discussed in the next chapter. It is easy to select a Text Box in the total row and insert a count of rows, et cetera.

If groups are being used in the report (as they are in our example), subtotals may be desired. In our example report, sales documents are grouped per customer number.

When a group is added to a Tablix, a row can be added automatically at the bottom of the group for totals. In the Tablix Add a Group window, checking the box Add Group Footer provides an extra row at the end of the group for Group Totals.

In our example, we added the Group Footer when the group was created.

To add a row to a group for totals, place the cursor in the Text Box that holds the field that data is grouped by. For example, if rows are grouped by customer number, place the cursor in the field holding the customer number group ID. Right click in this space and select Insert Row -- Inside Group -- Below. The row that is added will appear at the end of the list of data rows in the group.

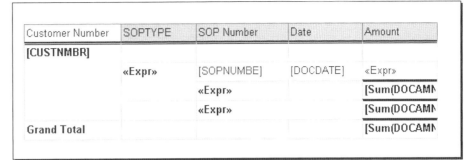

| Customer Number | SOPTYPE | SOP Number | Date | Amount |
|---|---|---|---|---|
| [CUSTNMBR] | | | | |
| | «Expr» | [SOPNUMBE] | [DOCDATE] | «Expr» |
| | | «Expr» | | [Sum(DOCAMN |
| | | «Expr» | | [Sum(DOCAMN |
| Grand Total | | | | [Sum(DOCAMN |

Put the cursor in the Text Box under the numeric column that is to be subtotaled. Select the table icon and pick the numeric field. Again, a SUM([*fieldname*]) placeholder will be inserted. The total of the selected numeric field for the rows in the group will appear in this space when the report is rendered.

Of course, the field should be formatted. Place a line above the subtotal (top border, of course) format the data as numeric (or currency if the currency symbol should be displayed).

# V.D.    Creating a Matrix Report

A Matrix Report looks like a spreadsheet pivot table. Data is grouped in two directions, down and across, and summary information appears in the body of the table. In our earlier report where we listed customers and document types, we listed on the table report the actual transactions. If we only need totals or a count of the documents and do not particularly need the details, a matrix report can be useful.

| Customer / Type | Quote | Order | Invoice | Backorder | Return | Total |
|---|---|---|---|---|---|---|
| AARONFIT0001 | 0 | 40 | 44 | 2 | 0 | 86 |
| ADAMPARK0001 | 0 | 3 | 5 | 0 | 0 | 8 |
| ADVANCED0001 | 0 | 2 | 2 | 1 | 0 | 5 |
| ADVANCED0002 | 1 | 2 | 0 | 1 | 0 | 4 |
| AMERICAN0001 | 0 | 3 | 3 | 0 | 1 | 7 |
| ASSOCIAT0001 | 0 | 1 | 1 | 0 | 0 | 2 |
| ASTORSUI0001 | 1 | 19 | 20 | 0 | 0 | 40 |
| ATMORERE0001 | 0 | 1 | 0 | 1 | 0 | 2 |
| Total | 10 | 263 | 283 | 7 | 2 | |

The data items appearing in the top row (the column headings) and in the first column (the row headings) are the grouping fields. The data appearing in the cells in the center are aggregated data. In the example shown, the numbers represent the Count of Sales Documents. The Sum of Document Amounts could just as easily be displayed. The functions of Sum and Count are called Aggregation Functions.

And, of course, across the bottom and down the far right column appear totals of the data in the cells.

**Where is the Matrix Report Tool?**

SSRB

Insert Tab → Data Regions → Matrix

Microsoft Visual Studio 2008

Toolbox → Matrix

# V.D.1.    Starting a Matrix Report

Creating a Matrix report is just as easy as creating a Table report (perhaps easier). Most of the tasks of formatting the report (selecting a Dataset, headers, footers, parameters, sorts et cetera) are the same as they are when creating a Table report. The difference occurs in placing data in the pasteboard in the body section of the report.

A matrix report can be built using either the Report Wizard or simply by using the Report template. By now, use of the Report Wizard should be second nature to the readers. We will discuss the manual creation of a matrix report.

Create a new object in the Project by clicking Project → New and select the Report template. The desktop will change to show the standard report designer panes. Right click on the Datasets folder in the Report Data pane to assign a Shared Dataset to the report or create an embedded Data Source and Dataset as desired. These processes are identical to the processes described earlier in this chapter for table reports. Refer to those sections for instructions.

## V.D.2. Placing a Matrix on the Pasteboard

The Matrix tool in the Toolbox pane is used to place a matrix object on
the report Pasteboard. Drag the tool to the
pasteboard and drop it there. An initial 2x2
matrix will be drawn with a Text Box for the
column group field, the row group field and
the aggregated data.

## V.D.3. Selecting Grouping Fields

Table reports start by inserting data and then
optionally grouping that data. Matrix reports
assume that data is being grouped both by the row and by the column.
The fields to be used to group the data must be dropped into the Columns and Rows Text Boxes.

Open the Dataset, display the fields, and drag and drop the appropriate
fields to the Columns or Rows Text Boxes on the matrix. For example,
to show summary data for each customer on one row, drag the customer
number field to the Rows Text Box. To have a column for each sales
document type, drag the document type field to the Columns Text Box.

Note that in MS Dynamics GP, document types are stored as codes.
A function might be preferable to translate the codes into words. See
Accolade's companion manual SSRS Advanced Functions for lists of
functions, including one that will translate codes into words.

# V.D.4.     Placing Data in the Matrix

Data can be placed in the matrix by dropping the desired field into the data Text Box. However, since the data will be grouped, an aggregation function must be applied. It is better to use an expression.

Right-click in the data Text Box in the matrix. From the Text Box menu, click Expression to open the Expression Builder.

In the Expression Builder window, click on the plus sign ( + ) to expand the Common Functions group. Then click on the Aggregate function. A list of aggregation functions will be displayed in the Item pane.

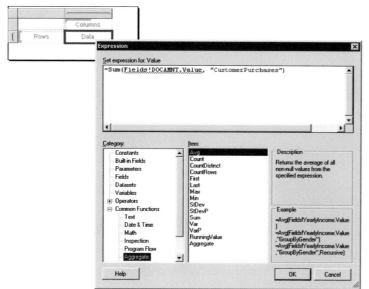

The individual aggregation functions are described in detail in Chapter VI. Two of these functions are worth mentioning at this point: Sum and Count.

The Sum function displays in the data Text Box the sum of the values that appear in fields specified in the group of rows or columns. If the expression Sum(DOCAMT) is placed in the data Text Box, the sum of the document amounts for each grouping will be displayed.

The Count function allows the report designer to display the number of rows/columns that are aggregated in the Text Box. For example, if the expression Count(SOPNMBR) is entered in the Text Box and the grouping is by customer number and document type, each data Text Box displayed on the final report will contain the count of the specific type of document for the specific customer.

At this point, do not select an aggregation function. In the Expression Builder Category pane, click on the Datasets item. The list of Datasets will be displayed in the Item pane. In the Values pane, the various fields in the highlighted Dataset will be shown. Notice, however, that each field in the listing already has an aggregation function associated with it. Sometimes the pre-selected aggregation function is the one the report designer wants to use. Frequently, the aggregation function needs to be changed.

Select from the list of values the Sum(DOCAMNT) to place the sum of the sales transaction amounts in the data Text Box. Run the report to see the results. Of course, formatting should be applied to insert currency symbols, commas and the correct number of decimal places.

# V.D.5.    Putting Totals on the Matrix

Totals can be added to both the right side of a matrix, providing a total for the row, and to the bottom of the matrix, providing a total for each column.

To put totals for each column across the bottom of the matrix, place the cursor on one of the rows of the matrix and right click.  From the menu select Insert Rows Outside of Group-Below.  Place the cursor in the Text Box that contains the data to be totaled and right click again. Make sure the data placeholder is not highlighted and the Tablix menu is displayed.  Select from the Tablix menu Add Total Row.  The proper aggregation function and field will be inserted into the Text Box below the totaled field.

The user can also add totals without first creating the row or column to hold the totals.  Right click again on the data Text Box and select Add Total Column.  Not only will the total be added to the report but the column needed to hold the column will be added with the title "Total".

Preview the report to see the effects of inserting the totals.  Of course, formatting should be applied as described earlier in this chapter.

**Where is the List Report Tool?**

**SSRB**

Insert Tab → Data Regions → List

Microsoft® Visual Studio 2008

Toolbox → List

# V.E.    *Creating a List Report*

A List form report produces a list of the records selected in the query. The data fields, however, are not necessarily arranged in a tabular format. The List Tool defines an area on the pasteboard and any field from the Dataset can be placed anywhere in one large space.

Examples where a List form report might be useful include address labels, shipping labels, forms et cetera.

To create a report using the List tool, place the List tool on to the pasteboard. In SSRB, double click on the List tool icon. In Visual Studio, drag the List tool to the pasteboard. A Dataset Properties window will open allowing the report designer to select or create a Dataset and, if necessary, a Data Source. The List box will then appear on the pasteboard.

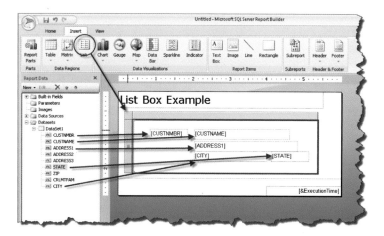

The List Box area can be re-sized as needed to fit the need. If address labels are being generated, size the List Box to the label. If a form is being created, size the List Box to the full size of the form.

Place fields as needed inside the List Box area. Unlike a Text Box, multiple fields are placed free form inside the List Box. Technically, each field is placed inside a Text Box and the Text Boxes holding the fields are then arranged as needed inside the List Box.

List Boxes can be duplicated on a report page easily. If, for example, address labels are being printed and the sheet of labels contains 33 individual labels three across and eleven down, the List Box can be selected as a single unit by clicking on its edge, copied with the Control-C key or the Clipboard Copy function and then placed again on the pasteboard by using the Control-V key or the Clipboard Paste function. The additional copy can be moved into the desired position. When the report is run, each copy of the List Box will display a different record from the Dataset!

# V.F.    General Report Formatting

The following sections discuss some of the major report formatting options such as page headers and footers, the selection of specific records using report parameters, sorting data et cetera.  Specific formatting of fields and data is discussed in Chapter VI.

# V.F.1.    Adding a Page Header

Having data on a sheet of paper is nice.  But most people want a title and dates at the top of the report pages.  Some firms also place the company name and other information in this space.  Also, the column headings in the table only appear at the top of the column on the first page of the report.  To repeat the column headings on each page, they must appear in a page header.

A page header is repeated at the top of each page of the report.  To add a page header, right click on a blank spot on the pasteboard to show the Pasteboard menu.  From that menu, select Insert and then Page Header. A new section will be added to the top of the pasteboard.

To add fixed text such as a report title, place a Text Box from the Toolbox into the Page Header.  Use the rulers (right click on the pasteboard and select View/Rulers) to center the title.  Click in the Text Box and type the desired title.  Use the menu options at the top of the Designer to set the font size, weight (bold), and to center the title in the Text Box.

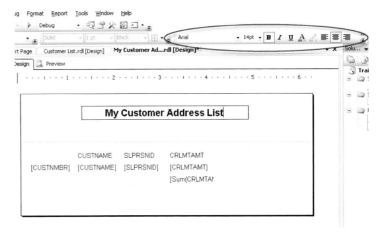

Data from the Built-in Fields folder in the Report Data pane can be added to the Page Header by dragging the desired field to the Page Header and placing the item in the desired place.  When these items are dragged and dropped, a Text Box is automatically added to frame the item. Page numbers, total page counts and the name of the user that is running the report can all be added to the Page Header.

Notice anything missing from the list of Built-in Fields?  There is a field named Execution Time but no date field!  In MS-SQL, date and time information is contained in a single field in the tables.  Thus, the Execution Time data element includes the date.  Adding this value to the report will print a Date/Time such as:

12/31/2011  12:45

To show only the date, an expression must be used.

From the Toolbox, place a Text Box in the Page Header at the place where the report print data should appear. Right click in the Text Box and select Expression. The Expression Builder window will open.

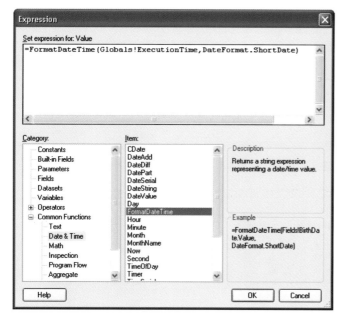

Initially, the Set Expression box will simply contain an equals sign. In the Category area, expand the Common Functions and select Date & Time. In the Item area, double click on FormatDateTime. The FormatDateTime function will be added to the Set Expression box. Type an open parentheses.

In the Category area, select Built-in Fields and double click on Execution Time. The phrase "Globals!ExecutionTime" will be added to the expression.

Type a period (.) followed by "DateFormat.". After typing the period, help should arrive listing several different Date/Time formats. Select ShortDate or simply continue to type in the phrase. Make sure to type the closing parentheses. If ShortDate was selected, then the date will appear like:

12/31/2011

The functions in the Expression window are Visual Basic functions.

## V.F.2.     Adding a Page Footer

Page Footers are added to a report in exactly the same manner as the Page Header above (only Page Footer is selected from the View menu!). Page Footers are frequently used to hold page numbers and confidentiality statement, the report storage location and other such status information.

# V.F.3.    Adding Report Parameters

Report Parameters are used to allow the users that run the reports to select specific groups of rows to be printed.  For example, when printing a list of customers, one user may want to see all of the customers assigned to a specific sales representative.  While this can be designed into the report Dataset, using a parameter allows one user to run the report for one sales person and then run the report again for a different sales person without re-coding the report.

There are two steps required to add parameters to a report: define the questions that will be asked of the users then apply a filter using the results from those parameters.

## V.F.3.a.    Defining Parameters

The questions that should be asked to the user running the report are defined in the Report Data pane in the Parameters folder.  Click on the folder, select Add Parameter and the Report Parameter Properties window will display.

Creating a parameter question is as simple as giving the object a **Name**, entering a **Prompt** to be displayed when the report executes and selecting a few characteristics.  In total, four screens provide a large number of additional functions, but only the **General Screen** must be completed.

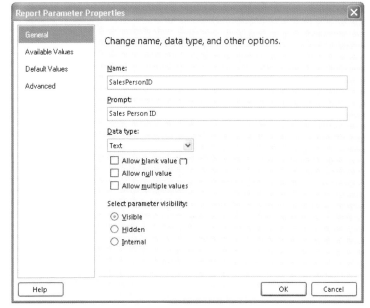

The **Data Type** pull down list allows the report designer to specify the type of information the user must enter when the prompt is displayed.  Valid types are:

**Text** -- Any characters can be entered.  The characters entered will be treated as a string.

**Boolean** -- When the report is executed, two options will be offered next to the prompt: True and False.  The user will be allowed to select one.

**Date/Time** -- Date/Time fields in MS-SQL are special fields that require data formatted in a specific manner. A report designer cannot simply use a text format and allow users to enter a date. Use this data type instead. When the report is run, a text field is displayed next to the prompt and a Date Picker ( ) icon is presented. The user can click on the Date Picker icon and select the desired date.

**Integer** -- Whole numbers without decimal points are entered for this data type.

**Float** -- Selecting this data type allows the user to enter a value with a decimal point.

The **Allow Blank Value** check box, if marked, allows the input field to be left blank.

The **Allow Null Value** check box, if marked, allows single value Data Types (boolean, integer, et cetera) to be left blank.

The **Allow Multiple Values** checkbox, if marked, allows the user running the report to enter multiple values for a parameter. If the filter that will be built uses an IN comparison, multiple options can be entered or selected. (Note: IN comparisons must be built in the Dataset query!)

The **Select Parameter Visibility** options allow the report designer to specify whether users will be able to see the parameters. It sounds strange, if parameters are being created, why not show them? There are several reasons.

Sometimes, reports are executed automatically with parameter values fed directly to the report by the software that launches the report. The user does not need to view the parameters and confirm them. Hidden runs the report with predefined parameters but the user can change the parameters if desired. Internal runs the report with pre-loaded parameter values and does not allow the values to be changed.

Normally, the parameters are set to Visible.

As mentioned earlier, only the General screen needs to be completed to define a Parameter. However, three additional screens are available to further refine the use of parameters in a report.

The **Available Values Screen** allows the report designer to specify a list of values to be selected from a pull down list when the parameter prompt is displayed.

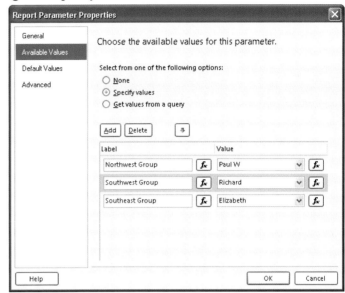

There are three options on this screen: None, Specify Values, and Get Values from a Query.

If **None** is selected, no list of values will be displayed. The user will need to manually enter a value into the prompt field when the report is run.

The **Specify Values** option allows the report designer to specify a list of values to appear in the pull down list. As seen in the adjacent screen, two columns of information are provided. In the first column, the phrase that will appear in the pull down list is entered. In the second column, the value to be used in the filter statement is specified. For example, using the information shown in the adjacent screen, the user will see a list that offers the Northwest Group, Southwest Group, and the Southeast Group. If the user selects the Southwest Group, the filter will select records where the salesperson ID is Richard.

The **Set Values from a Query** option on the Available Values screen allows the pull down list of selections to be completed using a query in a Dataset.

Typically, a special Dataset is defined to provide a list of values for a parameter. The value to be listed in the pull down list may appear in the data table multiple times. For example, using our customer list example, one sales person may be assigned to multiple customers. Simply using a query that lists all records and displaying the salesperson ID field will cause each salesperson to appear in the list multiple times. A DISTINCT clause is needed.

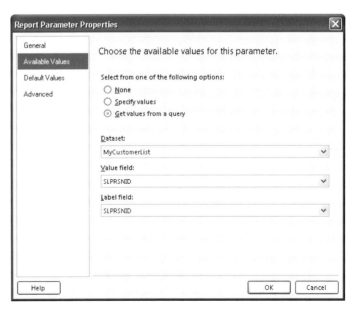

Create a special Dataset for the available values list. In the Query Designer, select only the one field needed for the pull down list. If a separate field is to be used for the Value and Label fields, select both fields. Edit the SQL statement to add a DISTINCT clause and a Group By.

Using a Group By clause causes all of the records in the table to be grouped by the selected field. In our example below, the contents of the table are grouped by the salesperson ID. Only one record will be returned for each salesperson ID.

If a separate field will be used to display a list of values, the contents of that field must be aggregated into one value. In our example below, we used the Max function to select the largest name for each salesperson ID.

```
SELECT DISTINCT SLPRSNID, Max(Name) AS NameList
FROM   RM00101
GROUP BY SLPRSNID
```

The above SELECT statement will return a list with one row for each different salesperson ID and containing a field with the name of the sales rep. This data can be used in defining the pull down list of available values for the parameter.

In the Report Parameter Properties Available Values screen, when Get Values from a Query is selected, select from the pull down lists the Dataset, the Value field and the Label field. The contents of the Label field will be displayed to the user when the report is executed while the contents of the Value field will be used in the filter statement to select the appropriate rows.

The Default Values screen allows the report designer to specify default values for the parameters. In most cases, a single default value is specified. If the parameter allows multiple selections, then multiple default values can be specified.

Just like the Available Values screen, default values can be specified by the report designer on this screen or a query can be built to return a set of defaults. The options work exactly like the corresponding options on the Available Values screen.

The Advanced screen allows the report designer to define when or if the Dataset for a report should be updated. Generally, when a report is first rendered, the data is read from the tables, cached and then displayed to the user. For some reports, it may be desirable or necessary to update the rendered report when the values associated with the parameter are changed. The parameter must be referenced in the query used to extract the data. This reference can be in the form of a filter, for example.

Options for refreshing data when the parameter changes include:

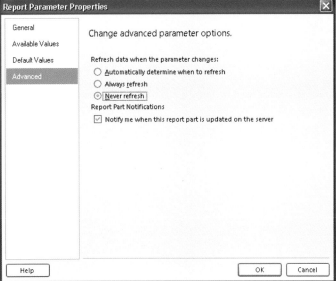

**Automatically Determine when to Refresh** -- This allows the system to determine when the data needs to be refreshed. This is the default setting and is also the recommended setting.

**Always Refresh** -- Causes the system to extract new data anytime the parameter changes.

**Never Refresh** -- Do not update the data until the cache expires. Caution must be exercised when selecting this option as it can result in invalid data being presented to users. It can be useful to report designers in a rapidly changing database that are trying to apply formatting to a new report. If the data is constantly changing, noticing the effects of formatting changes can be difficult and marking this option can result in the same data being displayed with each rendering. USE EXTREME CARE when using this option.

Multiple parameters can be defined for a report. For example, parameters may be used to select all records for a single sales rep and then only those records in a specific state. The report, when generated, would only show records that match both the sales rep ID entered and the state entered.

Another use of multiple parameters allows a range of records to be selected. Create a Starting and an Ending parameter field. The user can then enter a beginning and ending range. The filter created must use both of these parameters to select records between the two values entered.

## V.F.3.b.    Creating a Parametrized Filter

Once the Parameters have been created, a filter must be applied to the Dataset. This is accomplished using the Dataset Properties Filters screen and the Expression Builder. In the Report Data pane, select

Dataset and open the Dataset Properties window. Select the Filters screen.

The value entered by the user in a Parameter field must be compared to data in a field in the tables from the Dataset. A filter is created to make this comparison. If the filter evaluates to True, the data is displayed on the report, otherwise, it is omitted. To create a filter, click the Add button on the Filters screen.

A set of 4 fields will be added to the Filters list.

The **Expression** field is used to select the Dataset field to be matched. Using the pull down list box, a list of fields selected in the query is shown. Select the desired field.

The Function Icon ( ) allows a function to be written around the data fields. For example, the report designer may want to select all records where the ZIP code starts with "3". Clicking on the function icon opens the Expression window. See the section below on the use of the Expression window.

The Comparison Type field tells the filter how to compare the Expression to the Value. For example, when using Greater Than or Less Than operators, considering the expression to be Text versus an Integer can yield different results. Valid Comparison Types are:

**Text** -- The field or expression is considered to be text, even if the text is composed of numbers.

**Boolean** -- The field or expression is evaluated as either true or false. Any value that equals 0 is considered false, other values are considered True.

**Date/Time** -- The field or expression is considered to be a SQL Date/Time value.

**Integer** -- The field or expression is considered to be an integer.

**Float** -- The field or expression is considered to be a float value with decimal points.

An example of the importance of the Comparison Type field is seen when lists of numbers are used. If a text comparison is performed, the text 2 is considered greater than the text 15. However if an integer comparison is performed, the number 2 is less than the number 15.

The Operator field determines how the Expression is compared to the Value. Valid operators are:

= -- The Expression must equal the value for the filter to be evaluated as True.

<> -- The Expression must be different from the value for the filter to be evaluated as True.

**Like** -- The Expression must match the fixed portion of the value. For example, if the value is expressed as RL%, any Expression starting with RL followed by any characters will cause the comparison to be evaluated as True.

> -- The Expression must be greater than the Value field for the filter to be evaluated as true.

>= -- The Expression must be greater than or equal to the Value field for the filter to be evaluated as true.

< -- The Expression must be less than the Value field for the filter to be evaluated as true.

<= -- The Expression must be less than or equal to the Value field for the filter to be evaluated as true.

**Top N** -- The data is sorted by the Expression field and a specified number of records is selected from the top of the list. The number of records to be returned by the Data Source is specified in the Value Field.

**Bottom N** -- The data is sorted by the Expression field and a specified number of records is selected from the bottom of the list. The number of records to be returned by the Data Source is specified in the Value Field.

**Top %** -- The data is sorted by the Expression field and a percentage of the total number of records is selected from the top of the list. The percentage to be returned by the Data Source is specified in the Value Field.

**Bottom %** -- The data is sorted by the Expression field and a percentage of the total number of records is selected from the top of the list. The percentage to be returned by the Data Source is specified in the Value Field.

**In** -- The data found in the field specified in the Expression field must appear in the list of values entered into the Value field.

**Between** -- The Value field is split into two fields and the value found in the field specified in the Expression field must be between the first and last values entered in the two Value fields.

The name of the parameter to be matched must be entered into the Value field. Simply typing the name, however, will not work. The Expression Builder must be used to insert the parameter name. Click on the function button next to the Value field to open the Expression Builder. In the window, select Parameters in the Categories column and then select the desired parameter from the list in the Values field.

Click OK to save the formula. If several parameters have been defined, it may be necessary to create several filters.

When all of the filters have been defined as desired, click OK on the Dataset Properties window to close the window and save the filters.

## V.F.3.c.  Running the Report with Parameters

When previewing a report with parameters, Visual Studio will present the parameters to the user and allow them to enter data in the field or select responses from a list (if a list of Available Values was created). Simply make the appropriate entries and click the View Report button on the pane.

## V.F.3.d.  Data Considerations with Parameters

When restricting the data that appears on a report using parameters, the report designer needs to consider how data is stored and what will be compared. When most people look at, for example, a PO number in the data table, they see PO12345. What they do not realize is that the PO is stored in a 17 character field and the remaining spaces in the field are filled with spaces.

If a user types a PO number into a parameter field, they will type only the readable characters and not type the spaces. When this data is compared against the data in the table, with PO numbers padded with spaces, no match will be found! (And this applies to Sales Order Numbers, Item Numbers, Employee Numbers, Class ID's, et cetera).

If the user is going to be typing an identifier into a parameter field, the data typed in must be compared to the field values with all extra spaces trimmed off. This is accomplished using the Trim function. In the Dataset Properties Filters screen, use the Function editor next to the Expression field to apply the Trim function.

1.  First, use the pull down list to select the desired field.

2.  Click the Function icon to open the Expression Builder.

3.  Type the phrase Trim (between the equal sign and the field name and put a closing parentheses) at the end of the field name as shown.

4.  Click the OK button to save the expression.

5.  Complete the filter, comparing the expression to the Parameter.

Now when a user types in 'PO12345' the system will take the value in the PO field ( 'PO12345          ') and trim it to 'PO12345', a value that can match what the user enters.

On the other hand, if a list of available values is associated with the parameter and the user is required to select a value from the list, the list of available values will include the extra spaces. For example, a PO selected from the list of available values will keep the spaces and look like 'PO12345       '. Now, when that selected value with the spaces is compared to the matching field in the filter, the spaces in the data field are needed and the Trim ( ) statement is not needed.

The final issue arises when a user can pick from a list or enter a value for a parameter. Here, the user could enter just the characters of the identifier and not the spaces. In this case, both the field used in the Expression field of the filter AND the parameter itself in the Value field should have the Trim ( ) function applied. In this manner, both fields will have any possible blanks stripped and matches will occur as expected.

# V.F.4.    Fixing Header Information

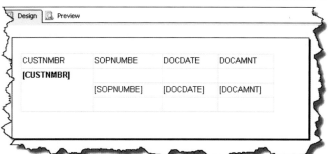

Well formatted reports have clear and meaningful column headings. When a data item is dropped onto a Text Box in the Table, a column heading is automatically generated. The system uses the data field names as column headings. Most of the time, these should be changed. Also, there is significant formatting that can be applied to make the column headings look much better.

The first step to creating attractive and meaningful headers is to edit the text in the header areas. Simply click on the column name (not in the Text Box that holds the name but on the name itself) and edit the phrase. It's real easy to make the column names meaningful. Additional formatting can be applied to the headers in several ways.

The column names can be selected and the text controls at the top of the Visual Studio desktop used to apply attributes. Bolding or Italics can be applied, the type face changed, the font size changed, even underlining applied (although there are better ways to draw a line between the headers and the data).

The Tablix Property page contains some options that apply to row headers. Click on an empty spot in the table to show the Table Frame. Right click in one of the blocks of the frame and from the menu that is displayed and select Tablix Properties. The important options are found on the General screen.

The Row Headers section on the General screen offers two options:

**Repeat Header Rows on Each Page** -- Checking this box will cause the header rows of the table (or matrix) to be repeated at the top of each page. This box should be marked by default.

**Keep Header Visible While Scrolling** -- Checking this box will cause the header rows of the table (or matrix) to remain on screen when the report is viewed (rather than printed). This works similar to the Freeze Panes option in an Excel spreadsheet.

Using the Text Box Properties, the report designer can set the fill color, put borders around the header boxes or just on the bottom (creating a line between the column titles and the data, and change the font characteristics). However, these changes must be made for each Text Box in the header row, one by one. But there is a better way.

Each object in the Project has a page of Properties. The settings on the properties windows update this table of information. But the properties can also be updated by selecting the object and opening that object's Properties window. AND...several Text Boxes can be selected at one time and the properties for all selected objects changed at one time.

Here is how:

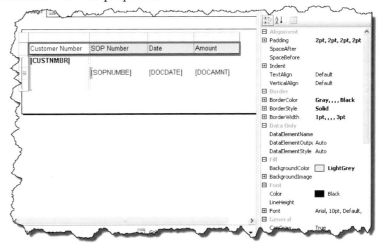

1.     Put the cursor in some empty space in the Text Box at the far left of the row of column titles and click. A frame is drawn around the one box indicating that the Text Box is selected.

2.     Put the cursor in some empty space in the Text Box at the far right of the row of column titles. Hold down the shift key and click the mouse again. All of the Text Boxes in the row will be selected.

3.     In the View menu, select Properties Window (or hit the F4 key) and the Properties Window will open. This window reflects only properties common to all selected objects (the row of Text Boxes for the column headers in this case).

4.     Locate Border Color in the list of properties. It typically defaults to Lite Grey. Click the Plus Sign ( + ) icon to the left of the property and a list of sides will be shown. The border color can be set for all sides by changing the color in the Default property or different sides can have different colors. Often, the Default is set to White while the Bottom is set to Black. This draws a line under the column headers.

5.     To change the border from a solid line to another style, expand the Border Style property. The Default setting can be changed or any specific side edited. Options include Dashed, Dotted, Solid (or single) and Double.

6.     To change the thickness of the border, edit the BorderWidth property. As before, each side can be set individually or a Default value can be set to control all 4 sides.

7.     The fill color for all of the selected Text Boxes can be set using the Fill property.

8.     The font characteristics can be changed for all of the selected Text Boxes using the Font properties.

# V.F.5.  Selecting Data

Parameters were used earlier in this chapter to show a method of allowing the user to select specific rows to appear on the report. It may be desirable or even necessary to restrict the rows pulled into the report permanently.

In our report, for example, we are showing both Orders and Invoices. Typically (but not always) orders become invoices. If we only want to know what was sold and what was returned, we need to limit or filter the rows selected for the report. This is accomplished using the Dataset Properties Filters screen.

The Filters screen is discussed in detail in Chapter IV.C.1.d. of this

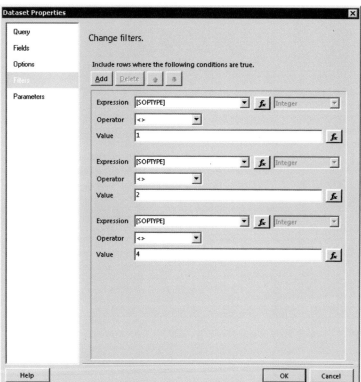

chapter. In this section, we are going to discuss a different use of the Filter screen, restricting the data available to the user.

As was explained earlier, filters can be applied to restrict the rows pulled for the report. When multiple filters are used, each and every individual filter must evaluate to TRUE for a row for that data to be made available to the report.

If a report is to be printed and, for example, only invoices in the sales transaction history file are to be printed, a filter restricting records to those where the document type (SOPTYPE) is equal to 3 (MS Dynamics GP's code for invoices). If, as in our example, we want invoices and returns, we cannot enter two filters where one selects records where the document type is Invoice and a second filter where the document type is Return. No records would be returned since no record is both an invoice AND a return.

In the example shown, we reversed the logic and selected records where the document type is different from quotes, orders, and back orders. This means that both invoices and returns will find all filters true and will be selected to appear on the report.

# V.F.6.     Sorting Data

Sorting ensures that data appears in a prescribed order, usually Alphanumeric and either ascending or descending.

Rows can be sorted on multiple fields. Contact information, for example, sometimes has First and Last Names in separate fields. Simply sorting by Last Name is not sufficient as there are quite a number of people that share the same last name. Thus, by sorting first on the Last Name and then on the First name, a properly organized list can be printed.

If data is grouped, the groups are printed by default in ascending alphanumeric order. For example, in our sample report of customers and their transactions, the transactions are grouped by the customer number. Customer numbers will appear on the report in ascending alphanumeric order. The sort order can be changed for groups and their contents.

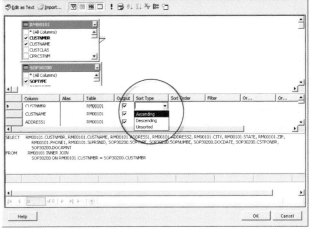

Data in a report can be sorted at a couple of different levels. Most of theses levels actually relate to groups.

Rows returned by the Dataset can be sorted through commands entered in the Dataset Query itself. In the Query Designer, select the fields to be sorted. In the Sort column, select Ascending or Descending to indicate the direction of the sort.

If more than one field is to be used to sort the data (such as our Last Name, First Name) indicate the sort order in the Sort Order column. Using our example, Last Name would be marked 1 (as the first sort field) and First Name would be marked 2 (as the second sort field).

The next level where sorting can occur is the Detail Group. When rows returned from the Dataset are placed on the report, they are actually placed in a Group named Details by default. In the Row Groups pane, select the Details group and right click. Open the Group Properties window and select the Sorting screen.

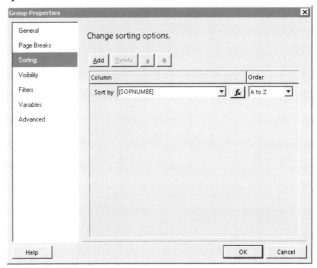

To sort the rows in the group, click the Add button to add a sort column to the screen. Two fields and a Function ( 𝑓ₓ ) icon are added to the screen. In the first field, select from the pull down list the datafield to be used to sort the rows. Alternately, the Function icon can be clicked to open the Expression Builder where an expression can be used to select the data used to sort the rows. In the Order field, select either A to Z or Z to A to sort the rows in ascending or descending order.

Multiple fields can be used to sort the rows by adding more than one set of sort criteria to the screen. The topmost field in the list is the primary sort field. For example, to sort a list of customers by Last Name then First Name, the Last Name field would be selected first in the topmost set of criteria followed by the First Name.

When rows on a report are grouped, the group is automatically sorted by the selected Grouping fields. For example, when we added a group by customer number to our report, the customer number list was sorted in ascending order. This is accomplished by the system automatically adding a set of sort criteria to the Sorting screen of the Group Properties window for the group by fields. By default, the rows are sorted in ascending (A to Z) order. The sort order can be changed and additional fields added to the sort list. Removing the grouping fields from the Sort window or moving them out of the topmost position is not recommended.

# VI.  *Formatting Text and Data*

# VI.  *Formatting Text and Data*

Visual Studio provides a large number of features that allow a report designer to create a well formatted and easy to read data presentation. In the earlier pages of this manual, we have discussed many of the formatting options.  In this chapter, we will attempt to create a comprehensive list of formatting tools and explain their use.

Some parameter pages have been discussed in other sections.  For example, the Report Parameter Properties are discussed in Chapter V under Adding Report Parameters.  This chapter will focus on fonts, lines, spacing, data placement, et cetera.

# VI.A.  *Common Property Screens*

In many of the objects used to build reports in SSRS, properties windows contain screens that are identical between different objects.  For example, when an object such as a Text Box, a Tablix or an Image can be bordered, the Border screen works the same regardless of the object type.  Rather than repeating screen images and text over and over again, we are listing the common Property Screens first.  In the sections that follow, individual objects will be discussed and, when a common screen such as the Border screen applies, this section will be referenced.

# VI.A.1.    Border

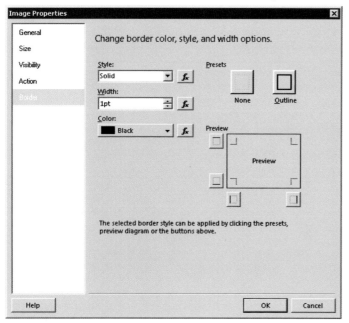

The **Properties Border** screen allows a border to be drawn around the object. Before applying the border to the Text Box, the Style, Width and Color fields should be set. Then apply the border by clicking either on the Presets or by clicking one or more of the Preview buttons.

The **Style** of a border can be Solid, Dotted, Dashes, or Double lines. The **Width** or weight of the line can be any value from 1/4 of a point up to 24 points in 1/4 point steps. Use the Up and Down arrows on the field to locate and select the desired line weight.

By default, most Text Boxes are surrounded by a Light Grey 1point line. If no lines are desired, these must be removed.

Lines from the Toolbox cannot span multiple objects. If a line across several objects is needed, then the Border option must be used. Create a border on the top or bottom only across the several objects. The same rule applies for lines running up and down across several objects.

Object types that support this property include:

- Text Boxes

- Tablix (tables and matrixes)

- Images

# VI.A.2.    Sorting

Sorting ensures that data appears in a prescribed order, usually Alphanumeric and either ascending or descending.

Rows can be sorted on multiple fields. Contact information, for example, sometimes has First and Last Names in separate fields. Simply sorting by Last Name is not sufficient as there are quite a number of people that share the same last name. Thus, by sorting first on the Last Name and then on the First name, a properly organized list can be printed.

If data is grouped, the groups are printed by default in ascending alphanumeric order. For example, in our sample report of customers and their transactions, the transactions are grouped by the customer number. Customer numbers will appear on the report in ascending alphanumeric order. The sort order can be changed for groups and their contents.

Data can be sorted in the Dataset as part of the query that returns the rows to the reports. That style of sorting is specific to the Dataset object. Please review the section of this manual on Datasets for information on sorting inside a query.

The next level where sorting can occur is the Detail Group. When rows returned from the Dataset are placed on the report, they are actually placed in a Group named Details by default. In the Row Groups pane, select the Details group and right click. Open the Group Properties window and select the Sorting screen.

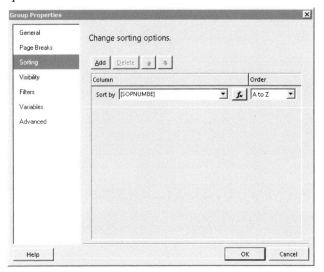

To sort the rows in the group, click the Add button to add a sort column to the screen. Two fields and a Function ( $f_x$ ) icon are added to the screen. In the first field, select from the pull down list the data field to be used to sort the rows. Alternately, the Function icon can be clicked to open the Expression Builder where an expression can be used to select the data used to sort the rows. In the Order field, select either A to Z or Z to A to sort the rows in ascending or descending order.

Multiple fields can be used to sort the rows by adding more than one set of sort criteria to the screen. The topmost field in the list is the primary sort field. For example, to sort a list of customers by Last Name then First Name, the Last Name field would be selected first in the topmost set of criteria followed by the First Name.

When rows on a report are grouped, the group is automatically sorted by the selected Grouping fields. For example, when we added a group by customer number to our report, the customer number list was sorted in ascending order. This is accomplished by the system automatically adding a set of sort criteria to the Sorting screen of the Group Properties window for the group by fields. By default, the rows are sorted in ascending (A to Z) order. The sort order can be changed and additional fields added to the sort list. Removing the grouping fields from the Sort window or moving them out of the topmost position is not recommended.

Object types that support this property include:

- Tablix (Table and Matrix)

- Groups

# VI.A.3. Filters

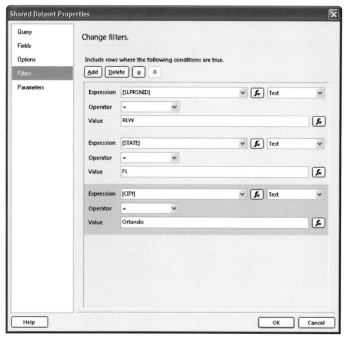

The Filters screen allows the report designer to limit the rows selected to appear on a report. The filters can be hard coded (only select sales for rep RLW) or parameter based (let the user enter a sales rep ID when the report is executed and compare the data in the parameter against the sales rep field in the data.)

The value entered by the user in a Parameter field must be compared to data in a field in the tables from the Dataset. A filter is created to make this comparison. If the filter evaluates to True, the data is displayed on the report, otherwise, it is omitted. To create a filter, click the Add button on the Filters screen.

A set of 4 fields will be added to the Filters list.

The **Expression** field is used to select the Dataset field to be matched. Using the pull down list box, a list of fields selected in the query is shown. Select the desired field.

The Function Icon ( 𝑓ₓ ) allows a function to be written around the data fields. For example, the report designer may want to select all records where the ZIP code starts with "3". Clicking on the function icon opens the Expression window. See the section below on the use of the Expression window.

The Comparison Type field tells the filter how to compare the Expression to the Value. For example, when using Greater Than or Less Than operators, considering the expression to be Text versus an Integer can yield different results. Valid Comparison Types are:

**Text** -- The field or expression is considered to be text, even if the text is composed of numbers.

**Boolean** -- The field or expression is evaluated as either true or false. Any value that equals 0 is considered false, other values are considered True.

**Date/Time** -- The field or expression is considered to be a SQL Date/Time value.

**Integer** -- The field or expression is considered to be an integer.

**Float** -- The field or expression is considered to be a float value with decimal points.

An example of the importance of the Comparison Type field is seen when lists of numbers are used. If a text comparison is performed, the text 2 is considered greater than the text 15. However if an integer comparison is performed, the number 2 is less than the number 15.

The Operator field determines how the Expression is compared to the Value. Valid operators are:

= -- The Expression must equal the value.

<> -- The Expression must be different from the value for the filter to be evaluated as True.

**Like** -- The Expression must match the fixed portion of the value. For example, if the value is expressed as RL%, any Expression starting with RL followed by any characters will cause the comparison to be evaluated as True.

> -- The Expression must be greater than the Value field for the filter to be evaluated as true.

>= -- The Expression must be greater than or equal to the Value field for the filter to be evaluated as true.

< -- The Expression must be less than the Value field for the filter to be evaluated as true.

<= -- The Expression must be less than or equal to the Value field for the filter to be evaluated as true.

**Top N** -- The data is sorted by the Expression field and a specified number of records is selected from the top of the list. The number of records to be returned by the Data Source is specified in the Value Field.

**Bottom N** -- The data is sorted by the Expression field and a specified number of records is selected from the bottom of the list. The number of records to be returned by the Data Source is specified in the Value Field.

**Top %** -- The data is sorted by the Expression field and a percentage of the total number of records is selected from the top of the list. The percentage to be returned by the Data Source is specified in the Value Field.

**Bottom %** -- The data is sorted by the Expression field and a percentage of the total number of records is selected from the top of the list. The percentage to be returned by the Data Source is specified in the Value Field.

**In** -- The data found in the field specified in the Expression field must appear in the list of values entered into the Value field.

**Between** -- The Value field is split into two fields and the value found in the field specified in the Expression field must be between the first and last values entered in the two Value fields.

The name of the parameter to be matched must be entered into the Value field. Simply typing the name, however, will not work. The Expression Builder must be used to insert the parameter name. Click on the function button next to the Value field to open the Expression Builder. In the window, select Parameters in the Categories column and then select the desired parameter from the list in the Values field.

Click OK to save the formula. If several parameters have been defined, it may be necessary to create several filters.

When all of the filters have been defined as desired, click OK on the Dataset Properties window to close the window and save the filters.

Object types that support this property include:

- Datasets

- Tablix (Tables and Matrixes)

- Groups

# VI.A.4.     Visibility

The Visibility screen allows objects to be defined and hidden. Typically, most objects in a report should be displayed and should be visible. However, in some cases, Groups, Rows, Columns, Text Boxes et cetera may need to be hidden from view under specific conditions.

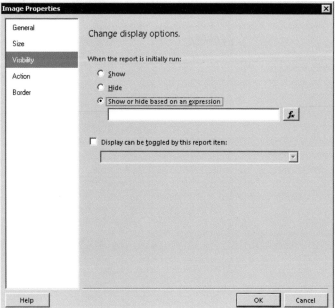

For example, a message (text in a Text Box) may be printed on a report only if the customer's account balance is past due. In this case, the Text Box would be placed on the report and hidden if the customer's balance is current.

Another example involves the display of an appropriate message. The report designer might want to print an easily read message indicating how far past due the customer is. In this case, three or four Text Boxes, each containing a specific message (such as "Over 30", "Over 60",

"Over 90", "Account on Hold") are placed in the same space on the report, one on top of the other. All are hidden by default with code that shows the appropriate message.

The Visibility screen is basically the same for each object that supports the property.

Three radio buttons control when the object is displayed:

**Show** -- The object always appears on the report.

**Hide** -- The object is always hidden or not shown on the report.

**Show or Hide Based on an Expression** -- The object will be shown or hidden based on an expression. When the expression returns TRUE, the object will be hidden. If the expression returns FALSE, the object will be shown. Expressions are constructed using the Expression Builder. Constants of True and False are provided in the Expression Builder to be returned to control the visibility of the object.

Other objects in the report can be used to control the visibility of the current object. For example, a different object can use an expression to calculate a True or False value. That report object can then be used to control the display by checking the box next to the prompt Display Can Be Toggled By This Report Option and then selecting the report object in the pull down list.

Object types that support this property include:

- Text Boxes

- Tablix

- Images

- Groups

- Rows

- Columns

# VI.A.5.    Fill

The Fill property screen allows the background of several different objects to be filled with a selected color and/or image. The application of the fill color, even the color itself and/or the image used can be controlled with an expression if desired.

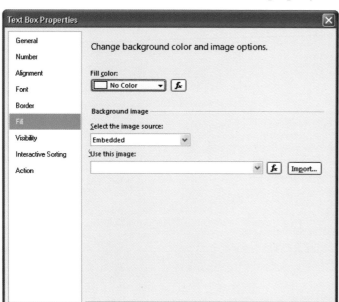

There are two areas in the Fill screen: the color and the image area.

A Fill Color can be selected from the pull down list. Clicking on the arrow opens a display of 40 standard colors. Any one can be selected as the background color by clicking the color on the display. If a finer color designation is needed, click on the More Colors option. The Select Color window will be displayed.

The Select Color window allows colors to be selected from three different sources or RGB (Red, Green, Blue) or HSB (Hue, Saturation, Brightness) color schemes can be used to create the desired color by setting the appropriate values.

On the left side of the Select Color window, a pull down list allows the report designer to pick a Color Selector. Picking one of these items displays a matching color chart. The report designer can pick the fill color by selecting one of the color options from the color pallet or touching the desired color on the color wheel or color square.

On the right side of the Select Color window, the report designer can select to use either RGB or HSB color schemes and then set the appropriate parameters.

In all cases, the selected color will be displayed in the Color Sample pane.

When the desired color has been identified, click OK to select the color and return to the Fill Properties window.

A function button opens the Expression Builder, allowing a formula to be written to set colors based on criteria or data available to the report. For example, a formula can be written that will set the background color to Yellow if the customer's balance is 30 days or more overdue. Multiple tiers can be defined, using several colors for several levels of severity in the aging.

Constants in the Expression Builder associated with the color field represent colors to be displayed. Conditional statements can then be written (using these predefined constants) that say "IF DOCAMT >50000 THEN ORANGE" which will change the fill color to orange if the document amount is greater than $50,000.

The lower half of the Fill Parameter screen allows the report designer to select an image to appear on the report.

Images from three different sources can be used: External, Embedded and Database.

**External Images** require an acceptable image file to be located in a folder on the system accessible to all individuals that may run the report or properly filed in Sharepoint. When External is selected as the Image Source, the system will display one field where a fully qualified URL is entered to define the location of the image. For example, if the image is located on the server, the URL may be in the form:

*http://<servername>/folder1/folder2..../image.jpg*

If the image is published in a Sharepoint server, the URL may be in the form:

*http://<SharePointServerName>/<site>/folder1/folder2..../image.jpg*

**Embedded Images** are imported into the Project as part of the current document. The report designer can use the Report Data pane, click on Images and import the desired image.

When Embedded is selected in the Image Source, a single field is offered with a pull down list of the images imported into the Report Data Image folder. Select the desired image from the list. (If a new image needs to be imported, an Import button opens a file browser. Locate the new image and it will be automatically imported into the Report Data Image folder.)

**Database Images** are stored in one of the tables of the database and exposed to the report through the Dataset.

When Database is selected as the Image Source, two fields are displayed. In the first field, the database field containing the images is selected. In the second field, the image type is selected.

Object types that support this property include:

- Text Boxes

- Tablix

- Images

# VI.A.6.    Action Screen

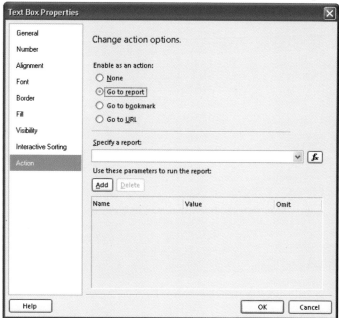

The **Action Properties** screen allows the report designer to define an action to be taken when a user displays the report on screen and clicks the object.

The default action is **None**. And, if a report is designed primarily to be printed to paper, this is really the only valid option. However, if reports are typically used as on-screen displays, the Action properties allow the report to be linked to other objects.

The **Go To Report** option allows the user to launch a second report from the current one. When this option is marked, the report designer must select one of the reports created in the current Project.

In many cases, the new report to be launched will have parameters that control the execution of the report. When the current report launches a second report, it can provide the appropriate data for the parameters, Click the Add button under the Use These Parameters to Run the Report prompt to insert a set of fields for each parameter in the target report.

In the parameter Name field, click on the pull down arrow to display a list of the parameters in the target report. Then, in the value field either enter a specific value or select a value that appears on the host report from the pull down list. Of course, the Expression builder may be used to generate the value by clicking on the Function ( $f_x$ ) icon next to the value field.

Values must be defined for each parameter in the target or second report.

Object types that support this property include:

- Text Boxes

- Images

# VI.A.7.    Shadow Screen

The **Shadow Properties** screen allows the shadows available around some objects to be configured.  Two options are available.

**Shadow Offset** -- Use the scrolling controls to increase or decrease the size of the shadow applied to the object.

**Shadow Color** -- Clicking the pull down arrow opens a color picker window.  The report designer can select the color of the shadow using this option.

Functions can be written for either of the options.  A function for the Shadow Offset must return a value that can be used as the shadow size while the function for the Shadow Color must return a color.

# VI.A.8.    3D Effects Screen

The **3D Options Properties** screen allows the report designer to apply 3D effects to certain report objects such as bar charts et cetera.  Applying 3D effects to a chart can turn a plain flat display into a more attractive display of the data.

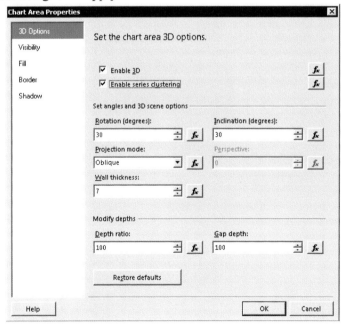

**Enable 3D** --  This box must be checked to enable 3D effects.

**Enable Series Clustering** -- If more than one series of data points is used in the chart, by default each series will occupy a row in the 3D rendering.  To show the series bars side by side, check this box.

**Set Angles and 3D Scene Options Group** --The options below determine the angles  applied to the 3D effects.  Apply them carefully!

**Rotation (degrees)** -- This parameter rotates the entire 3D display side by side.  It is akin to walking past a building to get a different view.  The default value is 30 degrees.

**Inclination (degrees)** -- This value defines the tilt to the 3D projection. It is akin to climbing up a latter to get a different view of an area. The default value is 30 degrees.

**Projection Mode** -- Projection mode allows the report designer to specify whether the chart should appear to get smaller in areas that appear further away. Options are Oblique (no spatial projection), or Perspective (apply projection)

**Perspective** -- If Perspective is selected as the Projection Mode, this field allows the report designer to specify the how much smaller "distant" areas are compared to "near" areas of the chart. The default adjustment is 0.

**Wall Thickness** -- In 3 dimensional bar charts, for example, a wall is drawn behind, under, and to the left of the chart. This parameter allows the report designer to specify the thickness of the wall. The default value is 7.

### Modify Depths Group

**Depth Ratio** -- Specifies the depth of each bar in each series in the 3D rendering. The larger the number, the thicker the bar.

**Gap Depth** -- This number specifies the depth of the gap between rows of bars in the 3D rendering. Larger numbers result in larger separation between bars.

**Restore Defaults Button** -- When things get really messed up, click this button to restore the 3D settings to their default values.

# VI.A.9.   Number Screen

The **Text Box Properties Number** screen allows for the formatting of numeric data.  This includes integers, floating numbers, currencies, dates and times, percentages et cetera.  Scientific notation and custom formats are supported.

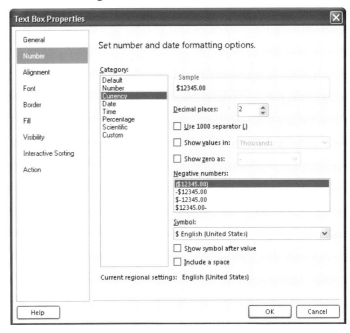

The default option for numeric formatting is that no formatting will be applied.  Data will be displayed in its native form.  If a field had 10 whole places and 5 decimals defined, then all 10 digits to the left of the decimal and 5 to the right will be displayed.

The **Number Category** provides options for the formatting of numbers not considered currency values.  Options in the Number Category include:

**Use Regional Formatting** -- The regional format defined when the desktop operating system was installed or last configured is used.  The current Regional Settings are displayed at the bottom of the window.

**Decimal Places** -- The number of decimal places up to the precision of the data can be specified.   If more decimal places are selected than are supported by the data, the extra places will be filled with zeros (0).

**Use 1000 Separator** -- Checking this box inserts the Thousands Separator when appropriate.  The separator to be used is defined by the Regional Settings and is displayed to the right of the prompt.

**Show Values In** -- Checking this box allows the report designer to select either Thousands, Millions or Billions.   The data in the field will be rounded to the specified level.  Extra zeros will not be shown.

**Show Zero As** -- Checking this box allows data with a value of zero (0) to be shown as either a blank field or a dash.  Once the box is checked, the report designer can select either option from a pull down list.

**Negative Numbers** -- Five options are offered for the presentation of negative numbers. They may be enclosed in parentheses ( ), shown with a leading minus sign, shown with a leading minus sign and a space, shown with a trailing minus sign, or a space followed by a trailing minus sign.

The **Currency Category** provides all of the same options as the Numeric Category plus three additional fields.

**Symbol** -- The symbol that designates the value as a currency value can be selected from this pull down list. A significant variety of characters is provided which should cover most currency systems in the world. By default, currency amounts will show the default symbol for the Current Regional Settings. If the Regional Settings are English (United States) for example, the default symbol will be the English dollar sign ($).

**Show Symbol After Value** -- Checking this box will show the currency symbol after the numeric value rather than before. Leaving the box unchecked shows the symbol before the value.

**Include a Space** -- Checking this box includes a space between the currency symbol and the numeric amount.

The **Date** and **Time Categories** each provide a list of formats that the report designer can select to provide dates and/or times printed in a desired manner. The 36 different formats offered should satisfy most report designers. Otherwise, an expression can be created for those really strange date or time formats.

The **Percentage Category** automatically multiplies the number by 100 and adds a percentage sign to the end. Thus .25 becomes 25%. If decimal places still are important, they can be shown with values such as .25125 showing as 25.125%. The number of decimal places to show can be specified. Also a check box places a space between the value and the percent sign.

The **Scientific Category** shows numbers in scientific notation. Thus very small numbers such as 0.000123 can be shown as 1.23E+004. The number of decimal places shown can be specified.

The **Custom Category** allows the report designer to type in a format string to control the display of the numeric data. For example, if the report designer enters 000009.99 as the format and a value of 12.34 is displayed, it will show as 000012.34, showing the leading zeros. This is useful in printing checks where the blank space needs to be consumed to avoid alterations.

# VI.A.10. Font

The **Text Box Properties Font** screen allows the report designer to specify the font characteristics for the information displayed in the Text Box.

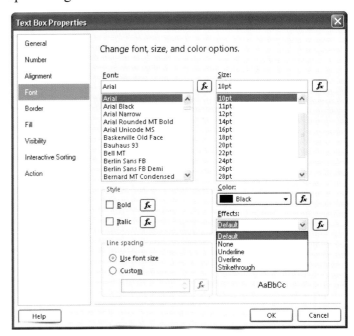

In the **Font** scrolling list box, a list of font **Faces** is shown. All of the fonts installed on the local workstation are shown and any may be selected. Report designers should be careful when selecting font faces. If a special face is installed on the report designer's machine but not on the machines of other users, the report probably will not look as expected. If reports are to be rendered on other machines, be sure to use a common font face.

The font **Size** can be specified by selecting a value from the Size scrolling list. A value can also by typed in, assuming that a TrueType face is selected (most fonts are TrueType today). An expression can be used to calculate the font size.

The **Style** of the font can be changed from regular to Bold and/or Italic by checking the appropriate box in the Style area of the screen. Again, an expression can be created that returns a True or False value to automatically change the style based on values in the report.

An almost infinite range of colors (limited by the monitors and printers used to render the report) can be selected. The Color pull down list shows a table of basic color selections. Clicking on the More Colors option opens the Select Color window with color pickers, RGB and HSB value specifications.

An expression can also be used to generate a standard color value, allowing the color of the text to be controlled by other information in the report. For example, if customer invoices are being displayed, past due invoices can be printed in Red, if desired using the Expression Builder.

Several **Effects** can be applied to the font. These include Underline, Overline, and Strikethrough. Again, the Expression Builder can be configured to select one of these effects based on a value in the report data.

**Line Spacing**, the space between lines printed in a Text Box can be controlled. A font size has a standard spacing associated with it and by default this standard spacing is used as long as the User Font Size option remains marked. If the Custom option is marked, the report designer must enter a value in points for the spacing between lines. And, yes, the Expression Builder can be used to calculate these gaps.

# VI.B.   ToolBox Items

The Toolbox is a pane with a number of icons that allows items to be dropped onto the pasteboard, providing significant design abilities to the report designer.  The Toolbox, if not present on the desktop, can be opened by selecting it in the View menu.

Some of the icons are simple such as adding lines and rectangles to a report.  Others, such as the Table, Matrix, Subreport and Text Box are quite powerful.

Each of these tools is described in detail in this section.

## VI.B.1.   Pointer

The Pointer tool is used to select other objects in the report.  Select the Pointer tool by clicking on the Pointer ( ➤ ) icon.  The cursor will change to the pointer shape.

## VI.B.2.   Text Box

The Text Box is the basic framing tool for any data (variable or constant) displayed on the report.  Every element on the pasteboard, the titles, the dates, page numbers, the various fields from the Datasets, et cetera are encapsulated in Text Boxes.  Even the structures of Tables and Matrixes are simply groups of Text Boxes linked into a single structure.

The Text Box tool allows a single Text Box to be dropped onto the pasteboard.  The user can drag-and-drop the Text Box ( ▭ ) icon, or right click on the pasteboard and select Text Box in the menu.  A Text Box will be placed on the pasteboard.  For such a simple object, the formatting options are significant.

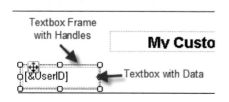

Textbox Frame with Handles

**My Custo**

[&UserID]     Textbox with Data

Clicking on the edge of the Text Box displays the Text Box Frame with handles and the directional arrows.  The Text Box can be moved using the cursor to drag it to the desired space or by clicking the directional arrows on the keyboard.  The Text Box can be resized by grabbing one of the handles with the mouse and pulling it in the desired direction.

Other formatting options are accessed by right clicking in the empty space inside the Text Box.  The Text Box menu is displayed.

The Layout option on the Text Box menu allows the user to move the Text Box forward or backward in the stack of objects that may share the same space on the pasteboard. A Text Box may be placed in the same space with an image and the designer wishes the data in the Text Box to appear on top of the image rather than be hidden behind it. Click Bring Forward to move the Text Box one layer toward the top or Bring to Front to move the Text Box to the top of the stack of objects. Send Backward and Send to Back work the same way but place the Text Box under other objects.

The Expression option on the menu opens the Expression Builder window to allow the report designer to create an expression to provide data to be displayed in the Text Box. The use of the Expression Builder is explained later in this chapter of this manual.

The Text Box Properties option on the menu opens the Text Box Properties window. There are nine screens to the Text Box Properties window.


## VI.B.2.a.    General Screen


The **Text Box Properties General** screen shows the Text Box name, the source of the Value displayed in the text box, ToolTip help for on-screen displays and options that control the growth and shrinkage of the Text Box.

All Text Boxes have a name automatically assigned. It may be as simple as Text Box42 (the 42nd Text Box placed on the report) or the name of the field displayed in the Text Box.

The Value field can hold a constant, such as the name of the report or any other prompt or label that appears on the report, data from the Dataset or an expression. If the Value field contains a label such as [&*fieldname*], then the contents of the field *fieldname* from the Dataset will be displayed in the space. If the Value field holds the results of an expression built in the Expression Builder window, it will display the text <Expr>.

The Expression Builder can be used to create an expression, the results of which will be displayed in the Text Box. Click on the Function ( $f_x$ ) icon to open the Expression Builder.

The functions in the Expression Builder allow the report designer to display parts of fields, change the fields to all upper case or all lower case, display selected values based on the contents of other fields (such as the phrase "CREDIT BALANCE" if a customer balance is a negative value or a credit) and much more.

# VI.B.2.c.    Alignment

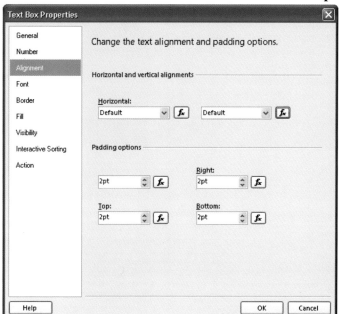

The **Text Box Properties Alignment** screen controls the alignment of the information displayed in the Text Box as well as padding between the data and the edge of the Text Box frame.

Two fields on this screen control the Horizontal and Vertical alignment of data inside the Text Box:

**Horizontal** -- Options include the default for the type of data, General the same as the default setting, Left, Center and Right.

**Vertical** -- Options include the default for the type of data, Top, Middle or Bottom. In a large Text Box, for example, a block of text might need to be displayed at the top of the box expanding down or in the bottom of the box expanding up.

Padding is the amount of space between the information displayed in the Text Box and the edge of the box itself. By default, two points of padding surround the information. Seldom is extra padding needed but having the option provides some interesting opportunities.

For example, if a report is designed that shows components on a Bill of Material and all levels of the BOM are shown, it is convenient to indent the components based on their level. An expression can be written that takes the component level (minus 1) and multiplies it by 10 to generate the left padding value. This would cause each component to be indented 10 points per level down the BOM.

## VI.B.2.d.　Numbers Screen

The **Text Box Properties Numbers** screen defines the way numbers are shown in the text box.

The Number screen is a common property and is discussed in detail in Section VI.A. of this chapter.

## VI.B.2.e.　Font

The **Text Box Properties Font** screen defines the way text is displayed in the Text Box.

The Font screen is a common property and is discussed in detail in Section VI.A. of this chapter.

## VI.B.2.f.　Border Screen

The **Text Box Properties Border** screen allows a border to be drawn around the Text Box.

The Border screen is a common property and is discussed in detail in Section VI.A. of this chapter.

## VI.B.2.g.　Fill Screen

The **Text Box Properties Fill** screen allows the report designer to apply a background color or image to a Text Box.

The Fill screen is a common property and is discussed in detail in Section VI.A of this chapter.

## VI.B.2.h.    Visibility Screen

The **Text Box Properties Visibility** screen allows the report designer to control if and when the Text Box appears on the report.

The Visibility screen is a common property and is discussed in detail in Section VI.A of this chapter.

The Expression Builder is very helpful in this respect, allowing programmatic control of the display of information on the report.

The Visibility screen is a common property and is discussed in detail in Section VI.A of this chapter.

## VI.B.2.i.    Interactive Sorting Screen

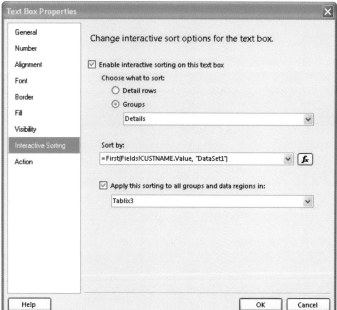

The **Text Box Properties Interactive Sorting** screen allows the report designer to pass the ability to sort data and the direction of the sort to the end user. When an end user runs the report to the screen, up and down arrows will be displayed on the selected object. The end user (not the report designer but the person running the report) can then click on an arrow and sort the data as desired.

Check the box labeled Enable Interactive Sorting on this Text Box to enable sorting by the user. Until this box is checked, no other fields on the screen are active.

In the Choose What to Sort options, select to sort either the Detail Rows or the Groups. If Groups is selected and more than one group is defined on the report, the report designer needs to specify which group level the user may sort.

In the Sort By field, pick the field that will control the order of the data when sorted. For example, if the Customer Number field is selected, when the user sorts the data it will be sorted by the Customer Number. The user can control whether the data will be sorted ascending or descending but the report designer picks the field to sort by.

Unless the next box is checked, the sorting option applies only to the current group or data area. When the Apply This Sorting to All Groups And Data Regions In box is marked, the report designer can offer the sorting option to all groups and data regions by selecting the desired range in the pull down list.

## VI.B.2.j.    Action Screen

The **Text Box Properties Action** screen allows the report designer to define an action to be taken when a user displays the report on screen and clicks the Text Box.

The Visibility screen is a common property and is discussed in detail in Section VI.A of this chapter.

## VI.B.3.    Line

Lines are useful formatting tools that can be used to separate sections of reports, visually break groups of rows into a section for each detail record and otherwise make the report more readable.

To place a line on a report, drag the Line ( ＼ ) icon from the Toolbox onto the pasteboard. Place the cursor at the desired starting location for the line and pull the line across to the desired ending location. (A line can also be inserted by right clicking in the desired starting location and selecting Insert →Line. A short line will be placed on the pasteboard. Drag the endpoints to the desired locations.)

**Table versus Tablix**

There are two primary report styles supported by Visual Studio and SSRS: tables and matrixes. Many of the functions, features, and parameters for a table apply to a matrix. Thus, Microsoft invented a new word to refer to a reporting structure on the pasteboard, the Tablix. A Tablix can be either a table or a matrix report, depending on how the grouping is controlled.

Tables are grouped by rows only and details are printed. Matrixes have data grouped by rows and columns and aggregated data is displayed.

Lines are formatted using pull down lists in the menu area of the Designer. First, make sure the line is selected by clicking it with the mouse. The line handles will appear at each end of the line. Then use the pull down lists to select the desired values. Lines can be solid, dashed or dotted. Their weight can be adjusted from 1/4 point to 6 points (a point is 1/64th of an inch), and they can be rendered in a wide variety of colors, including black, the default.

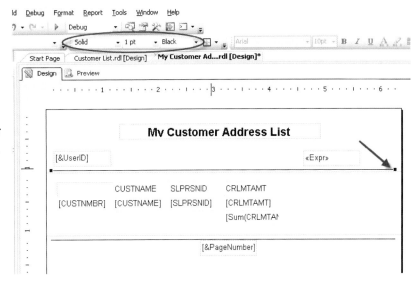

# VI.B.4.    Table/Tablix

The Table tool allows the report designer to specify the number of columns of data to appear on the report, the individual data elements to be printed, and the heading to appear over each column.  It is a shortcut to building clean tabular reports.

A table report layout is placed on the pasteboard by dragging and dropping the Table ( ▥ ) tool onto the pasteboard.

The use of the Table tool to format a table report is discussed in detail in Chapter V of this manual.  However, in the next few pages, we will discuss the options available for a Table placed on the report using the Table tool.

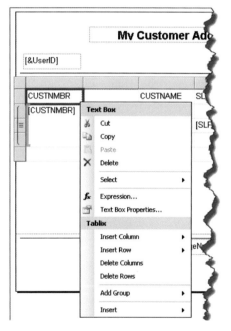

# VI.B.4.a.    Tablix Menus

Most of the formatting options and parameters for a table or matrix report are launched from a Tablix Menu.  Once a table (or matrix) has been placed on the pasteboard, right clicking in different areas of the object opens different menus.  Different options are available on each of these different menus.

If the cursor is placed in a Text Box in the Tablix and right clicked, the Text Box/Tablix combination menu is displayed.  This menu contains options for both the Text Box object and the Tablix object.

If the cursor is placed over one of the blocks of the frame around the tablix (click on the tablix to show the frame), and right clicked, the Tablix menu is shown with a few select option.  One of these options, however, provides access to the Tablix Properties window.  The screens of this window will be discussed below.

Tablix objects also have a Properties Page.  Properties Pages often provide additional options to the report designer but are not as easy to use as properties displayed on the Properties Window.

# VI.B.4.b.    Adding/Deleting Columns/Rows

Using the Tablix menus, the report designer can easily insert new rows or columns into the table.  If a new row is inserted into the Details area, then each row will be printed for each row of data returned from the Dataset.  If a row is inserted above or below the Details area, it is available for column headings or report totals.

If a table report is grouped and rows are inserted, the report designer must select to insert the row inside or outside the group.  If the row is inserted inside the group, it belongs to the group data.  Outside of the group, it belongs to the column headings or totals area for the group.

Columns are added in the same manner.

Columns can also be added by dragging a data item from the Reports Data Dataset area onto the Tablix and placing it on a line between two columns.  A new column will be created between the two existing columns.

# VI.B.4.c.    Setting Column Width/Row Height

Setting a column width can be simple or precise.  And there are two different ways to accomplish the task.

The simple way to adjust a column width is to grab the line on the right edge of a column in the Text Box Frame and move the line.  The column width will grow or shrink when the line is pulled to the right or left.

To accurately adjust the column width, the Column Properties Page must be used.

In the Tablix object, click to expose the Table Frame.  Click on the desired column in the Table Frame.  If the Properties Pane is not already displayed, select either View → Properties Window or click the F4 button.  Locate in the Properties Pane the Size group.  Click on the Plus Sign ( + ) next to the Size prompt to show the Size Parameter set.  In the Width parameter, set the desired within inches or fractions of an inch ( ie 1.75in ).  This allows the width of the column to be set accurately.

Row height can be controlled in the same manner.

## VI.B.4.d.    Setting Type Parameters

Font characteristics are easily set for individual text boxes using the Font Screen in the Text Box Parameters window. However, using that screen requires the report designer to set the font characteristics for each Text Box individually. When a large number of Text Boxes appear on the report, this can be time consuming.

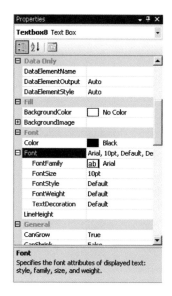

The Tablix (the entire collection of Text Boxes) has it's own Properties Pane. In this Properties Pane, font characteristics can be set that will be the default values for all Text Boxes. Note that these values MUST be set before any specific formatting is performed for individual Text Boxes.

Click on the Tablix area on the pasteboard so that the Table Frame is displayed. Make sure that the Properties Pane is shown or hit the F4 key (or select View → Properties Window). Scroll down the Properties Pane for the Tablix until the Font Group is seen. Click on the Plus Sign ( + ) next to the Font Group to expand the list of properties. Set each of the font properties as desired. These new settings will be applied to all Text Boxes in the Tablix.

## VI.B.4.e.    The General Properties Page

Most (but not all) of the properties for a Tablix can be set in the Tablix Properties window. This formatted window provides 4 screens with fields to be used to set the parameters. The four screens are the General, Visibility, Filters and Sorting.

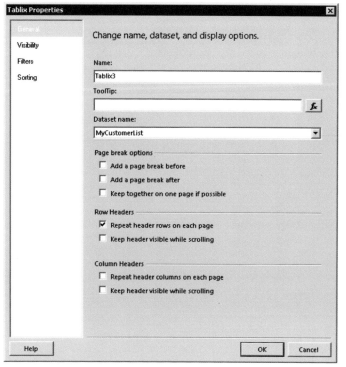

The **Tablix Properties General** screen provides access to properties of the Tablix used to name the object, set page break options and set Row and Column Header options.

### Page Break Options

Three check boxes are provided to allow control of page breaks:

**Add A Page Break Before** -- Checking this box causes the system to insert a page break before rendering the Tablix object.

**Add a Page Break After** -- Checking this box causes the system to insert a page break after rendering the Tablix object.

**Keep Together on One Page If Possible** -- If possible, the system will render the Tablix object and keep it on one page. If necessary, a page break will be inserted before the Tablix data area to allow enough room to render the Tablix on a single sheet of paper.

## Row Headers

The Row Headers area provides two check boxes that control the display/printing of the headers that appear down the left side of the Tablix.

**Repeat Header Rows on Each Page** --When the report is printed, the Row Headers that appear to the left of the data area will be repeated on each page if the report requires more than one page to print the entire width of the report.

**Keep Header While Scrolling** -- If the report is rendered on screen and this box is checked, the row headers will remain on screen as the data area of the Tablix is scrolled side to side.

## Column Headers

The Column Headers area provides two check boxes that control the display/printing of the headers that appear across the top of the Tablix.

**Repeat Header Columns on Each Page** -- If the report is printed, the Column Headers are printed across the top of each page of the report.

**Keep Header Visible While Scrolling** -- If the report is rendered on screen and this box is checked, the column headers will remain on screen as the data area of the Tablix is scrolled.

## VI.B.4.f.    Visibility

The **Tablix Properties Visibility** screen provides options to control the display or hiding of the Tablix. This screen is a common format screen and described in Section VI.A. of this chapter.

## VI.B.4.g.    Filters

The **Tablix Properties Filters** screen allows the report designer to filter the rows that will appear on the report. The Filters screen is a common screen and is described in detail in Section VI.A. of this chapter.

## VI.B.4.h.    Sorting

The **Tablix Properties Sorting** screen allows the report designer to define the manner in which rows of data are sorted. The Sort screen is a common screen and is described in detail in Section VI.A. of this chapter.

# VI.B.5.    Matrix

The Matrix tool ( ▢ ) places a 2x2 matrix on the pasteboard allowing the report designer to group the rows in two directions and show summary information. As was seen in the prior chapter, the matrix allows Group By fields across the top and down the left side.

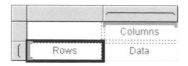

Additional columns and rows can be inserted into the Matrix object both inside and outside the groups. Rows or columns inside the groups are repeated for each group while rows or columns outside the groups are not repeated and used either for headers or totals.

Clicking the mouse on any cell in the matrix displays the table frame. On a matrix, the table frame contains parentheses that indicate the row and column groups. This table frame is not printed on the final report but is a useful tool for building the report. Right clicking on a cell in the matrix opens a Text Box/Tablix menu. Right clicking on one of the cells of the Table Frame opens a Tablix menu only with some different options than the combination menu. Right clicking on the block in the upper left corner of the Table Frame opens a menu with even another group of options.

The Matrix tool supports all of the functions of the Table tool. The difference is the grouping of data. In a Table report, data can be grouped by rows. In a Matrix report, data can be grouped by rows and columns.

Cells or Text Boxes in the body of a Matrix report do not display detail data. Since the data is grouped in two directions, only summary information can be displayed. The data in the body of a Matrix report is summarized by one of the aggregation functions described later in this chapter.

For example, if rows are grouped by customer number and columns are grouped by sales document type, then the data cells can contain a sum of the amounts of each document type for each customer. Or, the cells can contain a count of each document type for each customer.

If multiple columns or rows are inserted into the group, the report can show both a count of documents and a total amount of the documents per document type for each customer.

Multiple groups can be used. In our example of customer sales documents, the documents can be grouped by customer and then the customers grouped by territory. Now, a list of territories is presented with the customers in each territory listed. The summary data for customers can show the dollar amount of each type of sales document. Subtotals by Territory are available as well as a grand total at the bottom of the report.

All of the menus and properties described in the Table tool section of this chapter apply to the Matrix tool. (That is why Microsoft calls the report area a Tablix, a combination of a table and matrix.) Refer to the Table tool section of this chapter for information on the property pages available.

# VI.B.6.    Rectangle

The Rectangle tool ( ☐ ) in the Tool Box allows the report designer to place a rectangle on the report. A rectangle can be placed on the pasteboard surrounding either of the report tools (the table tool or the matrix tool) or inside any Text Box.

To place a rectangle around the report data, place the rectangle on the pasteboard first and then place the report layout tool (table or matrix) inside the rectangle. If the rectangle is added to the report after the report layout tools, the report data could be rendered outside of the rectangle.

Note: It is better to use the border properties of the report tool to draw an outline around data in the report.

The properties of the Rectangle are set either through setting fields in the menu area of the Report Designer or set through Properties page. Click on the Rectangle object and ensure that the Properties page is displayed (hit the F4 key or select View → Properties Window). Locate the desired properties and edit as desired.

**Usable Image Types**

At the time of this writing, the following image types could be used in a report. Additional types may be added as software updates are released.

- bmp
- jpg
- jpeg
- gif
- png
- x-png

# VI.B.7.    List

The List tool ( 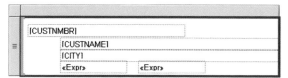 ) provides a data space that is repeated for each row returned from the Dataset.  Inside the List box space, multiple Text Boxes can be placed free form to display data elements.  The List tool places a Tablix with no predefined grouping other than the detail rows group.  All of the properties of a Tablix apply to the List object.  (Review the Table tool for Tablix properties.

An example of the use of the List Tablix is shown.  In this example, the customer number is followed by the customer name and parts of the address in a format similar to an address label,  This information is printed on the report for each record returned from the data set.

Text Boxes with data or labels, expressions, et cetera can be placed free form in the list box.

# VI.B.7.    Image

The Image tool supports the placement of images on a report and provides a set of property pages to control the formatting of the image.  The actual images can be stored in a common folder, embedded in the report itself or in the database.

If an image is dragged from the Report Data Images folder onto the report, the Image Properties accompany the image.  If the user drags the image tool onto the report, they need to specify the actual image and source.

# VI.B.7.a.   General Screen

The Image Properties General screen allows the image to be named, provide a ToolTip to be displayed if the report is rendered to a screen and to select the source of the image.

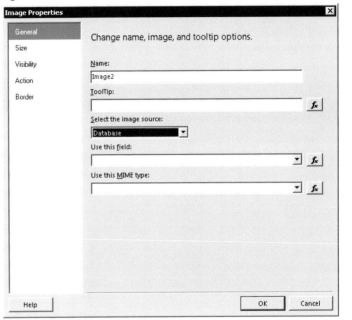

The **Name** field is used to provide a name for the specific placed image on the report. The name is useful for locating the object should the Parameters pane be needed to adjust the parameters of the image.

The **ToolTip** appears when the user hovers the cursor over the image when the report is displayed on screen.

Images from three different sources can be used: External, Embedded and Database.

**External Images** require an acceptable image file to be located in a folder on the system accessible to all individuals that may run the report or properly filed in Sharepoint. When External is selected as the Image Source, the system will display one field where a fully qualified URL is entered to define the location of the image. For example, if the image is located on the server, the URL may be in the form:

*http://<servername>/folder1/folder2..../image.jpg*

If the image is published in a Sharepoint server, the URL may be in the form:

*http://<SharePointServerName>/<site>/folder1/folder2..../image.jpg*

**Embedded Images** are imported into the Project as part of the current document. The report designer can use the Report Data pane, click on Images and import the desired image.

When Embedded is selected in the Image Source, a single field is offered with a pull down list of the images imported into the Report Data Image folder. Select the desired image from the list. (If a new image needs to be imported, an Import button opens a file browser. Locate the new image and it will be automatically imported into the Report Data Image folder.)

**Database Images** are stored in one of the tables of the database and exposed to the report through the Dataset.

When Database is selected as the Image Source, two fields are displayed. In the first field, the database field containing the images is selected. In the second field, the image type is selected.

# VI.B.7.b.  Size Screen

The **Image Properties Size** screen provides controls that manage the size of the image on the report.

In the Display section of the screen, four option buttons are provided:

**Original Size** -- The image will be displayed on the report at its original size.

**Fit to Size** -- The image will be re-sized to fit the space it is being placed in.

**Fit Proportional** -- The image will be re-sized to fit in the allowed space but it will be re-sized maintaining the original proportions of the image. This prevents distortion of the image.

**Clip** -- Selecting this option causes the image to be trimmed or cropped to fit inside the space provided.

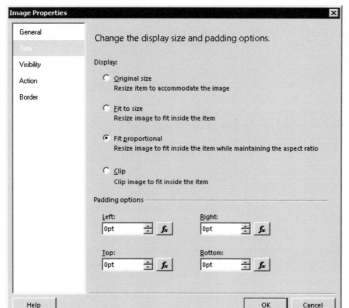

In the Padding Options area, four fields are provided to control the padding between the edge of the area that holds the image and the image itself. Padding is the space between the edge of the area and the object (in this case the image).

The default padding is 0 points (a point is 1/64th of an inch). The padding can be set independently for the Left, Right, Top and Bottom of the area. As well, the Expression Builder can be used to calculate a padding value.

## VI.B.7.c.    Visibility

The **Image Properties Visibility** screen provides options to control the display or hiding of the Tablix.  This screen is a common format screen and described in Section VI.A of this chapter.

## VI.B.7.d.    Action Screen

The **Image Properties Action** screen allows the report designer to define an action to be taken when a user displays the report on screen and clicks the image.

The Visibility screen is a common property and is discussed in detail in Section VI.A. of this chapter.

## VI.B.7.e.    Border Screen

The **Image Properties Border** screen allows a border to be drawn around the image area.

The Border screen is a common property and is discussed in detail in Section VI.A. of this chapter.

# VI.B.8.    Advanced Tools

The advanced tools are discussed in the next chapter.  These items include:

- Sub-reports
- Charts
- Gauges
- Mpas
- Data Bars
- Sparklines
- Indicators

# *VI.C.  Body Properties*

The Body parameters window is opened by right clicking in the body area on the pasteboard and selecting Body Properties.  There are two screens:  Fill and Border.

## VI.C.1.    Fill Screen

The **Body Properties Fill** screen allows the report designer to apply a background color or image to a Text Box.

The Fill screen is a common property and is discussed in detail in Section VI.A. of this chapter.

## VI.C.2.    Border Screen

The **Body Properties Border** screen allows a border to be drawn around the image area.

The Border screen is a common property and is discussed in detail in Section VI.A. of this chapter.

# *VI.D.  Header Properties*

The Header Properties window is opened by right clicking in the Header area of the pasteboard and selecting Header Properties.  There are three screens to this window:  General, Fill and Border.

## VI.D.1.  General Screen

The **Header Properties General** screen allows several print options to be set for the report header:

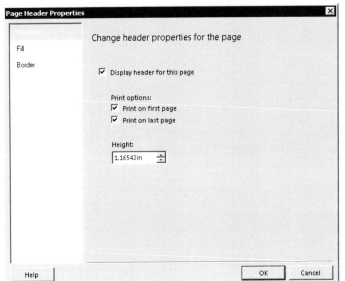

**Display Header for this Page** -- The page header is normally inserted by clicking on the Insert Header option on the Body menu.  If this box is un-checked, the header is removed.

**Print on First Page** -- Checking this box causes the header page to be printed on the first page of the report.

**Print on Last Page** -- Checking this box causes the header page to be printed on the last page of the report.

**Height** -- The height of the header area appears in this field.  The height can be set to a desired value by adjusting the value in this field.

## VI.D.2.  Fill Screen

The **Header Properties Fill** screen allows the report designer to apply a background color or image to a Text Box.

The Fill screen is a common property and is discussed in detail in Section VI.A. of this chapter.

## VI.D.3.  Border Screen

The **Header Properties Border** screen allows a border to be drawn around the image area.

The Border screen is a common property and is discussed in detail in Section VI.A. of this chapter.

# VI.E.  Footer Properties

The Footer Properties window is opened by right clicking in the Footer area of the pasteboard and selecting Footer Properties. There are three screens to this window: General, Fill and Border.

## VI.E.1.    General Screen

The **Footer Properties General** screen allows several print options to be set for the report Footer:

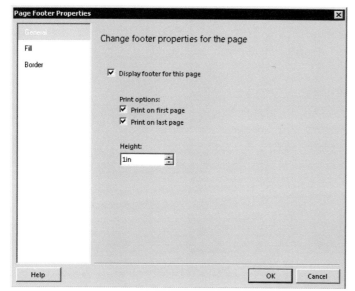

**Display Footer for this Page** -- The page footer is normally inserted by clicking on the Insert Footer option on the Body menu. If this box is un-checked, the footer is removed.

**Print on First Page** -- Checking this box causes the footer page to be printed on the first page of the report.

**Print on Last Page** -- Checking this box causes the footer page to be printed on the last page of the report.

**Height** -- The height of the footer area appears in this field. The height can be set to a desired value by adjusting the value in this field.

## VI.E.2.    Fill Screen

The **Footer Properties Fill** screen allows the report designer to apply a background color or image to a Text Box.

The Fill screen is a common property and is discussed in detail in Section VI.A. of this chapter.

## VI.E.3.    Border Screen

The **Footer Properties Border** screen allows a border to be drawn around the image area.

The Border screen is a common property and is discussed in detail in Section VI.A. of this chapter.

# VI.F.  *Group Properties*

Grouping in reports allows certain types of information to be printed together. When a Tablix is associated with a Dataset, by default, a Details Group is defined and placed in the report. This allows all fields from each row of information returned from the Dataset to be placed on the report together.

Other groups are added by the report designer as needed. For example, if a list of sales documents is grouped by Customer Number, then all of the sales documents are grouped together in Customer Number order. All of the rows for one entry in the group will be printed before any of the next group of rows is printed (i.e., all sales documents for one customer number will be printed before starting on the list of sales documents for the next customer.)

For more information on groups and their use, review Chapter V of this manual.

Each group has its own set of properties, including the default Details group. The Group Properties window is opened by right-clicking on the desired group in the Row or Column Groups pane and selecting Group Properties.

## VI.F.1.  General Screen

The **Group Properties General** screen allows the group to be named and the Group By expression(s) to be specified.

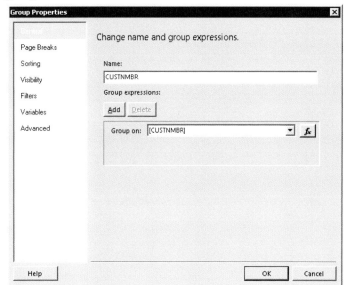

The **Name** of the group is displayed in the Row/ Column Groups panes and in the Properties Pane, allowing the report designer to locate the desired group when modifications are to be made to the properties. If data is being grouped on a field from the Dataset, the field name is the default group name.

The **Group On** field holds an expression that details how the rows are to be grouped. Typically this is a field from the Dataset but an expression can also be constructed. If a new group is being constructed, select the desired field from the pull down list or create an expression using the Expression Builder by clicking on the Function ( $f_x$ ) icon.

Multiple fields can be used to group the records. Simply click on the Add button to insert additional grouping fields.

# VI.F.2. Page Breaks Screen

The **Group Properties Page Break** screen allows the report designer to determine whether or not page breaks should occur between instances of the group. For example, if the data is being grouped on Customer Number, there should be a page break between each Customer Number. Three check boxes are provided on this screen:

**Between Each Instance of A Group** -- If this box is checked, a new page is started between each new set of group data. The next two check boxes are not active unless this box is checked.

**Also At The Start of A Group** -- If this box is checked, a new page is started before the first group of data on the report.

**Also At The End of A Group** -- If this box is checked, a new page is turned at the end of the last group on the report. This is helpful to "turn the page" before printing totals. For example, if a commission report is grouped by sales rep, clicking this box starts a new page before the totals are printed, allowing pages of information to be given to each rep without sending anyone the company totals.

# VI.F.3. Sorting Screen

The **Group Properties Sorting** screen allows the report designer to define the manner in which rows of data are sorted. The Sort screen is a common screen and is described in detail in Section VI.A. of this chapter.

# VI.F.4. Visibility Screen

The **Group Properties Visibility** screen provides options to control the display or hiding of the Tablix. This screen is a common format screen and described in Section VI.A. of this chapter.

# VI.F.5. Filters Screen

The **Group Properties Filters** screen allows the report designer to filter the rows that will appear on the report. The Filters screen is a common screen and is described in detail in Section VI.A. of this chapter.

# VI.F.6. Variables Screen

The **Group Properties Variables** screen allows the report designer to specify one or more variables and establish a value for those variables. When the first row of the group is printed, the variables are evaluated and they are not re-evaluated until the next group of rows is printed. The variables evaluated in the group can be used in child groups of the parent group and allow the passing of information between groups.

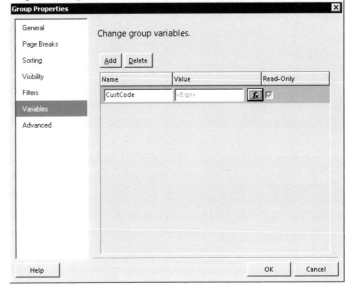

To create a variable:

1.    Click the Add button to add a set of fields for a single variable.

2.    In the Name field, give the variable a name.

3.    In the Value field, enter the value of the variable. If desired, an expression can be created using the Expression Builder. Click the Function ( 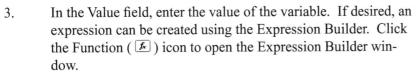 ) icon to open the Expression Builder window.

As many variables as may be needed can be created.

# VI.F.7.    Advanced Screen

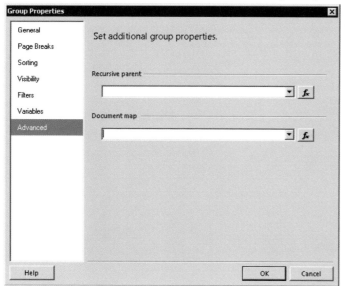

The **Group Properties Advanced** screen allows the report designer to specify the Recursive Parent and the Document Map field. Recursive Hierarchy reports are supported in SSRS. The Recursive Parent field is one of the controlling fields for these reports. Recursive Hierarchy reports (such as organization charts) are discussed in Chapter VII of this manual.

When reports are long, locating specific information can be challenging. A Document Map can be handy.

When a report is rendered on screen and is configured to display a Document Map, a window on the left side of the screen lists the field or expression that identified data in the report. Selecting a specific entry in the Document Map and clicking will move the report output directly to the associated information.

For example, if a list of customer sales transactions prints hundreds of pages, having a Document Map on screen can be helpful. In the Document Map field of the Advanced Group Properties screen, select the Customer Number field. When the report is rendered on screen, a list of customer numbers that appear in the report is found on the left side of the screen. Clicking on one customer number will skip directly to that customer in the report.

The Expression Builder can be used to generate more meaningful Document Map labels. If the data is grouped by Customer Number, the report designer may want the customer name to also appear in the Document Map. Use the Expression Builder to create a string consisting of the customer number plus the customer name.

## *VI.G.  Row/Column Visibility*

From time to time, rows or even columns may need to be hidden. Rows and columns can be permanently hidden or hidden based on other values in the report.

Right click on the row or column in the Table Frame and select from the menu Row Visibility (or Column Visibility). This opens the Visibility Property window. The visibility screen is a common screen and is described in full in Section VI.A. of this chapter.

# VII. Sub-reports, Charts, Et Cetera

# VII. *Sub-reports, Charts, Et Cetera*

Both the SSRB and the Visual Studio report builder provide a number of enhanced controls that enable report designers to insert sub-reports into reports, place a variety of different styles of chart and graphical representation of the data points, insert maps showing locations or distributions of addresses, gauges, even indicators to single out special circumstances such as customers on hold or inventory items below reorder points.

Many of these controls are complex with a large number of parameters. Gauges, for example allow the report designer to specify the range of the gauge, the color and shape of the gauge, the type of indicator, the color of the indicator, et cetera. However, they do provide a means of easily creating a reporting dashboard. Imagine, for example, a sales "report" that, rather than showing lines of data, showed a gauge for each product line or type and the current or past 4 month's sales levels for that product line. Clicking on the gauge could then open a "report" showing gauges for each product. Further clicking would produce a list of customers that purchased that item during that time. This is possible using these tools!

Most of these enhanced controls will be discussed in this chapter.

**Fewer
Sub-reports?**

SQL Server Report Services and
the report designer tools have
been structured to make optimal
use of SQL stored data. With
the use of views as virtual tables,
the need for sub-reports has been
minimized. However, they are still
well supported by the tools.

# VII.A. Subreports

Sub-reports allow the inclusion of a report within a report. There are
times when the structure of the data in the tables does not allow a single
report to present all of the data. By the time a query is structured that
pulls all of the data points together, some desired data may be omitted. For example a list of customers can have a sub-report that shows
open orders by the customer. If all customers are to be printed and just
open orders, a sub-report can be used to pull in orders when orders are
present.

Think of a sub-report as a frame within a web page. Additional data
from other sources can be displayed within the sub-report.

Any report can be printed inside another report as a sub-report. The
sub-report must be published to a Report Server and generally is found
in the same folder in the Report Server as the calling report.

The concept behind sub-reports allows a child report to be executed
by a parent report. The parent report goes through it's selected list of
records and displays the information from each record on the report.
Then, for each record in the parent report, the sub-report is executed
and specific information, usually related to the current row of the parent
report, is displayed. After the sub-report has executed, the parent report
displays the next row of its data and again calls the sub-report for the
new row. This process repeats until the parent report has completed
displaying its selected data.

Reports and their sub-reports are related by parameters. In the Properties window of the sub-report in the main report, data from the main
report is fed to the parameters of the sub-report to ensure the correct
data is displayed in the sub-report. For example, if a report lists customers and a sub-report lists open orders for those customers, the report
and sub-report are linked by Customer Number. In this manner, as each
customer is printed on the main report, the sub-report can be executed
to show only the open orders for that one customer. When the next
customer is printed on the main report, the sub-report is again executed
for the new customer number.

The process of including a sub-report in a parent report is simple.

1.  Create, test and deploy the report that will be the sub-report.
    Make sure the parameters that will limit the data displayed in
    the sub-report are included in the document. For example,
    if the sub-report is to show open orders for each customer, a
    parameter asking for a customer number must exist in the sub-
    report and restrict selected records to those for the customer
    number entered during testing.

2.	The sub-report must be deployed to the Report Manager or Share Point Server.

3.	Create the parent report and list the records that contain the information needed in the sub-report's parameters. Following our example, if the sub-report will need a customer number, the parent report must step through a list of customers and have the customer number available.

4.	Insert the sub-report into the parent report.

5.	Open the sub-report properties, go to Parameters and link the fields in the parent report to the parameters in the sub-report list of parameters.

6.	Done!

While that sounds simple, let's walk through the process now in some detail. Let's assume that a decision has been made that a sub-report is needed to properly format or select the data needed on the complete report.

Write the sub-report first. Create the necessary Data Sources, Datasets and place the desired data on the pasteboard. Create parameters that will select the desired data each time the parent report launches the sub-report.

Following our example, if the parent report will list customers and the sub-report will list orders for the customers, then write a report that will list orders. The parameters for this report will select orders for one customer. During testing, the report designer will be required to enter the ID of a customer and only orders for that customer will be displayed. Re-launching the report and entering a different customer ID will display orders for the new customer ID.

Test the report that will become the sub-report and make sure the information desired is shown and the parameters work as expected. Note that it is not necessary to provide any Available Values or Default Values for the parameters in the sub-report. These options make it easier for end users to select the desired values. The parent report and not an end user will be passing data to the sub-report's parameters.

Thoroughly test the sub-report. Then deploy the report to the Report Server or Share Point Server. Place the sub-report in the same folder that will house the parent report. Sub-reports MUST be deployed to the Report Server or Share Point Server before they can be inserted into the parent report. Reports saved in a Visual Basic Project or stored by SSRB to a folder cannot be inserted into the parent report unless they and all of their components (Data Sources, Datasets, Images et cetera) are deployed.

**Sub-Report Terminology**

**Complete Report** -- This is the entire finished report, containing the parent report plus any sub-reports needed to provide the complete picture.

**Parent Report** -- The outside or base report that is executed or launched by the end user. The parent report calls sub-reports.

**Sub-Report** -- A child report called by each and every row on a Parent Report that displays additional information.

**Parameters** -- A set of questions that one report must have answered before it will run. For example, if a report looks through customer data but should only print information for one customer, the report must ask that the customer be identified.

**Linkage Parameters** -- A set of questions that a sub-report must have answered before it will return the desired information. Linkage Parameters work exactly like regular parameters when a sub-report is launched by itself. When a sub-report is launched by a parent report, the data needed by the sub-report's parameters is fed to the sub-report by the parent report. The parameters in the sub-report are then called Linkage Parameters.

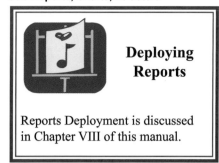

**Deploying Reports**

Reports Deployment is discussed in Chapter VIII of this manual.

Create the parent report that will eventually launch the sub-report. Each record selected on the parent report must include information that will be fed to the sub-report's parameters. It is not necessary to print this data on the parent report but the data must be available in the Dataset.

Create and apply any parameters that are needed to limit the records selected and displayed by the parent report. These parameters for the parent report do not apply to the sub-report. They simply limit the records selected from the parent report's data set and limit the rows that can be displayed on the parent report.

Test the parent report and make sure it is working as desired. It is not necessary to deploy the parent report at this time.

Up to this point, the creation of each of these two reports employs only skills learned earlier in this manual. Now comes the new steps.

In the parent report, insert into the Details Group a row that will hold the sub-report. If necessary, to provide enough width for the sub-report's data, merge two or more cells of the new row.

Right click on the cell in the report table that is to hold the sub-report to display the Text Box/Tablix menu. At the bottom of the menu, select the Insert option and pick Sub-report from the sub-menu. This will insert a sub-report place holder in the cell of the parent report.

Right click on the <Sub-report> placeholder. The Sub-report/Tablix menu is displayed. In the Sub-report section, select Sub-report Properties. The Sub-report Properties window will open. There are four screens for this window: General, Visibility, Parameters and Border.

The General screen of the Sub-report Properties window allows the
report designer to provide a name for the
sub-report object, select the report to be used as
the sub-report and to control the display of the
border on page breaks.

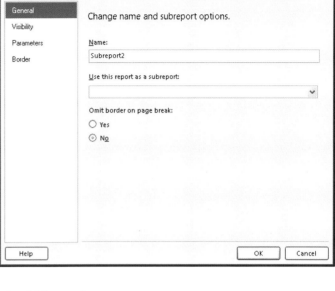

Options on this screen include:

**Name** -- The name specified here is used to
locate the properties windows for the
sub-report. Each sub-report must have a
unique name. The contents of this field
are displayed on the pasteboard but not
on the final report output.

**Use This Report as a Sub-Report** -- Opening the pull down list for this field will
display a list of reports that have been
deployed to the Report Server or to the
Share Point Reports. Select the report that should be used as
the sub-report.

**Omit Border on Page Break** -- If the Yes option is selected, and a
sub-report is rendered across a page break, the bottom border
of the sub-report on the first page and the top border on the
next page will not be drawn.

The Parameters screen is used to establish the linkage between the
parent and child reports. This is where the fun
begins. The linkage established here allows the
sub-report to select records that are appropriate
to those displayed in the current row of the
parent report.

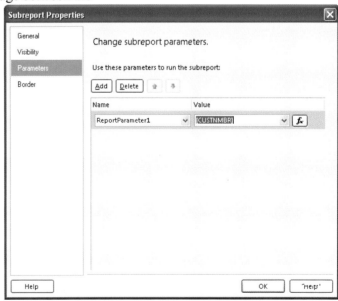

Click on the Add button to add a line to the
Parameter matching table. Use the pull down
list in the Name field to select a pre-defined parameter from the sub-report. In the Value field,
use the pull down list to display a list of fields
from the parent report's Dataset. Select the field
from the Dataset that matches the sub-report's
parameter.

A line must be added to the Parameters screen
for each and every parameter in the sub-report.
Any parameter that is not linked to a field in the
parent report will cause the system to ask the
user for a value. And this value will need to be entered for each and
every line on the parent report!

Constants or calculated values can be matched to parameters when appropriate. If, for example, the sub-report has a parameter asking for the type of document (1=quote, 2=order, et cetera), a constant value can be matched to the parameter to select only one type of document. If, for example, the constant value 2 is entered, only orders will be selected.

At this point, the complete report is ready for use. Of course, there are options available to help format the report and make it look better. This includes the Borders and Visibility screens.

These two screens work just like the common screens described in Chapter VI.A.. However, let's talk a bit about the Borders screen.

Borders screens are typically used to draw lines around an object and with the Borders screen in the Sub-Report Parameters window, the same is true. In this case, the border surrounds the entire sub-report.

Borders can be used to separate the details provided by the sub-report from the information provided by the parent report. Sub-reports, however, are typically longer than just a Text Box or two and can actually span multiple pages of the complete report. The question then is whether to draw the closing line at the bottom of the sub-report at the bottom of each page. This option appears on the General screen as described earlier.

Selecting Yes to omit the border on a page change leaves the bottom line of the border around the sub-report open and also does not draw the top line on the next page. Top and bottom borders are then only drawn at the actual top and bottom of the sub-report. If the report designer wants the box closed on each page, No must be selected for the option.

# VII.B. Charts

The Charts controls allow a report designer to represent data points graphically. For example, monthly sales totals can be printed on a report with one row of data representing each month with an amount representing the total dollar value of sales for each month. However, showing the same data as a series of vertical bars where each bar represents a month and the height of the bar represents the amount of sales for the period allows management to quickly see trends in sales.

Quite a large variety of chart types are supported by SQL Reporting. The configuration of a chart requires several steps. Each step includes property pages to allow the report designer to configure the chart. The steps are:

1. Gathering the Data

2. Select The Chart Type

3. Tying the chart to the data

4. Setting Labels and Scales

To begin the process of building a report that includes a chart, first create a report that displays the desired data. Later in the process, if the list of data is not wanted or needed, then it can be hidden by setting the appropriate visibility attributes.

Once the data is appearing properly, place the chart tool on the pasteboard by dragging and dropping the Chart Icon onto the pasteboard. The Select Chart Type window will open.

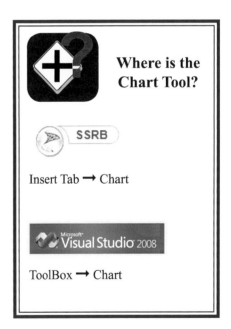

**Where is the Chart Tool?**

SSRB

Insert Tab → Chart

Microsoft Visual Studio 2008

ToolBox → Chart

# VII.B.1.   Select Chart Type

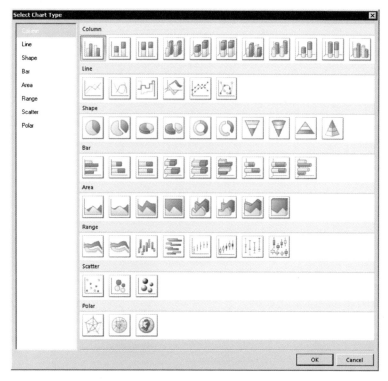

The Select Chart Type window displays all of the various chart types built into the reporting tool. Down the left side of the window is a pane that allows the report designer to select one specific type of chart. By clicking on one of the chart groups (Column, Line, Shape, etc) that group will be highlighted in the window.

Select the desired chart type by clicking on the icon that represents the type of chart to be used on the report. The chart will be placed on the pasteboard but still needs to be tied to the data and configured properly.

Each chart has a number of configurable properties. Placing the cursor on different areas and right clicking opens different menus and provides access to different property pages.

The adjacent graphic shows a typical chart icon placed on the pasteboard and most of the touch points that provide access to different property pages. Separate property pages exist for:

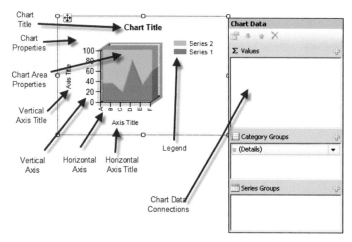

**Chart Title** -- Right clicking on the phrase Chart Title will open a menu that allows the Title Properties window to be opened. Use this properties window to edit the title.

**Chart Properties** -- Right clicking in the open undefined space of the chart icon opens a menu with several important options and access to two properties pages. Change Chart Type can be selected and the user will be taken back to the Select Chart Type window to pick a different chart style. Chart Properties can be selected to open the Chart Properties window. Also, the report designer can select to Add New Title, Add New Legend, or Add New Chart Area.

**Chart Area Properties** -- Right clicking in this area opens a menu that allows the Chart Area Properties window to be opened. Parameters that define the way the chart looks are controlled in this window.

**Vertical Axis Title** -- Right clicking in this area opens a menu that allows the Axis Title Properties window to be opened. The actual title, its alignment and font are defined in this window.

**Vertical Axis** -- Right clicking in this area opens a menu that allows the Vertical Axis Properties window to be opened. This window is used to define the way the range of values will be displayed on the Vertical Axis.

**Horizontal Axis** -- Right clicking in this area opens a menu that allows the Axis Title Properties window to be opened. The actual title, its alignment and font are defined in this window.

**Horizontal Axis Title** -- Right clicking in this area opens a menu that allows the  Horizontal Axis Properties window to be opened. This window is used to define the way the range of values will be displayed on the Horizontal Axis.

**Legend** -- Right clicking in this area opens a menu that allows the Legend Properties window to be opened. The position of the legend, the layout and other properties of the legend are defined in this window.

**Chart Data Connections** -- Data from the report is connected to the chart using this area. Rather than right clicking, however, the window is displayed by double clicking in the undefined chart area. The Plus sign icons on these panes are used to add data relationships as will be discussed shortly.

# VII.B.2.   Tie Data to the Chart

The Chart Data Panes are used to relate data from the report to the chart. Values to be displayed on the chart as well as the grouping of the data into the various columns (et cetera) are specified here.

Different Chart Styles display the data selected differently and can offer different options for the selection or summarization of data. But the basics of selecting data points are the same.

To select the data points to be graphed inside the chart, click on the Plus Sign (  ) icon at the right top edge of the **Summary Values** pane. A list of fields from the Dataset will be displayed. Select the desired data point. Multiple data points can be selected for many of the chart types. Each different value will be shown in a different color on the chart. How the data is represented depends on the type of chart selected.

Shown here are two different chart types (Column Bars and Stacked Ranges). In both charts, three data points are selected: dollar value of sales, number of invoices and number of returns.

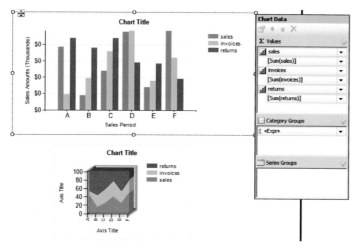

The data points were added to the charts by clicking on the Plus Sign icon and selecting each one by one. As each was added, it was assigned a color code in the default sequence. Sample data is shown on the chart representing the final layout of the chart. This sample data, however, is not taken from the report data but is random values that serve only to allow the report designer to see the desired chart layout.

The **Category Groups** pane is used to specify the horizontal (in the current example) axis of the chart. If the bar graph used horizontal bars, then the Category Groups would specify the vertical axis of the chart. A field from the Dataset or an expression can be used to group data. For example, if the report shows sales per period, then grouping the data by period would be appropriate.

Again, click on the Plus Sign icon to open a menu showing available fields from the Dataset. An additional option allows a function to be written to provide the Category Group points.

One final pane, the Series Groups pane, allows data from different ranges to be overlapped for comparison. For example, in the report shown, values for sales, number of invoices and returns are shown separated by period. If the periods cross several years, then selecting the year as the series will show data period by period and year by year for easy comparison. If only the sales dollars are shown and the data is limited to the current year and the most immediately prior year, then for period one, sales for the current year and the prior year would be shown side by side followed next by the pair of years for period two et cetera. Different colors are used for each series, of course, making it easy to compare one series (or year in the example) to the other series (or year).

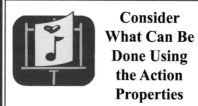

**Consider What Can Be Done Using the Action Properties**

Here is an idea...Generate a report using a chart or graphic to show the data. Then, using the Action Properties, allow the user viewing the report to double click and run a second report that shows the details behind the results!

# VII.B.3.　Set the Labels and Legends

Labels and legends are automatically applied to most charts and graphs. However, the report designer will need to edit some parameters (such as the chart name and the names of each axis) and may want to edit other parameters (such as the fonts, data representations et cetera).

There are (typically) six different labels that need to be edited on a chart:

**Chart Title** -- The name of the chart, position of the title, font, and a number of other parameters are specified in the Chart Title Properties window.  See below for a discussion of this window.

**Vertical Axis Title** -- The Vertical Axis Title is set by right clicking and opening the Axis Title window.  The fields and functions available in this window are described below.

**Vertical Axis** -- The Vertical Axis Properties window allows the report designer to control the labels found along the vertical axis of the chart.  See below for a discussion of this window.

**Horizontal Axis Title** -- The Horizontal Axis Title is set by right clicking and opening the Axis Title window.  The fields and functions available in this window are described below.

**Horizontal Axis** -- The Horizontal Axis Properties window allows the report designer to control the labels found along the horizontal axis of the chart. See below for a discussion of this window.

**Legend** -- The Legend Properties window allows the report designer to not only place a name above the legend but also control its placement and a number of other parameters.  See below for a discussion of this window.

**3D for More Attractive Charts**

Applying 3D effects to a bar chart can turn a plain flat display into an attractive 3D rendering.  When creating charts for executive presentations, consider using the 3D options available.

# VII.C. Gauges

Gauges are a special form of display. The speedometer, the fuel indicator and the oil pressure gauge on an automobile are all types of gauges. Each gauge takes a particular value or data point and represents that point as a marker of some type between the high and low possibilities.

Gauges in reports can be used for a number of purposes. In an inventory report, when a maximum and minimum stocking amount has been specified for an item, a gauge can indicate the current stock level between these two points.

Sales can be represented in gauges. If the firm has an expectation of sales up to a specific point, actual sales values can be projected on a gauge having a range from zero dollars to the maximum expected sales amount.

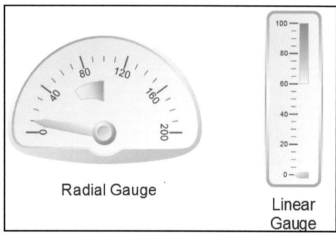

Radial Gauge

Linear Gauge

Unlike reports or charts, gauges represent one point of data. They do not show trends or histories of transactions. They simply show the state of a particular situation right now (or at the time the report is rendered). Gauges can show the current level of sales, not the collection of sales transactions that make up that number. A Gauge can show the current level of inventory, but not the history of item movements that lead to that point.

Like other reporting objects, gauges can have actions associated with them. If the report designer uses this feature, an end user could simply click on a gauge and run a different report that would show the history or accumulation of detail records that lead to the gauge value.

Individual gauges can be placed on reports or groups of gauges presented. Each gauge can present a different value to the end user. When a gauge is first placed on a report, a Gauge Panel is created. One or more gauges can be placed inside the Gauge Panel. Also, multiple Gauge Panels can be added to a report.

The SQL Reporting tools provide two different styles of gauges: radial and linear. Radial gauges are the typical speedometer style of display with a scaled background and a pointer that rotates to the current value. Linear gauges are more akin to the old fashioned thermometer where the indicator rides up or down to the correct scale value.

Selection of the correct gauge to use in a report involves aesthetics more than function. All gauges have configurable scales and pointers and can display the same range of values. While some linear gauges can display 2 or 3 values at the same time, the selection of a gauge often breaks down to the way the report designer or end user wants the report to look.

Placing gauges on a report is simple and (generally) involves three steps:

1.     Place the gauge on the report pasteboard.

2.     Attach data points to the gauges.

3.     Scale and dress the gauge.

# VII.C.1.     Placing Gauges on Reports

Placing a gauge on a report is simply a matter of dragging the gauge tool onto the desired location on the pasteboard.  Gauges can be placed directly on the pasteboard in the body area, within Text Boxes in a Table or Matrix, in the header area, or in the footer area of a report.

Once the Gauge Tool is dropped onto the report pasteboard, the Select Gauge Type window will be displayed.  In the pane to the far left, the two different styles of gauges are listed.  On the face of the window, all of the gauge options in both styles are displayed.  Selecting one of the styles in the left pane only changes the default highlighting in the body of the window.

To place any one style of gauge on the report pasteboard at the point where the Gauge Tool was dropped, simply double click the desired gauge in the selection window.  The selection window will close and the selected gauge will be displayed on the pasteboard.

# VII.C.2.     Attaching Data to Gauges

Remember that gauges represent data as a point in time.  That means that, generally speaking, data shown on a gauge is a summary or aggregation of records in most tables.  For example, a gauge showing the total number of open orders and/or the total dollar value of those orders does not show each and every order but the count of open orders and the sum of the document amounts for open orders. The Gauge control (the tool actually places a control on the report) makes the attachment of data easy as it automatically forces the aggregations.

Try this:

1.  Create a new report.

2.  Create a Dataset that shows the open orders. Include in the selected fields the order number, the order amount and restrict the selected records to only orders.

3.  Place two gauges on the report.

4.  In the Report Data pane, drag from the Dataset the Order Number to the dial of the first gauge and drag the Order Amount to the dial of the second gauge.

5.  Run the report.

Yes, it is that simple! The gauge control looked at each of the two pieces of data and determined that order numbers were not numeric and could not be added together so it counted them. It looked at the document amount field and determined that the amounts could be added together so it summed the values. The appropriate aggregation was automatically applied!

Now, the scales of the gauges may need to be adjusted. Labels need to be put in place. Actions, if desired added to the gauge. Colors of the gauge face, pointer and background set. But all of this is covered in the next section.

# VII.C.3. Configuring Gauges

Let's take a look first at the various different parts of a Gauge control.

The Gauge Panel is the control that holds one or more gauges on a report. The Gauge Panel allows a number of properties to be set one time and apply those properties to all gauges inside the panel.

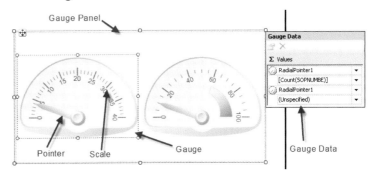

A Gauge is a single display control for one data point. Gauges can be radial or linear and contain several other components.

The Scale is the range of values that can be displayed on the gauge. Scales are configurable in terms of their range, the markers on the scale, label placement, number formatting, tick marks et cetera.

The Pointer is the marker that moves across the Scale to indicate the current value of the data point. If, for example, the gauge is configured to indicate the number of open orders, the pointer will point to the value on the scale that represents the current number of orders. Pointer styles, actions to be taken when the pointer is clicked, borders and shadows can be configured as well as other parameters.

While all of the parameters in each of the property pages will be discussed for gauges in the next section, let's take a look at some of the most important configurations for a gauge.

**Where is the Gauge Tool?**

SSRB

Insert Tab → Gauge

Visual Studio 2008

ToolBox → Gauge

The range of the Scale needs to be set. If, for example, the total order value is being monitored and the value can run from 0 to $200,000, having a scale that tops at $100 is useless. Right click on the scale area in the gauge area and select Scale Properties. The Scale Properties window will be displayed (see the next section for an image of this window). On the General screen, set the Minimum and Maximum values to set the range of the scale. If necessary, set the Multiply Scale Labels By field to produce more readable labels.

Unlike Charts, Gauges do not have built in labels. To attach a label to a gauge, drop a Text Box onto the report and enter the gauge label in the Text Box.

With just this little bit of work, gauges can be dropped onto a report, configured, and run. However, much more power and flexibility exists. In the next few pages, all of the properties of Gauges are discussed in detail.

# *VII.D. Maps*

**Customers per State**

1000 km
750 mi

Color Code -- Customers Per State
02 05 08 10 12 15 17 19 21 23 25 27 29 31 33 35 37 39 41 44 46 48 50 53 55
01 04 06 09 11 13 16 18 20 22 24 26 28 30 32 34 36 38 40 42 45 47 49 51 54 56

Looks nice, doesn't it.  This little map of customers per state took just 3 minutes to create using the maps feature of SQL Reports!  Maps like this can be created to show any map distributed data.  The number of invoices posted per state, the dollar value of sales per state, numbers of products sold per state, all can just as easily be produced using these reporting tools.  Data can even be posted county by county in the US states and other map galleries can be imported and used.

Maps in SQL Reporting are simply another control that can be applied to a report.  Yes, there are a number of parameters that can be adjusted to make the map look better, match the firm's color scheme, and show exactly what is needed.

Data coded by state is needed for state based maps. Data coded by county is needed to show county by county maps.  Country coded data is needed to show nation by nation maps (as well as importing a map from one of several sources).  However, when the data is available, the map tools will help organize that data and make including map based data on reports easy.

Putting map data on reports is easy.  Here are the steps:

1.      Create a data source that includes data that can be grouped by state, county or country (depending on the map to be used).  Note: SSRS and SSRB are delivered with US maps and US States with Counties.  Country maps are not provided and must be obtained from other sources.

2.      Place a map tool on the report.

3.      Relate the data to the map.

4.      Dress the Map.

Let's take a look at that map of customers by state as an example.  This one is really easy since the table used (the Customer Master Table -- RM00101 in MS Dynamics GP) already contains a field called State.  Of course, make sure that people are using real states in the state field.  I looked at one customer's data only to find that Japan was listed as a State!  Yes, clean data is important.

Create a new report in the reporting tool.  Create a simple Dataset that pulls GP data and references the customer table.  Make it simple and just include all the fields. We will only use the state field but these others will not be in the way.

Locate the Map tool and place it on the pasteboard for the report. Let's not do anything fancy here, we first need to learn how to use these tools. Fancy comes later.

Use the Map Wizard. Going through the property pages for the first time can be daunting. The Map Wizard takes us through the steps in the proper sequence.

Select the USA by State option for the new map. Select to embed map data in the report, take the default resolution, and select a Color Analytical Map from the options offered by the wizard. When asked, associate the map with a Dataset or create one accessing the customer master table.

The Wizard will present a screen used to match fields for spatial and analytical data. This screen allows the report designer to match fields in the data tables with the map. Select the StateName and in the far right side, use the pull down menu to locate the field name in the table representing the state where the customer is located.

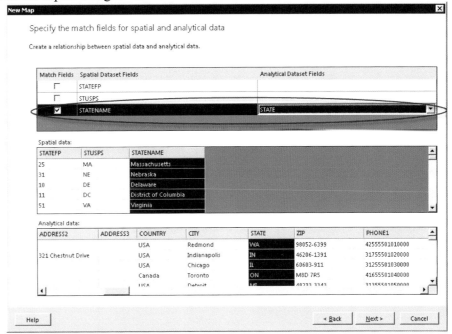

Click on the Next button. Pick a color scheme (Ocean does NOT work well for this unless you like shades of blue only) and click finish.

Play with this process a couple of times to see just how easy it is to create colorful and useful map based reports.

Now, lets look at some of the properties of maps and how we can really control what appears on the document.

As can be seen by flipping through the next few pages, there are quite a number of screens used to set properties on maps. As we demonstrated above, it is simple to place a nice looking map on a report. The property pages described below are then used to refine the map. It is not necessary to understand and/or manipulate all of these screens to place attractive looking maps on a report.

Many of the screens in the property windows below are common screens. Action, Fill, Border screens and more that are completely discussed in Chapter VI.A. are found in these windows. Please refer to that chapter for details on the common screens.

# VII.E.  Data Bars

Data Bars allows data to be visually compared to get an idea of the distribution of values between items.  It produces what is also called a trellis or table lens display.

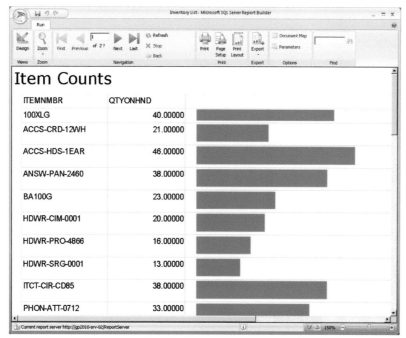

The sample Data Bar report shown displays a list of inventory items and the quantity on hand in numbers and in a relative bar.  The bar makes it easy to identify the items with the most or least quantity on hand.  Bar reports like this can be built, for example, to show high dollar value items, high versus low performing sales reps, high versus low performing sales territories et cetera.

Producing a report with Data Bars is again a simple process using the tools provided in the SSRB or Visual Studio report designer.  The application will even perform the necessary aggregation of data given a table with the appropriate fields.

A Dataset with the appropriate data points can be a listing of inventory items and quantities on hand, a list of sales reps and their accumulated sales in either dollars, number of sales or both.  Even the number of times a customer has placed an order or the average days to pay can be plotted using Data Bars.

To create a report with Data Bars:

1.  Select a Dataset containing a controlling field (such as the item number, the customer number, a sales representative ID) and a value to be displayed.

2.  Drop a Table on the pasteboard.

3.  In one column, place the controlling field.  In our example, the item number appears in the first column.

4.  Other columns are optional.  In our example, we included the quantity on hand as a numeric value in the second column.

5.  Drop the Data Bar icon into the cell to contain the bar and select the type of bar desired.

6.  With the Chart Data window displayed, click the Plus Sign icon ( + ) next to Values and select the numeric value to be charted.

By default, the Sum aggregation function will be associated with the data. If the Count, Max or Min or another aggregation is desired, use the pull down menu to the right of the aggregated value to open the list of aggregation functions and select the desired one.

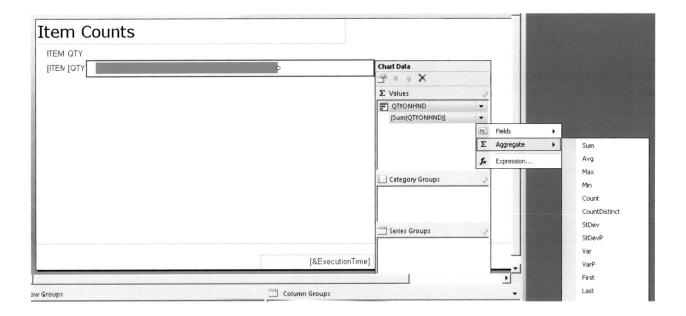

The Data Bar object has a number of parameters that can be used to limit the width of the bars, limit the data selected, include markers, borders and fill colors, even apply shadows and actions. See the ***SSRS Advanced Functions*** book from Accolade Publications for more information on these properties.

# VII.F.  Sparkline

Sparklines are an information graphically designed to show a relatively large amount of data in a small space.  Sparklines are commonly used to show trends in stock prices where each day or each hour represents a value and multiple data points are strung together in what appears to be a line moving sometimes up, sometimes down.

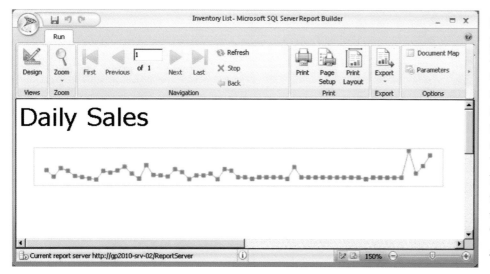

Sparklines are useful in presenting a number of key business indicators and trends.  For example, consider a Sparkline that shows in just a few inches the daily level of sales for each day for 6 months.  While Sparklines have been around for years, their electronic generation was defined by Edward Tufle in 2006 in his book ***Beautiful Evidence***.

Sparklines are as easy to build as Data Bars and other graphical displays.  The tool itself will perform the data grouping and aggregation. All a report designer needs to do is to specify the grouping fields and the style of aggregation.  Of course, a Dataset that contains a controlling value and a numeric value that can be aggregated based on the control value is required.  In other words, sales figures with a date allowing the sales amounts to be summed per day is a good candidate for a Sparkline display.

To create a Sparkline display of daily sales activity, for example:

1.  Select a Dataset that contains a grouping field (such as the date sales were invoiced) and a value to aggregate (such as the amount of the sale).  Note that it is not necessary to perform any aggregation in the Dataset as the Sparkline tool will manage the aggregation.

2.  Select the Sparkline tool and place the desired sparkline form on the pasteboard.

3.  In the Chart Data window, in the Category Groups block select the data element to be used to group and order data.  In our example, this would be the sale date.

4.  In the Chart Data Values block, select the data to be displayed. If the data is numeric, by default, the system will perform a

Sum aggregation on the data. If desired, use the pull down arrow to show a menu and select a different aggregation method. For example, management may want to see the number of sales per day rather than the total amounts. For that matter, two values can be shown with one showing the count of sales and the second sparkline showing the amount of sales per day.

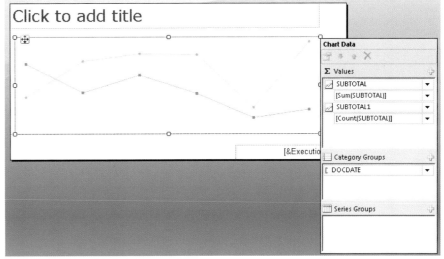

There are a number of properties associated with Sparklines that allow report designers to control visibility, fill colors, borders, and more. These detailed parameters are discussed in Accolade's companion book *SSRS Advanced Functions*.

# VII.G. Indicators

Indicators are icons that are used to indicate a state of the information appearing in the report. For example, if sales one day are higher than the average, a multi-star icon can appear while days with lower sales show fewer stars. Check marks versus stylized X's, sets of flags, even traffic lights (red, yellow, green) can be used as indicators. SSRB and Visual Studio have a sizable collection of indicators. And, it is even possible to add your own images to be used as indicators!

## Top Customers

| ID | Customer | Total Sales | |
|----|----------|-------------|---|
| ASTORSUI0001 | Astor Suites | 430,885 | ✓ |
| PLAZAONE0001 | Plaza One | 169,456 | ! |
| COHOWINE0001 | Coho Wintery | 150,667 | ! |
| VANCOUVE0001 | Vancouver Resort Hotels | 127,439 | ✗ |
| MAHLERST0001 | Mahler State University | 126,296 | ✗ |
| ALTONMAN0001 | Alton Manufacturing | 111,079 | ✗ |
| LAWRENCE0001 | Lawrence Telemarketing | 110,785 | ✗ |

The sample report shown lists all customers and their total purchases in a period of time. The customers are sorted showing the high purchasing or most valuable customers at the top of the list. The indicators are set to show check marks by the top 1/3, exclamation points by the second 1/3 and red X's by the low performing customers. These indicators provide a quick visual indicator of the break points between the groups of customers based on ranking.

Indicators are dropped into a Text Box in a Table just like any other data element. Once the Indicator tool has been dropped in place, the Indicator Properties page is used to map the break points.

When the indicator tool is dropped into a Text Box, the Select Indicator Type window will be displayed. The report designer can then select on of the standard indicator types from those shown. Note: if custom indicators are desired, select an indicator type that closely matches the array of images that are to ultimately be used. The use of custom indicators is discussed shortly.

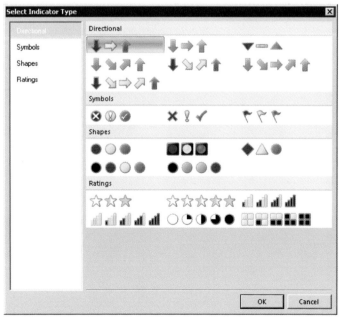

Once the type of indicator is selected, right click on the icon in the Text Box and open the Indicators Properties Window. A few fields must be comleted:

**Value** -- Indicate the field that will be used to control the display of the indicator. Typically the field is aggregated and, if a numeric value is selected, a Sum will be selected by default. It is possible to change the aggregation function.

**States Measurement Unit** -- Select either a Numeric range or Percentage range. The values of the next fields will be controlled by the selection in this field.

**Synchronization Scope, Minimum, and Maximum** -- If percentage is selected in the above field, these fields appear and control the range of values used to calculate the percentage position of each data point.

**List of Icons, Colors, and Ranges** -- This chart allows the report designer to select each icon in the group, assign a color to the icon, and a Start and End Range. If Percentage is selected in the States Measurement Unit, then the ranges must span from 0 to 100. If Numeric was selected, valid ranges of numeric values must be selected.

A new icon can be added to the group by clicking the Add button. A generic shape will be selected from those available but it can be changed by clicking on the pull down arrow. A color can also be assigned to the shape.

To add a custom image to the group of icons, first load the desired icons as images into the report. Then, from the shape pull down list, select image. Select the source of the image and the actual image name as described earlier in this book. This method is used to insert custom images into the group of shapes and all existing shapes can be replaced with a firm's desired group of icons!

There are other parameters such as Actions, Fill, Borders et cetera. Each of these additional parameter windows are explained in detail in Accolade's SSRS companion book *SSRS Advanced Functions*.

# VIII. The Report Manager

# VIII. The Report Manager

## VIII.A.  Overview

The SQL report building tools are great tools for creating reports. However, it does provide an opportunity to edit and change the reports, something that a report designer wants to prevent end users from doing!

SQL reports can be deployed to the Report Manager, a component of the SQL Server Reporting Services suite of tools. The Report Manager allows end users to execute reports, organize reports into logical folders, restrict certain users from running specific reports, and even subscribe to reports that will be run automatically.

Reports can also be deployed to a SharePoint Portal and run from the Reports Manager within Sharepoint.

In this chapter, we will focus on the standalone Reports Manager.

The Reports Manager is a web application that is launched (generally) by invoking a URL in the following form:

http://servername/Reports

where *servername* is the name of the MS-SQL server that hosts the reports server database. *Servername* may also include an optional port ID such as :80. Properly installed, the correct URL can be found by opening the Reporting Services Configuration Manager and viewing the Report Manager URL screen.

The URL used to launch the Reports Manager is found in the Reports Manager URL screen in the URLs: field. This field is actually a hot link and the user can click the link to launch the Reports Manager.

It is recommended, however, that the Reports Manager URL be used to create a desktop shortcut. Use the Reports Manager URL as the Location of the Item when creating a new Reports Manager icon. Now, a user only needs to click on the icon to launch the Reports Manager.

Read the section on Folder Security later in this chapter for information on controlling access to specific groups of reports.

A typical Reports Manager desktop is shown here.

The Report Manager shown has reports, Data Sources and folders displayed. Folders are used to organize reports. Rather than a user needing to wade through hundreds of reports on the Home page, they can click on the Sales Reports folder, then the Commissions folder in the Sales Reports folder and then select the appropriate commissions report.

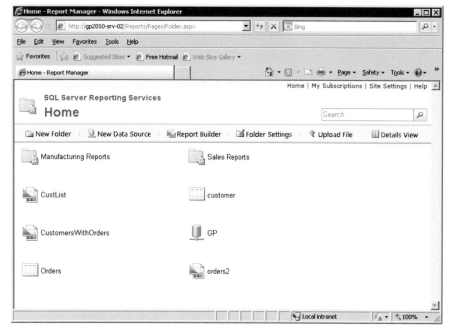

As can be seen, a tool bar provides users the ability to create New Folders, New Data Sources, launch the Report Builder, configure Folder Settings, Upload Files, or change the view from the Tile view shown to a Details view.

Each of these functions as well as the security to control access to the function will be discussed in this chapter. First, let's talk about how reports get to the Reports Manager.

# VIII.B.   Deploying Report Objects

When reports are created using either the SSRB or Visual Studio, the reports must be deployed to the Report Manager. If the tools are installed correctly, the URL of the Report Manager is already embedded in the configuration files. Deployment is then simple.

In SSRB, with the desired report open, click on the SSRB ribbon icon and select Publish Report Parts from the menu. If everything is configured properly, the system will deploy the report to the Report Manager or the SharePoint Reports folder, depending on which system the firm is using.

In Visual Studio, select the report to be deployed in the Solution Explorer. (If the report uses shared Data Sources or shared Datasets, those objects must be deployed as well. To deploy all parts, select the project name in the Solution Explorer.) Right click and select deploy. If everything is configured properly, the system will deploy the report to the Report Manager or the Share Point Reports folder, depending on which system the firm is using.

If deployment errors are encountered, consult with the firm's IT department to ensure the SSRS components are configured properly.

# VIII.C. *Navigating the Report Manger*

The Report Manager is a web based tool and, as such, web navigation rules apply. Users can open folders by double clicking on the folder icon. To return from a folder up to the prior level, click on the brower's back button or use the dynamic Path Bar to select the desired folder level.

For example, in the frame shown, the user is currently viewing the Commissions folder which is a sub-folder of the Sales Reports folder. The Sales Reports folder sits on the Report Manger Home screen. Clicking on Home will return the user to the Report Manager Home screen while clicking on Sales Reports will return the user to the Sales Reports folder.

To launch a report from the Report Manger, navigate through the folders to the folder that contains the report. When the report is located, double click on the report. The report will be cxccutcd. If the report requires it, the user will need to supply a valid user ID and password. If the report requires parameters, the user will need to enter the parameters to allow selection of the proper information.

To access the configuration menu associated with each object in the Report Manager, hover the cursor over the object until the pull down menu frame is displayed and click on the pull down arrow. The appropriate management menu will appear. Options on the various menus will be discussed in the sections on the individual options below.

# *VIII.D.* *Folders*

Folders in the Report Manager allow objects to be logically organized so that a user can quickly find a desired report among hundreds deployed. Folders can be created inside folders, creating a tree of folders. For example, a Sales folder can contain folders for Customers, Sales Orders and Commissions. The Sales Orders folder can contain folders for Open Orders and Historical Orders. Inside the Open Orders folder are reports that pull information from the Open Orders tables.

Access to some of these functions may be restricted by security!

## VIII.D.1.  Creating Folders

If a user has rights to create folders, the New Folder option appears in the web page's tool bar. Clicking the New Folder icon opens the New Folder screen in the Explorer. The following fields are available:

**Name** -- The name of the folder is entered here. This name will be displayed under the Folder icon in the Report Manager.

**Description** -- The text entered here will appear under the folder name in the tile view and in the Description column in the details view on the Report Manager. It can be used to explain the use of the folder

**Hide in the Tile View** -- If this box is checked, the folder will not appear in the tile view. Users can only see the folder in the details view.

Click the OK button to save the new folder. The new folder will be stored inside the current folder in the Report Manager. To create a sub-folder inside an existing folder, first navigate into the existing folder then click the New Folder button.

## VIII.D.2.  Folder Management Menu

Hovering the cursor over a folder and clicking on the pull down arrow displays the Folder Management Menu. Options in the menu include Move, Delete, Security and Manage.

# VIII.D.2.a. Moving a Folder

Selecting the Move option from the Folder Management Menu opens a folder selection screen. A Location field is provided where the user can type the desired location. However, that is not recommended as there is an easier way.

An explorer display of all of the tiered menus available in the Report Manager is provided. Expand the leafs of the explorer until the desired host folder is located. Click on that folder and click the OK button. The original folder will be moved to the folder selected in the explorer.

# VIII.D.2.b. Deleting a Folder

Select the Delete option from the Folder Management Menu to delete the selected folder. Make sure that any objects in the folder are already moved if they are to be retained. If a folder containing other objects or folders is deleted, the objects and folders contained in the folder are also deleted. There is NO undo!

# VIII.D.2.c. Security Menu Option

The Security Menu Option opens Folder Management with the Security screen selected. Folder Security is discussed in detail in Section VIII.I.

# VIII.D.2.d. Managing A Folder

Clicking the Management option on the Folder Management Menu opens Folder Management with the Properties screen selected.

The Properties screen displays the date and time the folder was first created and last modified along with the user ID that created and modified the folder. It also provides 3 fields that allow the folder name, description and view option to be edited or changed.

Once any changes to the folder name, description, or view option are made, click OK to save the changes. Changes take place immediately.

A Security tab is provided in the Folder Management option. Clicking this tab displays the Security screen. Folder security is discussed in detail in Section VIII.I. below.

# VIII.D.3.  Best Practices?

"Best Practices" is one of those terms that is thrown around a lot without any real definition.  "Best Practices" is supposed to be a definition of the rules that everyone should apply to ensure the firm is following the optimal operational concepts.  Unfortunately, what is "Best Practices" for one firm is not always "Best Practices" for another.  All we can do here is generalize.

If a firm has a small number of SSRS reports, say less than a dozen, placing all of those reports on the Home page of the Report Manager is quite sufficient.  There is no need to split the desktop into several different folders with sub-folders since each sub-folder might possibly hold only one report or less!  However, as the number of reports grows, the need to group reports becomes more important.

A hierarchal tree of report folders allows users to quickly browse through a Report Manager that holds hundreds to thousands of reports.  For example, starting with a Home page containing only a few folders, a user can select Sales Reports.  Then from that folder's display of sub-folders, the Customer Sales Analysis reports folder is selected.  Again, a group of folders is presented and the user can select the Sales by Customers folder.  Now, a dozen reports are shown.

In the scheme described above, over 7,000 reports can be stored, the user never sees more than 6 selections, and the desired report can be found in 5 clicks!

Special cases can be made for applications that launch SSRS reports.  If the firm is using a third party product that launches SSRS reports, a folder can be created for the special format documents/reports used by that application.  The top level folder can then be hidden in the tiles view, reducing the background noise shown to users but keeping all of the applications together.

- Home
  - Data Sources
  - Datasets
  - Forms Manager Forms
    - Check Forms
    - Purchase Order Forms
    - Sales Historical Orders Forms
    - Sales Open Order Forms
  - Inventory_Reports
  - Manufacturing Reports
  - Payables
  - Report Parts
  - Sales Reports
    - Customer Lists
    - Customer Sales Analysis
      - Sales by Customer Reports
      - Sales by Items Reports
      - Sales by Territory Reports
    - Open Orders

# VIII.E.    Report Management Menu

Hovering the cursor over a report icon and clicking on the pull down arrow displays the Report Management Menu.  Options in the menu include Move, Delete, Subscribe, Create Linked Report, View Report History, Security, Manage, Download and Edit in Report Builder.

Report Management provides a significant number of configuration options for reports launched from the Report Manager.  In most cases, the most common options are pre-selected for reports when they are deployed and do not need to be altered.  However, subscriptions, report chaining, the retention of history et cetera provide significant power for the user of the Reports Manager.

Some of these options are controlled by security and may not appear on all user's menus.

## VIII.E.1.  Move Reports

Selecting the Move option from the Report Management Menu opens a folder selection screen.  A Location field is provided where the user can type the desired location.  However, that is not recommended as there is an easier way.

An explorer display of all of the tiered menus available in the Report Manager is provided.  Expand the leafs of the explorer until the desired host folder is located.  Click on that folder and click the OK button. The report will be moved into the folder selected in the explorer.

## VIII.E.2.  Delete Reports

Select the Delete option from the Report Management Menu to delete the selected report.  The system will confirm that the report should be deleted.  Click OK to delete the report. There is NO undo!

**Login Credentials for Subscriptions**

Reports executed through a subscription must have the login credentials recorded inside the Dataset. The system will not have the opportunity to ask a user to login when the report is run on a schedule.

# VIII.E.3. Subscribe

Got users that want the same report run every morning and they want it waiting for them with their morning coffee? Got reports that take several hours to run but are required monthly? Or weekly? Got traveling executives that want their reports each Monday, where ever they are?

Subscriptions will do all of this easily! And, the users can be trained to create their own subscriptions! (Well, some of them can be trained...)

Subscriptions allow a report to be rendered on a schedule and to place that report in a folder, ready to be opened in a browser, or e-mailed to the user. E-mailed reports can be sent to groups of users with a re-directed reply-to address and they can be created and saved (or e-mailed) in a variety of formats.

The Subscription screen can be displayed by selecting Subscription from the Reports Management pull down menu or by selecting Subscription from the Reports Management screen and clicking on New Subscription. The screen is also executed when an existing schedule listed in the Reports Management Subscriptions screen or an existing report in the My Subscriptions list is selected and the word Edit is clicked.

The Subscription screen has two different layouts depending on the selection made in the Delivered By pull down list. Two options are available: Email and Windows File Share. Both screen options are shown and explained below.

Decide first how the report is to be delivered (email or file share).

# VIII.E.3.a. Report Delivery -- E-mail

When a report is to be delivered by e-mail, the delivery options allow the subscriber to specify the recipients, the sender, the method of attaching the report to the e-mail, format of the report, priority and more.

Fields in this portion of the subscription window include:

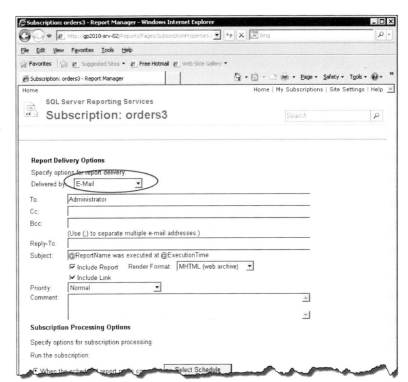

**Delivered by** -- This pull down list offers two options: E-Mail or Windows File Share. E-mail must be selected for the remaining fields to be displayed.

**To/Cc/Bcc** -- Enter the e-mail addresses of the individuals that are to receive copies of the report.

**Reply-To** -- An e-mail address of the person responsible for sending the report must be entered here. If there are any replies or bounced e-mails, they will be sent to this address.

**Subject** -- Enter a phrase that will be sent as the subject of the e-mail. Two special variables can be included in the subject line:

**@ReportName** -- This phrase is replaced by the name of the report.

**@ExecutionTime** -- This phrase is replaced by the date and time the report was executed.

**Include Report** -- If this box is checked, the report is included with the e-mail. If the rendering format is the Web Archive format and the receiving browser supports HTML 4.0 and MHTML, the report is included as part of the e-mail. Otherwise it is sent as an attachment. Note that the size of the e-mail or attachment is not checked. If the document is larger than the size e-mail system on either the sending or receiving side will accept, the e-mail will not be delivered. It is recommended that Include Link be checked for large reports.

**Render Format** -- If Include Report is marked, select the format of the report information from the following list:

- **XML file with report data**
- **CSV (comma separated values)**
- **PDF**
- **MHTML**
- **Excel**
- **TIFF**
- **Word**

**Include Link** -- If this box is checked, a copy of the report is archived and a link to the archived report is provided in the body of the e-mail. The recipient can click the link to view the report in their browser. This method of delivery is recommended for large reports.

**Priority** -- The e-mail is typically sent with Normal priority. Changing the setting of this option changes the priority of the e-mail. Options include:

- **Normal**
- **Low**
- **High**

**Comment** -- Text entered here will be sent with the body of the e-mail.

# VIII.E.3.b.  Report Delivery -- File Share

When a report is delivered using the Windows File Share option, fields are provided that allow the subscriber to specify the file name, path, and format of the report file. The subscriber must specify the destination for the report. Using Windows File Share, the reports are placed in a location where prospective readers of the report can browse and view the reports they want to see. This option is especially useful when a report takes a long time to run. The report can be run overnight and viewed immediately during the day.

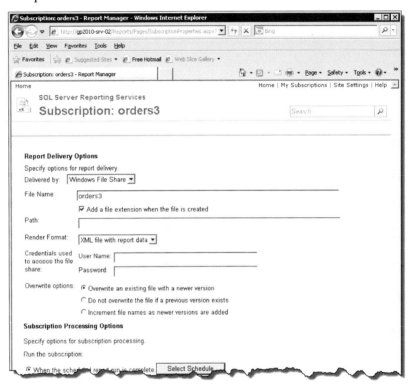

Fields in this portion of the subscription window include:

**Delivered by** -- This pull down list offers two options: E-Mail or Windows File Share. Windows File Share must be selected for the remaining fields to be displayed.

**File Name** -- Enter the desired name for the file that will be used to store the report.

**Add A File Extension** -- Check this box to have the system automatically add an extension to the file name above. The extension used will depend on the Render format selected below.

**Path** -- Enter a path in UNC format to the shared folder where the report will be stored. The UNC format is \\<*servername*>\<*reportsfolder*>. Include the double backslash at the beginning of the UNC path but do not add a slash to the end of the path.

**Render Format** -- Select the format of the report information from the following list:

- **XML file with report data**
- **CSV (comma separated values)**
- **PDF**
- **MHTML**
- **Excel**
- **TIFF**
- **Word**

**Credentials Used to Access The File Share** -- Enter a user ID that has full rights to the UNC specified above. The user name must be in the format <domain>\<user name>. Also enter the password for the specified user account. This user ID and password are used to obtain rights to place the rendered report into the specified file share.

**Overwrite Options** -- The following options tell the system what to do if another copy of the report already exists in the file share:

**Overwrite an Existing File with a Newer Version** -- The new version of the report file replaces the old version of the report. Only the most recent version of the report is found in the file share.

**Do Not Overwrite the File if a Previous Version Exists** -- If an older version of the report exists in the file share, the new report will not be saved. Only the older version of the report is available.

**Increment File Names as Newer Versions are Added** -- If this option is selected, reports are assigned a numeric suffix. The suffix is incriminated each time a new report is written to the share. Old and new versions of the report are available to be viewed. The system does no housekeeping and someone must examine the file share periodically and delete obsolete versions to avoid filling the drive with useless old report copies.

# VIII.E.3.c. Subscription Processing Options

Once either the E-Mail Delivery Options or the Windows File Share Delivery Options are completed, the subscriber must complete the Subscription Processing Options.

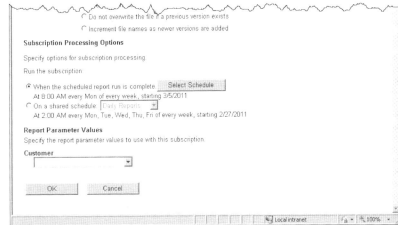

Fields in this section of the Subscription screen include:

**Run the Subscription when the Scheduled Report Run is Complete** --When this option is selected, the report will be run and a customized schedule is used.

**Select Schedule** -- This button is used to open the Schedule Details window, allowing a subscriber to specify a customized delivery schedule for the reports. See Section VIII.E.3.e. below for a description of the Schedule Details window.

**Run the Subscription On a Shared Schedule** -- When this option is selected, an existing shared schedule can be selected from the next pull down list. The report will be rendered on that schedule.

**Schedule Pull Down List** -- If Shared Schedule is selected above, this pull down list displays all of the report schedules defined in the Site Settings. The subscriber may select one of these predefined schedules for the report rendering.

# VIII.E.3.d. Report Parameter Values

If the report to be rendered requires parameters to be entered, the parameters from the report are displayed on the Subscription screen under the Report Parameters Values label. These parameters must be completed before the report subscription can be saved.

Note that login information for the Dataset is not requested. If access credentials allowing the report to read and display data from the tables is not embedded in the report itself, the report cannot be subscribed! If an error is displayed when trying to record a subscription that says that login credentials are required, contact the report designer and have the Dataset modified to include the credentials.

## VIII.E.3.e.  Select Schedule Option

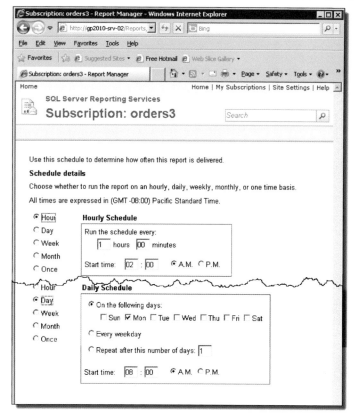

If a report is to be rendered and distributed on a Shared Schedule, that schedule must be defined before the subscription can be recorded. When a custom schedule is used for the report, the subscriber specifies the frequency and duration of the subscription. The Schedule Details window is displayed by clicking the Select Schedule button on the Subscription screen.

The Schedule Details area changes based on the time span selected. Time spans available are Hour, Day, Week, Month, or Once. The graphic shows each different configuration of the window depending on the option selected.

If **Hour** is selected, the gap between the regeneration or rendering of the report is specified in Hours and Minutes. Also, the Start Time is listed. When the start time passes, the report will be rendered and then it will be rendered again and again after the specified interval passes.

The Hour option allows reports to be updated automatically at almost any interval from 1 minute to 24 hours apart.

If **Day** is selected, the subscriber then marks the days the report should be rendered by either marking specific days, selecting Every Weekday, or selecting Repeat After This Number of Days and entering an interval. The start time is also specified.

The Day option allows the reports to be updated on specific days or at any interval from one day to 999 days.

If **Week** is selected, the subscriber then specified an interval in weeks between the updates to the report. The subscriber can select the day of the week the report will be rendered and the start time.

The Week option allows the report to be updated or re-rendered in intervals from 1 to 999 weeks apart.

The Month option allows the subscriber to cause the report to regenerate in monthly periods. The subscriber selects the particular months when the report should be rendered, the day of the week or the calendar day when the report should be rendered, and the start time for the creation of the report.

The **Month** option allows reports to be generated during specific months, on a particular week of the month and a specific day of that week, or on a specific calendar day. For example, the report can be rendered during the 3rd week of the month on Wednesday or it can be rendered on the 10th of the month.

The **Once** option allows a subscriber to set up a report to execute at a specific time of day and to run one time only. The user specified the start time for the report to be rendered. When the time passes, the report will be rendered and the subscription canceled.

At the bottom of the Subscription Scheduling screen, the subscriber can specify the start and ending date for the subscription.

Once all parameters are entered as desired, click on the OK button to save the schedule.

## VIII.E.3.f.  Saving the Subscription

When all of the parameters of the subscription have been entered, click the OK button to save the schedule.

If a customized schedule was used, the report will be produced at the next scheduled interval. If a shared schedule was used, the shared schedule must be active. It may already be active, especially if other reports are using the report. But it must be marked as active under the Site Settings before the report will be generated.

## VIII.E.3.g.  Editing a Subscription

Subscriptions may be edited when needed. Click on the My Subscriptions link at the top of the window and select the desire scheduled report by clicking on the Edit link. The Subscription window will open with the current parameters displayed. Make any necessary edits and save the subscription.

To delete a subscription, from the My Subscription screen, mark the check box to the left of the subscription and click the Delete icon on the tool bar.

# VIII.E.4.  Create Linked Reports

Reports in the Report Manager are assigned various parameters.  For example, security limitations may restrict a report to only one group of users.  If a second group needs to be able to run the report, a Linked Report is helpful.

Linked reports create a new virtual report using the report definition of another existing report.  This new virtual report can have its own settings and parameters.  Once a Linked Report is created, users with permission to do so can manage the Linked Report exactly like any other report.

To create a Linked Report, open the Report Management menu from the source report and select Create Linked Report.  Give the new virtual report a name and optionally, a description.  All of the report management options are available at this time.  See Section VIII.E.7. for information on the Reports Management options.

# VIII.E.5.  View Report History

The View Report History option on the Reports Management Menu opens the Report History screen.  On this screen is a list of the stored snapshots of the selected report.  If snapshots are retained, this allows a user to view prior versions of the report and look for data trends.

The report must be configured to take snapshots using the Snapshot options screen of Reports Management.  Optionally, the user can click New Snapshot and create a snapshot of the report.

# VIII.E.6.  Report Security

The Security Menu Option opens Report Management with the Security screen selected. Reports Security is discussed in detail in Section VIII.I.

# VIII.E.7.  Reports Management

Selecting Manage from the Reports Management menu opens the Reports Management screen collection.  In this window, a user can update the report name and description, view, edit and create subscriptions, change processing options, et cetera.  Many of the functions available off of the Reports Management menu appear as tabbed screens in this window.  Users can even Move reports, Create Linked Reports, Download and Replace reports from here.

The window opens by default with the properties window displayed.  Other screens are displayed by clicking on the screen name in the list on the left side of the screen.

## VIII.E.7.a.  Properties

The Properties screen displays the date and time the report was first created and last modified and the user ID that created and modified the report.  It also provides 3 fields that allow the report name, description and view option to be edited or changed.

Once any changes to the report name, description, or view option are made, click APPLY to save the changes.  Changes take place immediately.

## VIII.E.7.b.  Datasets

Report objects are separate components deployed to the Reports Manager.  While the report file is one object that refers to a Dataset, the Dataset itself is a separate object.  Selecting the Datasets option from the Reports Management screen allows a user to browse all Datasets deployed to the Reports Manager and select one appropriate to the report.

Typically, when a report is deployed, all components are deployed to the same folder in the Report Manger.  If the Report definition is moved to a specific folder, it may not be able to locate the associated Dataset.  For that matter, the Dataset can be moved to special folders that can be hidden but available to the report definitions.  The user deploying or moving reports must make sure that the Reports Manager knows where to find the Dataset for the report.  This screen allows a user to browse all Datasets in the Reports Manager and associate the appropriate one with the report, if necessary.

## VIII.E.7.c.  Subscriptions

The Subscription screen displays a list of subscriptions for the selected report.  New subscriptions can be added by clicking the New Subscription icon on the tool bar.  Existing subscriptions can be deleted by marking the check box to the left of the subscription and clicking the Delete icon on the tool bar.

See Section VIII.E.3. for detailed information on creating subscriptions.

## VIII.E.7.d.  Processing Options

The Report Processing Options screen allows users to configure the report data retention plans.  Report data can be collected and cached on a schedule and the report rendered from the cached information.  Report snapshots can be used to render the reports, if the system is capturing snapshots.  And the Report Timeout can be set.

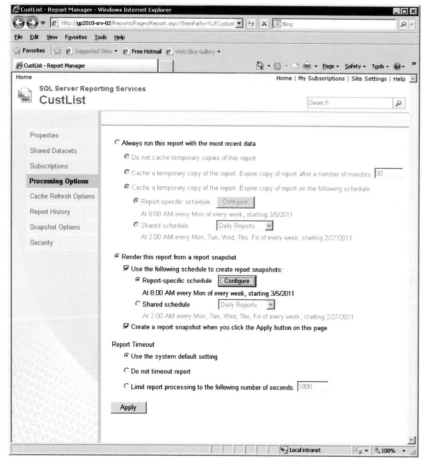

Two primary options are available that control the rendering of reports:  Always run the Report With the Most Recent Data and Render This Report from a Report Snapshot.

Selecting the first option, (Most Recent Data) causes the rendering engine to open the Data Source and pull new data from the tables.  This provides the user with the absolutely most recent and up to date data.  It also takes longer than the alternate option, Render... from a Snapshot.

Selecting to render the report from a snapshot instructs the report generator to pull the most recently stored snapshot of the data needed on the report and present that information to the user.  It is quicker and produces reports in less time but (a)  the data may not be as current and, (b) snapshots must be generated and stored.

Using snapshots of data is useful for reports that can take a long time to produce.  A snapshot can be created during off hours, when demands on the network and server are light, and stored for quick retrieval.  Now, when a user needs to view the report, rather than wait any significant amount of time and place a heavy demand on the server at peak hours, the data is pulled from the snapshot and delivered. If timeliness of data is not critical, this option can save considerable time.

Even when the option to run the report with the most recent data is selected, the system can be instructed to temporarily cache a copy of the report. This, again can save time and lighten system load. If, for example, sales teams frequently look at the daily sales reports between 8 and 10 am., the report can be marked to run with the most recent data. However, by enabling temporary caching, once the report has been created, a copy will be held for a specified amount of time, allowing the system to quickly show the report to the second, third, et cetera user much more quickly and without returning to the server.

The temporary caching options under "Always Run... With The Most Recent Data" include:

**Do not Cache Temporary Copies of this Report** -- Caching is turned completely off and each time the report is executed, data will be pulled from the server tables.

**Cache a Temporary Copy of this Report. Expire Copy of the report after xx minutes** -- The user specifies a number of minutes when the report configuration is set. When the report is rendered, if no cached copy exists, data is retrieved from the server. A copy of the report is held for the specified number of minutes in case another user wants to view the report.

**Cache a Temporary Copy of this Report. Expire Copy of the Report on on the Following Schedule** -- This option works like the previous option except much more sophisticated scheduling of the report retention is available. Options for retention match the options for subscribing to a report in that a "custom to this report" schedule can be defined or a pre-defined schedule selected.

If the option to render the reports from a snapshot is selected, the user configuring the option must specify a schedule for the creation of snapshots. While caching creates a copy of the data the first time the report is executed, rendering from a snapshot instructs the system to create and maintain a fresh copy of the report on a schedule. Scheduling of the creation of snapshots is identical to scheduling subscriptions to the report except that the data is recorded rather than distributed and held until a user requests a copy of the report.

Again, rendering a report from a snapshot produces a report quicker and allows a system manager to schedule the times when the report manager will pull data.

The Report Timeout option allows a system manager to limit the amount of time the Report Manager spends attempting to retrieve data and assemble the report before timing out and aborting the process. Normally, using the default system timeout is sufficient. In some cases, with complex reports or reports that pull a lot of data, system managers may want to restrict the amount of time that can be allocated to producing the report to limit loads on the server.

## VIII.E.7.e.  Cache Refresh Options

The Cache Refresh Options screen allows a system manager to establish caching plans that will pull data for a report into the system and hold the data for a specified length of time.

When a report requires parameters, the parameters can be specified as part of the cache plan. Different caching plans can be defined for the same report with different parameters specified. Thus, if different sales reps need analysis reports for their clients, data can be pulled and cached for each sales person during non-peak server times. Later, when the sales rep is ready to view their data, the information is pulled from cache, requiring much less processing time.

**Description** -- Enter a description for the cache refresh plan.

**Refresh the Cache According to the Following Schedule** -- A schedule for the cache refresh operation can be specified exactly like schedules for report subscriptions. Refer to the section on report subscriptions for information on creating schedules. Item specific schedules or shared schedules can be used.

**Parameters** -- If parameters are required for the item selected, the values for those parameters are specified in the Cache Plan for the item. This will cause the system to pull records that are required by the specific parameters. For example, if a report lists sales attributed to a sales rep and the sales rep is a parameter specified when the report is run, the sales rep must be specified at this time and information will be cached for that rep's sales. Additional caching plans can be created if information needs to be cached for other sales reps.

**Use Default** -- If parameters are required and a default value is specified in the report definition, checking this box will allow the report to execute immediately upon selection using the defaults provided.

# VIII.E.7.f.   Report History

The Report History screen is a list of the stored snapshots of the selected report.  If snapshots are retained, this allows a user to view prior versions of the report and look for data trends.

The report must be configured to take snapshots using the Snapshot options screen of Reports Management.  Optionally, the user can click New Snapshot and create a snapshot of the report.

# VIII.E.7.g.   Snapshot Options

The Snapshot Options screen allows the system manager to configure the frequency with which the Report Manager will create snapshot copies of report and the length of time the snapshots will be retained.

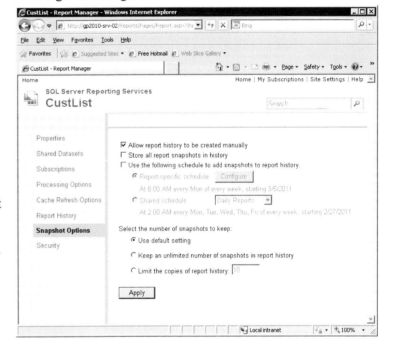

Options on this screen include:

**Allow Report History to be Created Manually** -- Checking this option will allow a user to browse to the Report History screen and click the button to create and save a snapshot of the report.

**Store All Report Snapshots in History** -- Checking this box will record a copy of the report in history every time it is rendered.

**Use the following Schedule to Add Snapshots to Report History** -- Schedules are assigned (either custom to this report or by selecting a pre-defined schedule) exactly like schedules are created for report subscriptions.  Rather than distribute copies of the report, however, a snapshot is created and stored.

**Select The Number of Snapshots to Keep** -- The options below allow the user to define the number of snapshots to retain

**Use Default Setting** -- The default setting for the Report Manager is used.

**Keep an Unlimited Number of Snapshots in Report History** -- Snapshots must be manually deleted if this option is selected.

**Limit the Number of Copies of Report History** -- If this option is selected, the system manager enters a value in the numeric field. When the number of snapshots exceeds that value, the system will delete old snapshots and retain only the number of copies specified.

If snapshots are used and automatically generated, it is STRONGLY recommended that the number retained be limited. Either set the global value or use the Limit the Number of Copies option.

## VIII.E.7.h. Security

See Section VIII.I for details on security.

## VIII.E.8. Download Reports

This option allows a user to select a report and export the report definition file to a local share. The report can then be moved to another system and uploaded. Make sure to move all of the objects associated with the report (the report definition, the dataset, et cetera)

## VIII.E.9. Edit In Report Builder

This option launches the SSRB (SQL Server Report Builder) with a copy of the report loaded. It allows the user, if permissions are granted to do so, to edit the report and re-deploy it to the Report Manager.

Clicking on this option automatically launches the SSRB. See the documentation earlier in this manual on using the SSRB.

## VIII.F. Launching Report Builder

Just like the option in the Reports Management Menu, this top level menu option launches the SSRB (SQL Server Report Builder). It allows the user with appropriate permissions to edit reports and re-deploy them. No report is automatically selected and the user must have rights and access to the original source code of the report.

Clicking on this option automatically launches the SSRB. See the documentation earlier in this manual on using the SSRB.

# VIII.G. Manage Data Sources

Just like reports, right clicking on a Data Source opens a Data Source Management menu. Most of the options perform the same functions as the Report Management menu. The Manage option, of course, has different functions.

The Properties screen of the Data Sources Management window shows

most of the information used to initially create the Data Source. Any of this information can be edited if necessary. Note that tools and wizards to make editing a Data Source are limited to other tools. A user must know what they are doing when editing Data Sources here. Also, changing the name or characteristics of a Data Source may make it unusable to any Dependent Items.

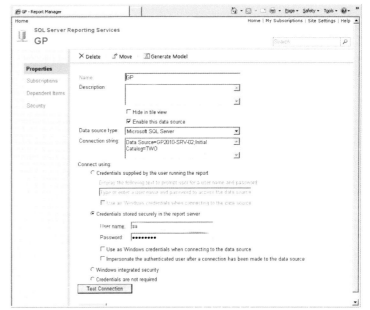

Refer to the section of this book on creating Data Sources in the reporting tools for an explanation of the fields on this screen.

Note the Dependent Items screen tab. This screen lists any items that are dependent on the Data Source. For example, Datasets are built on Data Sources. Changing the selected Data Source will change any reports tied to the Datasets listed in the Dependent Items tab.

One of the uses of this function is to change the database associated with the Data Source. Editing the Initial Catalog parameter in the Connection String will point the Data Source to a different database. The SQL name of the Database must be used, not the company name found on the login screen of a MS Dynamics application.

# VIII.H.   Dataset Management

Again, right clicking on a Dataset opens a Dataset Management menu. Most of the options perform the same functions as the Report Management menu.  The Manage option, of course, has different functions.

The Properties screen of the Dataset Management window shows the identification information for the Dataset.

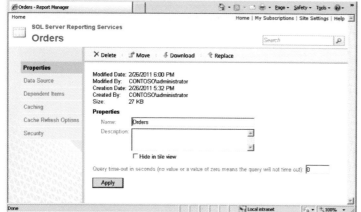

The Data Source tab on this window shows the Data Source to which the current Dataset is attached.  The Dependent Items tab on this window shows the Report Objects to which the Dataset is attached.  Between these two screens, a complete chain of linkage from the Data Source through the Dataset to the Report definitions can be seen.

# VIII.I. Report Manager Security

Report Manager security is designed to restrict access to specific reports or groups of reports to the appropriate individuals or groups of people in an organization. Since reports can be used to access any information in a database, and MS Dynamics databases contain not only inventory and stock planning but also receivables, payables, general ledger and even payroll information, it is important to most organizations to ensure that those users that can run reports can only see the information they need to see and are authorized to see. Since the Report Manager is a universal tool, available to all authorized to log into the network, some internal security mechanism must be available to limit users abilities to run and access specific reports.

The SSRS Report Manager is a component of the MS SQL product family and not specifically a part of the MS Dynamics family. It provides access to reports written using the SSRS report builders that create reports against MS-SQL databases and the MS Dynamics applications use the MS-SQL databases. However, since the Report Manger can host reports from applications other than MS Dynamics, security cannot be based on users defined in MS Dynamics. The Report Manager security is based on the broader security of the network or host system. Generally this means Active Directory users.

Objects in the Report Manager fall into two groups: report objects and folders. Report objects are the report definitions, Data Sources and Dataset definitions. Folders are structures inside the Report Manager that allow users or a system administrator to organize the report objects into logical groups. Report objects are then placed inside the appropriate folders.

Folders can contain other folders, forming a tree structure. For example, a Report Manager Home page may contain folders for Sales, Inventory, Purchasing, Corporate and Manufacturing. Inside the Sales folder, individual folders for Customer Reports, Commission Reports, Open Order Reports and Historical Orders exist.

The number of tiers of folders depends on the size of the firm and the number of reports hosted by the Reports Manager. Certainly, if less than a dozen SSRS reports are used by the firm, all of these reports can be hosted on the Reports Manger home page. However, with just three or four tiers of folders, thousands of reports can be hosted by the Report Manger, located and launched by a user with only 3-5 keystrokes.

More important, however, folders provide a mechanism for managing security and access to reports. The system administrator can control the security settings of individual reports, certainly. But setting access for each report is time consuming. Having access limited by folders allows a system administrator to define functional roles within the firm and establish access to folders based on a user's ID or the role of the user. Thus, all manufacturing users, for example, can be given access to manufacturing reports but prevented from accessing accounting reports. Then, whenever a new report is written for the manufacturing team, the report is dropped into the manufacturing team's folder in the Report Manager and inherits the rights of the folder. Any manufacturing employee that is a member of the role assigned to that folder can run the report.

As hinted above, when an object is created inside a folder, it inherits the security of the parent folder. If, for example, a folder is created on the Home screen of the Report Manger, by default, all individuals and groups that can execute the Reports Manager can browse into the folder. Objects placed into the folder, such as other folders or reports, also inherit the security of the folder and any user or group that has access to the parent folder can access the objects inside the folder if changes are not made.

Folder security enables the system administrator to assign specific rights of access to specific folders. Thus, access the Payroll folder, for example, can be limited to individuals in the payroll department, keeping manufacturing employees out of that folder.

As stated above, report objects dropped into a folder inherit the security settings of the folder. Generally this is the desired effect, allowing system administrators to control access by groups. However, under certain circumstances, a report in a folder may need to have its access restricted tighter than the security of the folder. Using payroll as an example, general payroll reports in the payroll folder are typically available to those people that run payroll. However, a payroll report listing only executive compensation may need to be restricted only to the head of the department or the CFO of the firm. The security of each report can be controlled independent of the host folder if needed.

Finally, the databases that provide information to the reports frequently have their own security system. MS-SQL does! Access to specific tables and even fields in the tables can be controlled in MS-SQL based on the users and roles in the network security system (Active Directory). Generally, this level of security is not used. However, in high security sites, the SQL DBA may elect to control access via SQL table security. If table level access is utilized, be very careful. Understanding which tables are associated with the various processes in the MS Dynamics Application requires a high degree of knowledge of the application. Restricting access to the wrong tables can have unexpected results.

# VIII.I.1. Site Security

Site security is used to control access to management and configuration functions of the Report Manager and the creation or use of shared schedules, using the Report Builder from the Report Manager, and setting default values for some server features.

A Local System Administrator default account is created with the Report Manger. Any other group or user needing system level security needs to have a role created. If the Local System Administrator role is deleted, Local System Administrators can still access and maintain the Report Manager.

To give others access to the Site Level functions:

1.     Select Site Settings from the Home Page of the Report Manger.

2.     Select the Security Tab to show the security page.

3.     Click on New Role Assignment to open the New System Role Assignment page.

4.     In the Group or User Name field, enter a valid network group or user ID. In an Active Directory network, this user or group must be a valid Active Directory user or group.

5.     Select the security role for the user or group. Options include:

    **System Administrator** -- Can view and/or modify system role assignments, role definitions, system properties and shared schedules.

    **System User** -- Can view system properties, shared schedules and use Report Builder.

6.     Click OK to save the new role.

# VIII.I.2.  Folder and other Objects Security

Security rights assigned to folders, reports, Data Sources, Datasets and any other objects are used to provide access to users to the objects in the Report Manager.  As stated above, unless they are changed, rights of folders, sub-folders, and objects in the folders inherit the rights of their parent object.

Default access is provided to the Local System Administrator.  Access for any other person or group must be assigned by the Local System Administrator and this access must be provided folder by folder or object by object.

Best practices suggests organizing reports and other objects in appropriate folder groups and assign specific rights to the folders.  Objects inside the folder will inherit the rights of the folder.  Thus, giving the customer service team rights to the Sales folder will allow members of that team to access and run any reports inside the folder.

Security for an object (a folder, sub-folder, report, et cetera) is assigned by right clicking on the object and selecting Security.  Manage can also be selected from the object's menu and then the Security tab selected.  Both paths lead to the same screen.

The Security screen will list all users and/or server roles that have rights to the folder.  If the folder is using rights inherited from it's parent, then a button will sit on the menu bar titled Edit Item Security.  Click the button to detach the item from it's parent's security.  Now buttons allow the user to add new security roles, delete existing roles, edit existing roles or revert to inherited security.

To add a user or role to the item...

1.  Click on the New Role Assignment button.  The New Role Assignment screen will be displayed.

2.  Enter into the Group or User Name field the name of a network user or network role (group of users).  Note that these are network users/roles and not MS Dynamics users.

3.  Select the Report Manger roles to assign to the network user or role.  Options include:

    **Browser** -- May view folders, run reports and/or subscribe to the reports.

    **Content Manger** -- Manages the content of the Report Server.  This includes report folders, reports and other resources.

**My Reports** -- Can publish reports and linked reports, manage folders, reports, and other resources in a My Reports folder.

**Publisher** -- May publish reports and linked reports to the Reports Manager.

**Report Builder** -- Can launch the Report Builder and view/ edit report definitions.

4.      Click OK to save the new role assignment.

To edit an existing role assignment, click the Edit hyper link in front of the role listing on the security screen.

To delete an existing role assignment, check the box in front of the role and click the Delete button on the menu bar.

# *VIII.J. Site Settings*

Site Settings are used to configure the Report Manger.  There are three screens used to configure the site settings:  the General screen, the Security screen and the Schedules screen.

## VIII.J.1.   General

The General screen of Site Settings allows a system administrator to

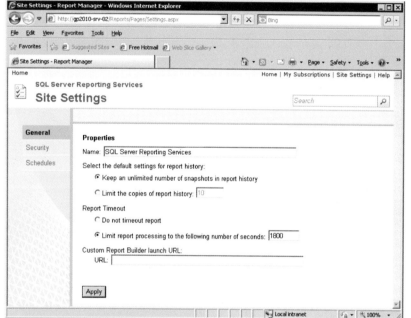

configure a few global settings. These include the title displayed at the top of the window, the report history and time out values.

**Name** -- Enter the name that is to be displayed at the top of the Report Manager window.  This allows a system administrator to customize the display for the firm.

**Select Default Settings for Report History** -- This allows a system administrator to keep an unlimited number of snapshots in history or limit the number of copies to a preset value.

**Report Time Out** -- This option allows a system administrator to instruct the Report Manager to wait forever for a report to complete running or to wait only a specific number of seconds and then to abort the report.  Normally, the system should not time out or wait for a significant amount of time (1800 seconds is 30 minutes!)  If reports are hanging, the number might be set shorter until the problem is diagnosed.

Click on the Apply button to save any setting changes.

## VIII.J.2.   Security

Site security is used to define the users or roles that have access to the site settings and configurations.  By default, Local System Administrators have access to the site settings.  Other users must be assigned rights as specified in Section VIII.I. above.

# VIII.J.3. Schedules

The Schedules screen of Site Settings allows a system administrator to create shared schedules to be used in the publishing of reports via subscriptions and generation of snapshots. Access the Schedules screen by clicking on Site Settings in the upper right corner of the Report Manager screen then selecting the Schedules tab on the left side of the display.

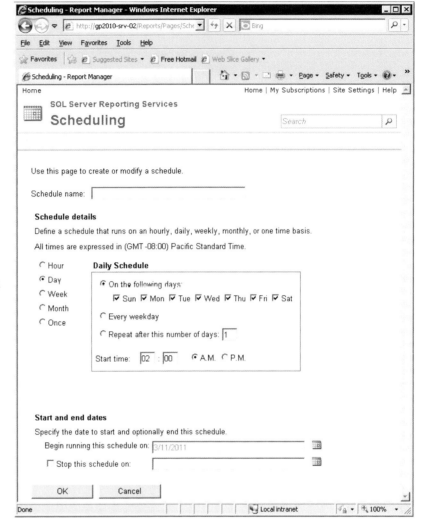

The first screen displayed will show a list of schedules. Existing schedules can be edited by selecting them (check the box next to the schedule) and clicking on the desired action. This includes deleting the schedule, pausing the schedule or resuming the schedule.

To create a new schedule, click on the New Schedule button. The screen shown here will be displayed. The fields available include:

**Schedule Name** -- Enter a unique name for the schedule. This name will appear in pull down lists when a shared schedule is selected for subscriptions, et cetera.

**Type of Schedule** -- The user can select to create a schedule that repeats each Hour, Day, Week, Month or Once only. Each changes the options available in the box to the right of the option list. See the section of this chapter on Subscriptions for an explanation of each set of parameters.

**Start and End Dates** -- Start and End Dates can be specified for the schedule. If dates are entered, the schedule will not execute until the Begin Running date and will optionally stop on the Stop This Schedule On date.

Click OK to save the schedule. The schedule can now be assigned to other subscriptions, et cetera.

# IX. Report Prep and Planning

# IX. *Report Prep and Planning*

## IX.A. *Designing the Report*

Before starting to write any report, it is important to design the report. Sometimes this is as simple as sketching the report on a piece of paper and sometimes a formal specification needs to be written and approved. If a report is being written to provide information needed by the report author, then simply sketching the report on a piece of paper may be sufficient. If a report is being written for others in the firm, the report author can save significant headaches by producing and getting approvals for a formal report specification.

A report author needs to know the intent and use of the report. Frequently, people requesting reports have a pre-conceived notion of what they want but do not have the ability to clearly relate their requirements to someone else. Sales reps may think in terms of pipelines and forecasts while a report designer thinks in terms of open quotes and orders in tables. Which transactions in the tables form pipeline documents may be a matter for discussion between the report designer and the ultimate user.

At a minimum, a report author needs to know what columns of information must appear on the report, how the information is to be sorted, if the information needs to be grouped, what groups are expected, and what totals and subtotals are required. If only a portion of the data from the tables are to be displayed on the report, what is the criteria used to select the records. And, will the criteria be the same every time the report runs or should the user be required/allowed to enter restrictions when the report runs.

Frequently, the ultimate user cannot express their needs in the terms needed by a report designer. Careful listening and analysis of the requirements, along with proposed report layouts and design documents allows a designer to repeat to the user what the designer heard the user say. Refinements can then be made to the specification.

From this information, the author can typically determine the databases and tables to be used, any formulas required to create columns, the user parameters to define and the basic layout of the report. The design document then becomes a measurement against which the performance of the report can be gauged. It also keeps the developer focused on the requirements of the requestor and keeps the requestor from blaming the developer when the developer generates incorrect data following the requestor's exact and specific instructions.

**Report Specification Template**

A sample report specification template can be downloaded from Accolade Publication's web site. Browse to www.AccoladePublications.com and visit the Free Stuff section.

The form of presentation of the data must be defined early in the process. Simply listing rows of data on a report and providing details to the user is a simple exercise. To summarize the data or to provide the data graphically in pie charts, bar graphs, sparklines, maps et cetera, requires some analysis and grouping of the data. Further, if the user wants to click on a data point on a graph and drill down into details, sub-reports may be required to support the drill downs.

Taking the time to formally document a report specification can seem to be a waste of time to many individuals. Experience proves, however, that the time taken to properly identify the end user's requirements and needs can reduce the time needed to refine the report over and over again until the document reaches it's final form. To identify the final form first makes the project successful more often.

## IX.B.  Report Specifications

The documentation of a report specification begins with an interview with the requesting user. With any luck, the requestor will have a sketch of their desired report. Identify the purpose of the report, the desired data to be presented, the method of presentation (list, graph, et cetera) and any totals or analysis that needs to be performed on the data.

The source of the information is important. While most report requestors will have absolutely no idea of the table structure of the data base involved, they will know the type of information that is to appear on the report. The report designer needs to ensure that the requests made by the user can be satisfied by the data in the tables. If the user wants information not stored in the tables nor attainable through analysis, the report cannot be produced. Modifications to the data may be needed or additional databases created and/or imported to generate the desired results.

Writing a report that produces a list of information based on dates, for example, can produce a useful listing. However, if the report always runs against a fixed range of dates, the useful life of the report is limited. If a report shows sales generated by a sales person, the report designer does not want to generate different versions of the report for each sales rep nor modify the report when new sales reps are hired. Report parameters should be carefully discussed that allow the user to run the report over and over again each time obtaining different sets of information.

After the user interview is over, the report designer prepares a formal specification document. This document should identify the data sources, the hard coded data select statements, the user optional selection statements, the sorting specifications for the data, the actual columns to be extracted and possibly displayed, any formulas needed to create new data elements (like an extended price created by multiplying a quantity ordered by the unit price) et cetera.

If data needs to be grouped for use in charts or graphs, the grouping and aggregation needs to be specified. If SQL views are needed to consolidate multiple databases, those need to be defined as part of the data source information.

If sub-reports are required, separate specifications for the sub-reports need to be written and the linkages between the primary and sub-reports identified.

Subtotals, totals and grand totals need to be defined.

The formatting of data in columns needs to be specified. Will dollar amounts show decimal quantities? How many decimals are needed in quantities? Are dates to show 2 or 4 digit years? Do codes in the data base need interpretation (1=Quote, 2=Order, et cetera)?

Once the data specification is created, the designer should prepare a pictorial representation of the report. It is difficult for many users to read a data specification and see in their minds an image of the report. A page showing the layout of data on the report using sample data or even XXX's and 9999's where data will appear will go a long way to helping a user visualize the report about to be written.

Finally, a summary narrative needs to be written to explain how the report will be launched, the options the user must enter to get the data they want, and any special presentations or analysis performed by the report, drill downs available et cetera.

This entire package is then presented to the report user for approval.


# IX.C.   Getting Spec Approvals


When a report specification is complete, it should be presented to the original requestor for approval. In many cases, the requestor will be overwhelmed by the presentation of the specification and will get lost in the details. Take the time to explain the specification to the user. It is important that the user understand what will be delivered to them or they will give a blanket "This looks Great!" approval and then hate the final version of the report when it does not show the information needed.

# IX.D.   Generating Sample Reports

As the report is being built, testing is important. While this sounds obvious, testing is not always easy. In the best case, data already exists in the tables for the report. In many cases, however, the report designer must build a test database and enter appropriate data into the tables.

It is important to have enough data in the tables, whether they are existing tables or a test database, to properly test the report. Otherwise, as the users run the report, they will find errors missed by the developer and faith in the report will fade. This is often followed by faith in the developer fading and work done on future reports will be questioned.

Knowing the intended use of the report allows the report designer to determine the amount of data needed to properly test the report. Make sure that all different scenarios are covered and that any analysis or drill downs in the report can be supported with the test data.

Finally, produce copies of the report and make a presentation to the users. Allow them to play with the sample data and run the reports several different ways. Chances are, they will find new ways to use the report or provide new requirements. Don't be surprised. Remember, most users find it difficult to express their exact needs, but they know what they want when they see it!

Be prepared to make revisions and changes.

# IX.E.   Making a Report Look Good

When a programmer is loading masses of data into tables, quick listings of rows with no headings or explanations may be sufficient to check the results of the imports. When the Board of Directors wants financial reports, they want well formatted information with supporting schedules, ratios, graphs, trend lines and presentation quality printing. Somewhere in the middle of these two examples, the rest of the world needs some basic formatting to make reading their reports easy. As a report designer, the better the reports look, the more satisfied a report user seems to be with the form of the report, even if the data shows horrible trends.

Presentation is important. More important than most report designers realize.

# IX.E.1.   Title Pages

Title pages are seldom seen on reports but can be nice. Some reports are designed to be printed and retained for several years. Having a title page provides a "cover" to the report.

A title page should be formatted like the title page of a book. The name of the report, date and time printed and parameters used to create the report are frequently printed on the title page.

# IX.E.2.   Page Header

The top of each page should have a nicely formatted header. The title of the report, date printed, company name and sometimes page number information is printed in the header. Parameters used to generate the report are also helpful and can be printed in the header.

# IX.E.3.   Column Headings

For columnar reports, do not overlook column headings. It is important that users know the names of the fields displayed on the data. The Column Headings should be repeated at the top of each page.

# IX.E.4.   Legends and Axis Labels

For graphical reports with charts and graphs, pay special attention to the legends and axis labels. Again, make sure the data on the report is properly labeled.

# IX.E.5.   Page Footer

The bottom of each page, in a well formatted report, should have a page footer. This space often contains the page numbers as well as any copyright or confidentiality notice.

# IX.E.6.    Summary Page

Like a title page, a summary page is not common.  However, many reports have complex sets of totals and summary information.  Commission reports are an excellent example where the body of the report will be split and distributed to each sales rep.  A summary page can be retained by the firm showing totals per sales rep et cetera.

# IX.E.7.    Page Numbers, etc

There are certain basic pieces of information that should appear on every report.  The presence of these elements allows a reader to identify certain vital parameters of the report.  Where they appear on the report is frequently up to the report designer.

**Page Numbers** -- It seems trivial to mention but all to often, report designers omit simple page numbers.  If a report is only displayed on screen and only contains a few lines of data, a page number seems insignificant.  However, reports tend to grow and get printed to paper.  Here, page numbers are instrumental in keeping the multiple sheets of paper in proper order.

Page numbers can appear in the header of the page but most often appear centered on the bottom of the page or on the bottom right corner of the page.  It is not necessary to print the total number of pages in a report (such as Page 24 of 75) but the inclusion of the word Page is often helpful.

**Date Printed** -- With the trend to on-screen displays of report data, the need for a date printed is frequently overlooked.  However, all too often an on-screen report is printed and retained.  When this happens, the ability to look at the document and know when it was printed is important.  The date printed can appear in the page header or page footer areas of each page and, if a title page is printed, on that page as well.

**Company Name** -- Even if the firm only uses one company name, print the company name on the report.  There are times when management will use a report to substantiate a loan application or make other regulatory filings.  Materials may be provided to vendors or customers.  Then, it becomes important to have the firm name prominent on the report.  The company name can appear in the page header and/or the page footer.  If a title or summary page is printed, it should appear there as well.

**Parameters** -- Months from now, when the report is reviewed, someone is going to wonder why all of the data from the tables is not listed. Printing the values entered for the user selected parameters on the top of the report provides this information. For example, if a report lists transactions between two specific dates, list the from and to dates in the report page header.

**Confidential Statement** -- Many firms print a confidentiality statement on the bottom of their reports. This most frequently is found in the page footer. If the firm or the firm's lawyers require this, do not forget it.

**Copyright Statement** -- Sometimes company proprietary information is printed on reports or documents. For example, in manufacturing firms, the manufacturing orders may include design specifications or drawings. The inclusion of a copyright notice is prudent. It is not necessary to find the circled c used in most copy right notices. A notice worked such as "(c) Copyright 2012, Accolade Publications, Inc." is legally sufficient in most cases. Consult with the firm's attorneys to confirm local requirements.

# IX.E.8.    Graphical Designs

SSRS in all of the current versions allows the inclusion of images in reports. The source of the images can vary from pre-loaded graphics for logos to database stored graphics. This ability provides some significant abilities to generate very attractive business documents.

Company logos have long been a staple of business documents. With SSRS, logos can be dynamic, printing different logos for different firms. Imagine a drop ship invoice with the purchasing firm's logo on the packing list!

In earlier chapters of this book, the inclusion of graphics in reports has been discussed. The use of this ability can provide some very attractive business documents.

# Index

## Symbols

3D Options Properties screen 163

## A

Action Properties screen 162
Active Directory 244
Add button 79
Add Filter icon 89
Add New Items 71
Add New Items window 71
Add New Item
    window 51, 64, 121
Add Relationship icon 31, 88
Advanced Group Properties
    screen 190
Advanced screen 140
Alias column 96
All Columns box 95
Applied Filters 89
Applied Filters pane 26, 70, 83
Arrange Fields window 31
Attach a Database File option 25
Auto Detect button 31, 87
Available Values screen 140
Available Values Screen 139
Axis Title Properties window 201
Axis Title window 203
Azure Data Source Connection
    Properties 67

## B

Best Practices 224
Blank Report 104
Body parameters window 184
Body Properties Border
    screen 184
Body Properties Fill screen 184
Border screen 184
Border Section 108
Borders screen 198
Build button 67
Built-In Fields 105
Button
    Query Builder 71

Buttons
    Add 79
    Auto Detect 31, 87
    Build 67
    Delete 79
    Design 28
    Down Arrow 79
    Edit as Text 26
    Edit Fields 88
    Group and Aggregate 85
    Import 75
    New Role Assignment 246
    New Schedule 249
    Query Builder 25, 69
    Query Designer 74
    Refresh Fields 75
    Run Query 91
    Shared Data Source 61
    Test Connec-
        tion 25, 42, 62, 65
    Up Arrow 79

## C

Cache Refresh Options screen 238
Category Groups block 212
Category Groups pane 202
Category pane 98
Chart Area Properties window 200
Chart Data Panes 201
Chart Data Values block 212
Chart Data window 210, 212
Chart Properties window 200
Charts 199
Chart Title Properties window 203
Chart Wizard 104
Check Boxes
    Save My Password 65
    Shared Data Source 63
child report 194
Choose a Style window 32
Choose the Layout window 32
Clipboard Section 106
Code Definition Window 52
Code View pane 52
Color Sample pane 160
Column column 96
Column groups 118
Column Headers 177
Column Headings 257

Column Properties Page 175
Columns 175
    Alias 96
    Column 96
    Output 96
    Sort Type 96
    Table 96
Commission reports 258
Commissions folder 220, 221
Common Functions group 132
Comparison Type
    field 80, 142, 143, 156, 157
Complete Report 195
Completing the Wizard
    window 45
Connection
    Properties 24, 42, 65, 67
Connection Properties winw 23, 2
    5, 42, 43, 59, 62, 64, 67
Connection String 42, 61, 62, 64
    , 65, 67, 241
Connect to a Database
    window 24, 42, 65
count function 86
Count function 132
create a Dataset 25
Create Linked Report 234
Credentials 63
Criteria pane 92, 96
Currency Category 166
Custom Category 166
Customer Account Balances
    table 31
Customer Number column 125
Customer Number field 28
Customer Sales Analysis reports
    folder 224
Customer Table 26

## D

Data Bar report 210
Data Bars 210
Database Images 161, 181
Database Name
    option 42, 60, 62, 65
Database Pane 84
Database View pane 26, 70
Database window 62
Data Connection Type window 67
Data elements 122

# X

# Y

# Z